Settings on the Dock of the Bay

A Collection of Recipes from
ASSISTANCE LEAGUE® of the Bay Area Texas

A Chapter of NATIONAL ASSISTANCE LEAGUE®

The cookbook committee expresses grateful appreciation to ASSISTANCE LEAGUE® of the Bay Area members and friends who contributed to Settings on the Dock of the Bay. *It is only through their efforts that this cookbook is possible. We regret that we were unable to include many wonderful recipes that were submitted due to similarity or availability of space. Every effort has been made to include only recipes that are thought to be neither previously published nor copyrighted. Should any published recipes inadvertently appear within this book, it is without our knowledge and it is unintentional.*

PHOTOGRAPHER: J. PAMELA CULPEPPER, CPP

LIBRARY OF CONGRESS CATALOG NUMBER: 98-074620
ISBN: 0-9668381-0-6

EDITED, DESIGNED, AND MANUFACTURED BY FAVORITE RECIPES® PRESS, AN IMPRINT OF

FRP

P. O. BOX 305142
NASHVILLE, TENNESSEE 37230
800-358-0560

DESIGNERS: BRAD WHITFIELD AND SUSAN BREINING

BOOK PROJECT MANAGER: LINDA A. JONES

PRINTED IN CHINA

FIRST PRINTING: 1999 10,000 COPIES
SECOND PRINTING: 2000 12,500 COPIES
THIRD PRINTING: 2005 7,500 COPIES

ABOUT THE COVER PHOTOGRAPH:
LAKEWOOD YACHT CLUB

Prior to 1900, the Rougers Hotel was located on the grounds of the present Lakewood Yacht Club. Colorful surreys from the hotel would pick up guests from the Southern Pacific train stations and bring them to the Rougers. Some of the Hotel's original oak trees and palms still stand near the club today. Withstanding the Great Storm of 1900, the Rougers operated until 1918 and was torn down in the 1930s. For more than 20 years the land stood vacant until, in 1955, Lakewood Yacht Club officially opened. The existing Bermuda-style clubhouse, situated on 35 acres on the north shore of Clear Lake, is the original structure. The club was developed by members of the Houston Yacht Club who wanted a facility solely for the use of power boaters. Currently, there is a 60/40 ratio of sailboats to power boats berthed at the Lakewood docks.

ABOUT THE BACK COVER PHOTOGRAPH:
WATERFORD HARBOR YACHT CLUB AND MARINA

This dock is located at Waterford Harbor, one of the Gulf Coast's unique boating communities. Built in 1987 on the south shore of Clear Lake, it offers the charm and elegance of a Williamsburg-style marina complete with narrow, red-brick lanes lined with live oaks and incandescent street lights.

⚓

PREFACE

ASSISTANCE LEAGUE® OF THE BAY AREA CELEBRATED ITS TENTH ANNIVERSARY OF PHILANTHROPIC SERVICE IN NOVEMBER 1998. ALBA BEGAN AS AN AUXILIARY OF ASSISTANCE LEAGUE® OF HOUSTON AND WAS CHARTERED AS A CHAPTER IN 1994. OUR GOAL HAS ALWAYS BEEN TO MAKE A POSITIVE DIFFERENCE, AND SINCE 1989, WE HAVE ACCOMPLISHED THIS THROUGH FIVE PHILANTHROPIC PROJECTS. OPERATION SCHOOL BELL®, ADOPTED AS THE NATIONAL ASSISTANCE LEAGUE® PROJECT, PROVIDES NEW SCHOOL CLOTHES TO CHILDREN IN NEED. OUR LOCAL SUCCESSFUL PROJECTS INCLUDE DOCENT PRESENTATIONS AND FUNDING FOR ARMAND BAYOU NATURE CENTER; SCHOLARSHIPS FOR ELEMENTARY AND INTERMEDIATE SCHOOL-AGED CHILDREN FOR THE SUMMER ENRICHMENT COURSES AT THE UNIVERSITY OF HOUSTON-CLEAR LAKE ("KIDS U"); TUTORING AND SUPPORT SERVICES FOR STUDENTS IDENTIFIED WITH SPECIAL NEEDS IN A NATIONAL SCHOOL DROP-OUT PREVENTION PROGRAM; AND HANDS FROM THE HEART, A PROJECT OFFERING MONTHLY INTERACTION AND THE WARMTH OF COMPANIONSHIP TO THE ELDERLY OF THE BAY AREA.

IN 1996, THE MEMBERSHIP VOTED TO PRODUCE A COOKBOOK WITH THE PROCEEDS GOING TO BENEFIT ITS PHILANTHROPIC PROJECTS. AS A RESULT, *Settings on the Dock of the Bay* WAS CREATED. THIS DELIGHTFUL COOKBOOK OFFERS A DISTINCT CULINARY AND VISUAL GLIMPSE OF THE BAY AREA.

AS A COMMUNITY, WE WILLINGLY ACCEPT THE CHALLENGES OF NATURE, SPACE, AND TECHNOLOGY. WE ARE AS ENTHUSIASTIC ABOUT THE OPPORTUNITIES WE OFFER THE WORLD THROUGH OUR SCIENTIFIC, EDUCATIONAL, AND MEDICAL DISCOVERIES AS WE ARE ABOUT THE ENTICING RECIPES SHARED THROUGHOUT OUR COOKBOOK. ALL OF US IN ASSISTANCE LEAGUE® HOPE YOU ENJOY THE SPECIALTIES OF OUR CUISINE AS YOU BECOME ACQUAINTED WITH THE WONDERFUL SPIRIT OF OUR DIVERSIFIED COMMUNITY.

ACKNOWLEDGEMENTS

*A*SSISTANCE LEAGUE®
*of the Bay Area expresses
much appreciation to those listed
below. We sincerely hope we have
not omitted anyone who has
contributed to* Settings on the
Dock of the Bay.

ARMAND BAYOU NATURE
   CENTER
BAY RUNNER GROUP, INC.
WAYNE BUCKHEIT
   Captain of the Legacy
KAREN BRODSKY CATE
FRANK CAMERA
   *Frenchie's Restaurant &
   Villa Capri*
NANCY CHEN
   Pennington-Chen Real Estate
MARY ALYS CHERRY
   The Citizen & Exchange News
ROGER CONNER, *FRP*®
PETER CRONK, *Select Images*
ZOE CUMMINS
VERVA DENSMORE
GUS DUNN, *Outback Steakhouse*

JAMIE DURAN, *Mallorcas*
MARY KAY AND PAULIE GAIDO
   Gaido's Restaurant
KARL GARCIA
   Cavanagh's American Grill
GEORGE GARTNER
DICK GREGG, JR.
LYNETTE MASON GREGG
ROBERT HESELMEYER
JIM HOLSTEIN
J. B. HOLSTEIN, CWC
HOUSTON YACHT CLUB
CHET JACHIMIEC
JOHNSON SPACE CENTER
SALLY JORDAN
   Jeremy's Books & Toys
MARY KEGG
   The Citizen & Exchange News
LAKEWOOD YACHT CLUB
LA MADELEINE® FRENCH
   BAKERY & CAFÉ
LANDRY'S SEAFOOD RESTAURANTS
CHERYL LEWIS ENTERPRISES
PAT LINDSEY, *Enzo's Pasta & Vino*
JOHN LOWERY, *Design At Work*®
MARILYN MIESKUC
CECI MIGLICCO

MINUTEMAN PRESS
PHYLLIS MOLLER
J. PAMELA PHOTOGRAPHY, INC.
CHRIS PERRY, *Perry's Italian
   Kitchen*
ROHM AND HAAS TEXAS
   INCORPORATED
DR. HAL ROSENTHAL
CHEF JOHN SCHWARTZ
   Bay Brewery
CHEF BRUCE ROSS
   Bay Oaks Country Club
ELIZABETH SCOTT
TOMMY TOLLETT
   tommy's Patio Café
UNIVERSITY OF HOUSTON-
   CLEAR LAKE
CHEF JESSE VERRETTE
   *South Shore Harbour
   Country Club*
WATERFORD HARBOR YACHT
   CLUB AND MARINA
LOIS WEBB, *Villa Capri*
WINDEMERE
WILLIAMS-SONOMA OF
   BAYBROOK MALL
PAT AND WENDELL WILSON

LEXUS
OF CLEAR LAKE

PHOTOGRAPHER

*J. Pamela Culpepper, CPP, President and owner of J. Pamela Photography, Inc. and a Community Associate
of our organization photographed the dock settings in this book. Located just a stone's throw from NASA,
J. Pamela Photography has documented the people and events of the Bay Area community for almost a
generation. Her practice has evolved to include photographing Presidents and First Ladies, athletes,
and actors. Culpepper, the recipient of local and regional awards, uniquely counts second marriages as a
studio specialty. J. Pamela, who has two grown daughters and one grandson, has been a longtime active
member of Clear Lake Presbyterian Church. Having earned two degrees from the University of Houston-
Clear Lake, she is currently serving as President of their Alumni association. Her partner in life and business
is husband Peter Cronk. We are deeply indebted to Pam for her generous gift of time and talent, but more
importantly for her vibrant spirit, which made this collaboration so rewarding.*

COOKBOOK COMMODORES

CHAIR *Barbara Rosenthal*   VICE-CHAIR *Mary Sue Holstein*

PROOFING EDITOR
Jan Parks
TESTING COORDINATOR
Mary Alice Dunn
VICE-CHAIR
Jeana Magness
RECIPE COLLECTION
Melinda Marcum

MARKETING CO-CHAIRS
Sharon Dillard and
Charlotte Teeter
NON-RECIPE TEXT
Ebby Creden
ART/DESIGN COORDINATOR
Laurie Jachimiec
SECRETARY
Joy Muniz

INDEXING
Ruth Beecher
TREASURERS
Lynn Brown and
Janet Watkins
COMPUTER
Atiya Abouleish

DOCK DESIGNERS

Carol Bergman
Linda Byrd
Belva Dewey
Donna Gartner

Cathy McDaniel
Pat Nichilo
Cathy Osoria
Jan Parks

Bertina Smith
Joy Smitherman
Barbara Visser

COOKBOOK COMMANDERS

APPETIZERS
Dana Brown and
Joy Smitherman
BEVERAGES
Mary Alice Dunn
BREADS
Sandra Sellers and
Gloria Cruz
BRUNCH
Linda Byrd
DESSERTS
Diane McLaughlin

ENTRÉES (BEEF)
Sharon Dillard
ENTRÉES (PORK AND LAMB)
Sheila Fichtner
ENTRÉES (POULTRY)
Connie Lopez
HOLIDAY
Joy Smitherman
RESTAURANTS
Casey Myers and
Charlotte Teeter

SALADS
Barbara Visser and
Lil Glynn
SEAFOOD
Donna Gartner
SIDE DISHES
Jeana Magness
SOUPS
Melba Heselmeyer and
Fran Gentry
WINES
Mary Kay Gaido

COOKBOOK CAPTAINS

Carol Bergman

Carol Bobo

Dana Brown

Linda Byrd

Nancy Chen

Barbara Coleman

Gloria Cruz

Belva Dewey

Pat Escue

Sheila Fichtner

Lynda Forsthoffer

Mary Kay Gaido

Donna Gartner

Fran Gentry

Rae Gillespie

Elizabeth Glenn

Lil Glynn

Louise Gregory

Jenny Hampton

Melba Heselmeyer

Suzanne Hicks

Kathy Incalcaterra

Lucy Jacobson

Emily Johnson

Carol Loomis

Connie Lopez

Johanna Mathera

Cathy McDaniel

Darla McKitrick

Diane McLaughlin

Casey Myers

Ulrike Nordhoff

Cathy Osoria

Sylvia Resch

Betsy Rogers

Marcia Safirstein

Sarah Sawin

Sandra Sellers

Bertina Smith

Joy Smitherman

Bernie Sullivan

Toinette Tillinghast

Pat Trampe

Barbara Visser

Nancy Watson

Owen Whitlock

Gloria Wong

LEAGUE PRESIDENTS DURING COOKBOOK PRODUCTION

1996–1997 Sharon Dillard

1997–1998 Linda Byrd

1998–1999 Melba Heselmeyer

1999–2000 Sarah Sawin

⚓

INTRODUCTION

WELCOME TO OUR BAY AREA-TEXAS STYLE. WHERE ELSE CAN YOU FIND THE PICTURESQUE FISHING VILLAGE OF KEMAH, THE HISTORICALLY CHARMING SEABROOK, OR THE SOPHISTICATED YACHTING COMPLEX OF LEAGUE CITY? THE KARANKAWA INDIANS ONCE WANDERED THE SHORES OF CLEAR LAKE AND MUD LAKE; THE PIRATE JEAN LAFITTE BURIED TREASURE ALONG THE GULF COAST; AND ONE OF THE PIONEERS OF RICE FARMING, H. KOBAYASHI, LEFT JAPAN TO SETTLE IN WEBSTER.

TODAY, OUR COMMUNITY TAKES PRIDE IN ITS ECONOMIC AND CULTURAL DIVERSITY. VISITORS DISCOVER FISHING AND SHRIMPING IN AREA WATERS, RE-LIVE THE BEAUTY OF PRIMITIVE FRONTIER LIFE ON THE PLAINS OF TEXAS AT ARMAND BAYOU NATURE CENTER, AND CRUISE THE WATERS OF ONE OF THE LARGEST INLAND SAILING CENTERS IN THE UNITED STATES. OUR COMMUNITY IS ALSO HOME TO ASTRONAUTS, SCIENTISTS, AND ENGINEERS WHO UNLOCK THE SECRETS OF THE STARS FROM THEIR TEXAS HOME, THE JOHNSON SPACE CENTER.

SET SAIL WITH US ON A CULINARY JOURNEY. SAMPLE A POTPOURRI OF FOODS REPRESENTING LOCAL AND INTERNATIONAL TASTES. AS YOU VISIT OUR ENCHANTING *Settings on the Dock of the Bay,* LET US HELP YOU PLAN A BEACH HOUSE COOKOUT, A SUMMER SUPPER, A DESSERT BUFFET, OR AN ELEGANT HOLIDAY COFFEE. CULINARY CHALLENGED? EXPERIENCED COOK? GOURMET CHEF? *Settings on the Dock of the Bay* REFLECTS YOUR STYLE AND EXPERTISE.

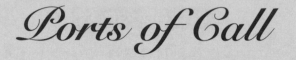

Ports of Call

Words on Wine

WINE PRODUCTION AND QUALITY ARE AT AN ALL TIME HIGH AND PEOPLE TODAY DRINK WINE AS OPPOSED TO COLLECTING IT, AND WELL THEY SHOULD. THERE ARE MORE GREAT WINES AT AFFORDABLE PRICES TODAY THAN ANYONE COULD TASTE IN A LIFETIME. A SEPARATE BOOK WOULD BE NECESSARY TO LIST EVERY WINE AND ITS COST. THE GOAL HERE IS TO DESCRIBE THE TASTE OF EACH GRAPE VARIETY, WHAT TO EXPECT FROM EACH ONE, AND WHAT FOODS BEST ACCOMPANY THEM. MOST IMPORTANTLY, IT IS NECESSARY TO KEEP IN MIND THAT WINE PREFERENCE IS AN INDIVIDUAL AND PERSONAL CHOICE.

LOOK FOR THIS SPECIAL WINE SYMBOL WHICH APPEARS THROUGHOUT THE BOOK. IT SIGNIFIES RECOMMENDED WINES FOR PARTICULAR TYPES OF FOOD. KEEP IN MIND THAT THESE ARE ONLY SUGGESTIONS. EXPERIMENTING IS HALF THE FUN WHEN DISCOVERING WHICH WINES YOU ENJOY WITH YOUR FAVORITE FOODS!

CHAMPAGNE

CHAMPAGNE—WHILE ALL CHAMPAGNE IS SPARKLING WINE—WINE WHICH HAS UNDERGONE NATURAL CARBONATION—NOT ALL SPARKLING WINE IS CHAMPAGNE. CHAMPAGNE IS VERY SIMPLY SPARKLING WINE FROM THE CHAMPAGNE REGION OF FRANCE AND IS STRICTLY REGULATED. CHAMPAGNE HAS AN INTERESTING HISTORY. IT WAS MADE ACCIDENTALLY BY A MONK NAMED DOM PERIGNON IN 1678. DOM PERIGNON, WHO WAS BLIND, STARTED MIXING DIFFERENT WINES AND PLACING THEM IN BOTTLES, UNEXPECTEDLY CAUSING THE STILL (NON-SPARKLING) WINE TO GO THROUGH A SECOND FERMENTATION. SINCE THE TWO PRODUCTS OF FERMENTATION ARE ALCOHOL AND CARBON DIOXIDE, THE BUBBLES WERE TRAPPED IN THE CORKED BOTTLES AND THUS, CHAMPAGNE WAS BORN. WHEN DOM PERIGNON DRANK HIS CREATION HE SAID, "COME QUICKLY, I AM DRINKING THE STARS." A POPULAR TECHNIQUE USED TO CREATE THE "BUBBLY" WAS THE ADDITION OF SUGAR, BUT THIS CAUSED SEDIMENT TO FORM IN THE BOTTLES.

THE SEDIMENT HAD TO BE REMOVED FROM THE BOTTLE BY DECANTING BUT THIS MADE

THE CHAMPAGNE LOSE HALF OF ITS EFFERVESCENCE. THIS WAS THE PROCESS USED UNTIL 1810,

WHEN VEUVE CLICQUOT TOOK HER KITCHEN TABLE TO THE CELLARS, DRILLED HOLES

IN IT, STOOD IT ON END AND PLACED THE BOTTLES—NECK FIRST—IN THE HOLES SO THE SEDIMENT

WOULD SETTLE ON THE CORK. THIS ALLOWED THE SEDIMENT TO EXPLODE OUT OF THE

BOTTLE WHEN IT WAS OPENED, A PROCESS NOW KNOWN AS "RIDDLING." CHARDONNAY AND

PINOT NOIR GRAPES ARE COMBINED TO MAKE CHAMPAGNE. IT IS THE PERFECT WINE TO SERVE AS

AN APERITIF BECAUSE THE OPENING OF THE BOTTLE IS A CEREMONY IN AND OF ITSELF.

CHAMPAGNE HONORS YOUR GUESTS. EVEN PEOPLE WHO DON'T GIVE MUCH

THOUGHT TO TASTING WINE WILL STAND AROUND FOR A MOMENT TO CONVERSE

ABOUT CHAMPAGNE. UNLIKE MANY WHITE WINES, CHAMPAGNE STANDS ALONE WITHOUT FOOD.

AND, OF COURSE, IT IS A PERFECT WINE FOR DESSERTS.

SAUVIGNON BLANC

SAUVIGNON BLANC (SOH-VIHN-YOHN-BLAHN) IS A WHITE GRAPE THAT IS HIGHLY CULTIVATED

IN FRANCE AND CALIFORNIA. THIS IS THE GRAPE THAT IS MIXED WITH SEMILLON TO MAKE UP

THE WHITE BORDEAUX WINES AND 100% OF THE SAUVIGNON BLANC GRAPE IS USED TO MAKE

SANCERRE AND POUILLY-FUME FROM THE LOIRE VALLEY. SAUVIGNON BLANC IS CONSIDERED TO BE

AN EXCELLENT FOOD WINE DUE TO ITS ACIDITY. THE ACID IN A WINE IS WHAT GIVES WINE ITS

BACKBONE AND ALSO ACTS AS A PALATE CLEANSER, WHICH IS WHY IT IS GOOD WITH FOOD.

THESE WINES ARE GENERALLY DESCRIBED AS GRASSY AND HERBACEOUS. THEY ARE CRISP,

FLAVORFUL WINES THAT GENERALLY SHOULD BE DRUNK YOUNG. THE RULE OF THUMB

IS TO SERVE THESE WINES WITH FOWL OR FISH. KEEP IN MIND THAT OUR CLIMATE ON THE

GULF COAST MAKES THIS A MOST REFRESHING WINE TO DRINK IN THE SUMMER MONTHS.

GEWÜRZTRAMINER

GEWÜRZTRAMINER (GUH-VURTS-TRAH-MEE-NER) IS AN UNUSUAL GRAPE
THAT PRODUCES WHITE WINES THAT ARE CHARACTERIZED BY A PUNGENT,
PERFUMED AROMA WITH A RICH AND OILY TEXTURE. THEY ARE USUALLY BOTTLED WITH A TOUCH
OF SWEETNESS TO OFFSET THE NATURAL BITTERNESS OF THE WINE. THE SONOMA STYLE
WILL HAVE A MUTED NOSE AND A SWEETER TASTE. BY COMPARISON, THE ALSACE WINE
WILL BE DRIER AND HAVE A MORE NATURAL NOSE AND FLAVOR.
ALSACE IS AN ANCIENT FRENCH PROVINCE BORDERING THE RHINE RIVER, NORTH OF SWITZERLAND.
THE VINEYARDS ARE ABOUT 20 MILES WEST OF THE RHINE AND EXTEND 70 MILES
ALONG THE LOWER SLOPES OF THE VOSGES MOUNTAINS. THERE ARE FOUR MAJOR VARIETALS
PLANTED IN ALSACE: RIESLING, GEWÜRZTRAMINER, SYLVANER, AND PINOT BLANC.
THE WINES OF ALSACE, SHIPPED IN TALL GREEN BOTTLES AND LABELED WITH THE NAMES
OF THE GRAPE VARIETIES ASSOCIATED WITH GERMANY, ARE OFTEN CONFUSED
WITH THE SLIGHTLY SWEET WINES PRODUCED IN THAT COUNTRY. ALSACE WINES
ARE COMPLETELY DRY, INTENSELY FLAVORED, AND MORE ASSERTIVE THAN THOSE OF GERMANY.

JOHANNISBERG RIESLING

JOHANNISBERG RIESLING (YOH-HAHN-IHSS-BERK REEZ-LING) IS THE FORMAL NAME
FOR ONE OF THE OLDEST GRAPES KNOWN TO MAN. THIS WINE IS NATIVE TO GERMANY'S
RHINE VALLEY BUT HAS BEEN TRANSPLANTED IN MANY DIFFERENT COUNTRIES.
IT HAS ALWAYS PRODUCED A SUPERIOR WINE IF GROWN IN COOL AREAS. THIS GRAPE IS CHARACTERIZED
BY A FLOWERY, FRAGRANT AROMA THAT HAS A DISTINCTIVE FRUITY ACIDITY. MOST OF THE CALIFORNIA
JOHANNISBERG RIESLINGS HAVE EVOLVED FROM AN AUSTERE AND DRY WINE TO A MORE DELICATE
AND AROMATIC STYLE WITH A TOUCH OF SWEETNESS BALANCED BY LIVELY ACIDITY.
THIS WINE IS BEST SERVED AS AN APERITIF OR DESSERT WINE.
FOR THE DARING, TRY THIS WITH CAESAR SALAD—IT IS WONDERFUL!

WHITE ZINFANDEL

WHITE ZINFANDEL IS NOT ACTUALLY A WHITE WINE, BUT RATHER WHAT'S CALLED A BLUSH WINE IN THE UNITED STATES AND A ROSÉ OR BLANC DE NOIR IN FRANCE. THE WINE MAKERS BRIEFLY LET THE SKINS OF THESE BLACK GRAPES SIT WITH THE PRESSED JUICE, THUS GIVING THE WINE ITS SALMON OR PINK COLOR. THIS WINE IS SWEET, SHOULD BE DRUNK YOUNG, AND GOES VERY WELL WITH SPICY FOODS OR ON ITS OWN.

CHARDONNAY

CHARDONNAY (SHAR-DN-AY) ALTHOUGH SOME ARGUE THAT THE RIESLING GRAPE PRODUCES THE FINEST WHITE WINE, IT'S CHARDONNAY THAT IS BEING EXTENSIVELY PLANTED THROUGHOUT THE WORLD BECAUSE IT HAS A GOOD BALANCE BETWEEN FRUIT, ACID, AND TEXTURE. NAPA VALLEY CHARDONNAYS HAVE A TENDENCY TO BE CLEAN AND CRISP WITH OAK OVERTONES FROM THE OAK CASKS IN WHICH THE WINES ARE AGED. SONOMA COUNTY CHARDONNAYS HAVE A TENDENCY TO BE RICH AND CREAMY. CARNEROS CHARDONNAYS HAVE A FULL BODY WITH FRUIT OVERTONES. ONE WOULD WANT TO PAIR A CLEAN, CRISP CHARDONNAY WITH A CREAM OR BUTTER DISH; A RICH AND CREAMY CHARDONNAY WOULD GO WELL WITH A MORE FRUIT-ORIENTED DISH.

WHITE BURGUNDY

WHITE BURGUNDY IS MADE FROM 100% CHARDONNAY. BURGUNDY IS A REGION THAT STRETCHES FROM DIJON TO LYONS, FRANCE AND INCLUDES CHABLIS. BURGUNDY'S ANNUAL WHITE WINE PRODUCTION ACCOUNTS FOR ONLY 0.75% OF ALL FRENCH WINE, WHICH EXPLAINS WHY IT IS SO EXPENSIVE. THE SPECIFIC APPELLATION (THE WINE'S PLACE OF ORIGIN) IS ON THE LABEL: "MACON-VILLAGES," "MEURSAULT," "POUILLY-FUISSE," AND "CHABLIS" ARE EXAMPLES. THE PRODUCER WILL ALSO BE ON THE LABEL BUT IN SMALL PRINT: LOUIS JADOT, JOSEPH DROUHIN, JOSEPH MATROT. THE LESS EXPENSIVE WHITE BURGUNDIES WILL TEND TO HAVE EXCELLENT FRUIT QUALITIES AND VERY LITTLE OAK QUALITIES. THE MORE EXPENSIVE WHITE BURGUNDIES WILL BE WELL-BALANCED, LUSH, AND WORTH THE MONEY.

PINOT NOIR

*P*INOT NOIR (PEE-noh NWAHR) IS A DISTINGUISHED AND CELEBRATED GRAPE. THIS IS THE RED GRAPE OF FRANCE'S BURGUNDY REGION. IT IS RESPONSIBLE FOR THE GREAT (AND EXPENSIVE) RED WINES FROM BURGUNDY'S COTE D'OR REGION. UNTIL RECENTLY, IT HAS BEEN A VERY DIFFICULT GRAPE TO CULTIVATE IN THE UNITED STATES. OREGON HAS BEEN MOST SUCCESSFUL AND SOME CONSIDER THE PINOT NOIRS COMING FROM THIS STATE TO BE THE BEST IN THE WORLD (EVEN BETTER THAN BURGUNDY!). THERE ARE ALSO SOME PINOT NOIRS FROM THE CARNEROS AND DRY CREEK APPELLATIONS OF SONOMA, ESPECIALLY SINCE 1994. THIS WINE COMPLEMENTS SEAFOOD VERY WELL.

BEAUJOLAIS

*B*EAUJOLAIS (BOH-ZHUH-LAY) THE BEAUJOLAIS AREA IS LOCATED IN THE SOUTHERN PART OF FRANCE'S BURGUNDY REGION. BEAUJOLAIS IS DIFFERENT FROM MOST OF BURGUNDY BECAUSE OF ITS FOCUS ON THE GAMAY GRAPE. THIS IS A FRESH FRUITY WINE THAT NEEDS TO BE DRUNK EARLY. THERE IS A SPECIAL CATEGORY OF BEAUJOLAIS CALLED "NOUVEAU" THAT IS RELEASED 7-9 WEEKS AFTER IT IS BOTTLED AND IS AVAILABLE TO THE PUBLIC ON THE THIRD THURSDAY OF NOVEMBER. IT IS A GREAT WINE TO SERVE WITH TRADITIONAL HOLIDAY DINNERS. THIS RED WINE BENEFITS FROM BEING SERVED CHILLED.

ZINFANDEL

*Z*INFANDEL (ZIHN-FUHN-DEHL) THIS IS A GRAPE THAT MOST PEOPLE ASSOCIATE WITH A WHITE WINE WHEN, IN FACT, IT IS A RED GRAPE AND MAKES A PEPPERY RED WINE THAT IS BECOMING QUITE POPULAR IN THE UNITED STATES. BECAUSE OF ITS TANNIC FLAVOR THIS WINE GOES WELL WITH BEEF DISHES. THE WHITE VERSION OF THE GRAPE, WHITE ZINFANDEL, IS ONE OF THE MOST POPULAR WINES IN THE UNITED STATES. BECAUSE OF ITS SWEETNESS, THIS WINE IS GREAT SERVED ON ITS OWN OR WITH SPICY FOODS.

MERLOT

MERLOT (MEHR-LOH) THOUGH COMMONLY REFERRED TO AS SIMPLY MERLOT, THIS RED-WINE GRAPE IS REALLY MERLOT NOIR. MERLOT IS ONE OF THE TWO PRIMARY GRAPES GROWN IN THE BORDEAUX REGION OF FRANCE, THE OTHER BEING CABERNET SAUVIGNON. MERLOT GRAPES HAVE LOWER TANNINS AND HIGHER SUGAR LEVELS THAN CABERNET SAUVIGNON. THEY ARE COMPLEX AND MEDIUM-BODIED WITH GOOD FRUIT FLAVOR. ALTHOUGH TRADITIONALLY BLENDED WITH CABERNET SAUVIGNON, MERLOT HAS FOUND ITS OWN MARKET AND IS CURRENTLY THE SECOND BEST SELLING GRAPE WINE IN THE UNITED STATES. THIS WINE GOES WELL WITH RED MEAT DISHES OR FISH/POULTRY DISHES WITH CREAM SAUCES.

CABERNET SAUVIGNON

CABERNET SAUVIGNON (KA-BEHR-NAY SOH-VIHN-YOHN) IF NOT THE KING, AS MANY ARGUE, CABERNET SAUVIGNON IS CERTAINLY THE MOST SUCCESSFUL AND POPULAR OF THE TOP-QUALITY RED WINE GRAPES. IT IS THE PRIMARY GRAPE OF MOST OF THE TOP VINEYARDS IN BORDEAUX'S MEDOC AND GRAVES DISTRICTS. IT IS ALSO THE BASIS FOR MOST OF CALIFORNIA'S SUPERB RED WINES. THIS REPUTATION FOR EXCELLENCE HAS LAUNCHED A CABERNET SAUVIGNON POPULARITY BOOM AROUND THE WORLD. CALIFORNIA CABERNET SAUVIGNONS WERE ORIGINALLY MADE FROM 100% CABERNET SAUVIGNON BUT IN RECENT YEARS MANY PRODUCERS HAVE BEEN BLENDING IN, AS IS DONE IN BORDEAUX. THE REASON FOR BLENDING IS TO MAKE CALIFORNIA CABERNET SAUVIGNONS MORE APPROACHABLE AT A YOUNGER AGE. CALIFORNIA WINE MAKERS ARE ALSO BEGINNING TO PRODUCE MERITAGE WINES. MERITAGE USES TRADITIONAL BORDEAUX GRAPES AND TRADITIONAL BORDEAUX LAWS TO PRODUCE THEIR WINES. THE MOST FAMOUS CALIFORNIA MERITAGE IS OPUS ONE, WHICH WAS PRODUCED AS A JOINT VENTURE BETWEEN ROBERT MONDAVI AND BARON PHILLIPE DE ROTHSCHILD, PROPRIETOR OF CHATEAU MOUTON ROTHSCHILD IN BORDEAUX. THIS WINE IS EXCELLENTLY PAIRED WITH HEAVY BEEF MEALS. FOR THE DARING, TRY A LIGHTER CABERNET WITH A DEEP, RICH, CHOCOLATE DESSERT—IT'S DIVINE!

MISSION STATEMENT

*N*ATIONAL ASSISTANCE LEAGUE® IS A VOLUNTEER ORGANIZATION DEDICATED TO PROMOTING EFFECTIVE VOLUNTEERISM THROUGH EDUCATION, SERVICE, LEADERSHIP DEVELOPMENT, AND FINANCIAL ACCOUNTABILITY. ASSISTANCE LEAGUE® OF THE BAY AREA IS A CHAPTER OF **NATIONAL ASSISTANCE LEAGUE®.**

*A*SSISTANCE LEAGUE® OF THE BAY AREA IS A NONPROFIT PHILANTHROPIC ORGANIZATION DEDICATED TO IMPROVING THE QUALITY OF LIFE IN THE BAY AREA BY PROVIDING SERVICES, EDUCATION, AND FINANCIAL ASSISTANCE TO AT-RISK POPULATIONS, INCLUDING CHILDREN AND THE ELDERLY.

*A*SSISTANCE LEAGUE® OF THE BAY AREA MOTTO
COMMITMENT — CONNECTION — COMMUNITY
CARING FOR THE CHILDREN — THE ELDERLY — THE ENVIRONMENT

All Aboard
Appetizers & Beverages

⚓

Seabrook Flats

This unique boat dock is located in Seabrook at the mouth of Hester's Gulley, a salt grass estuary and sea nursery, which flows into Galveston Bay. Beyond the mouth of the estuary is the Seabrook Flats where area fishermen go wade fishing for flounder, redfish and trout. Ospreys, egrets, herons, terns, brown and white pelicans, as well as the ubiquitous seagulls, also fish these waters.

Docker Party
All Hands on Deck
(A Progressive Dinner)

BLACK CAVIAR PIE, *page 126*
SUN-DRIED TOMATO TORTE, *page 29*
BEEF AND GORGONZOLA MEATBALLS WRAPPED IN PROSCIUTTO, *page 33*
ROASTED RED PEPPER AND ARTICHOKE TAPENADE, *page 25*
EGGPLANT IN PHYLLO SHELLS, *page 33*

BLANC DE NOIR OR SPARKLING WINE

GARDEN SALAD WITH BROILED GOAT CHEESE, *page 89*
MEDALLIONS OF BEEF TENDERLOIN WITH BORDELAISE SAUCE, *page 164*
SHRIMP AIOLI, *page 144*
FAR EAST BROCCOLI, *page 106*
TWICE-BAKED POTATOES, *page 110*
COUNTRY HOT ROLLS, *page 52*

CABERNET SAUVIGNON

ESPRESSO CARAMEL MOUSSE TART, *page 208*
PRALINE PECAN CHEESECAKE, *page 198*
POACHED PEARS WITH CRÈME ANGLAISE, *page 200*
SLICES OF SIN, *page 204*

BRUT CUVÉE OR SPARKLING WINE

Hot Pepper Queso

Yield: 20 servings

2 cups chopped onions

1 cup chopped green bell pepper

3 serrano peppers, chopped

1 jalapeño pepper, minced

1/2 cup (1 stick) butter

2 1/2 cups chopped tomatoes

2 (16-ounce) packages Mexican Velveeta cheese, cut into pieces

1 (10-ounce) can tomatoes with green chiles, drained

1 (7-ounce) can chipotle peppers in adobo sauce, drained, chopped

Sauté the onions, green pepper, serrano peppers and jalapeño pepper in the butter in a skillet until tender. Stir in the tomatoes. Place the Velveeta cheese in a large glass bowl. Microwave on High for about 5 minutes or until melted, stirring several times. Add the sautéed vegetables, tomatoes with green chiles and chipotle peppers and mix well. Microwave until heated through. Serve warm with tortilla chips.

CONSOMMÉ MADRILÈNE

For Consommé Madrilène, combine two 10-ounce cans beef consommé with 2 cans water in a large saucepan. Add one (28-ounce) can vegetable juice cocktail, 4 cloves, 1/4 teaspoon celery salt, 1/4 teaspoon onion powder or salt, 1/8 teaspoon pepper and a dash of garlic salt. Simmer for 30 minutes. Strain and serve hot.

—

Black Bean and Corn Salsa

Yield: 4 cups

1½ cups fresh corn from the cob or frozen whole kernel corn	1 garlic clove, pressed
1 cup canned black beans, rinsed	2 tablespoons lime juice
1 cup chopped red bell pepper	1 tablespoon chopped fresh cilantro
1 jalapeño pepper, seeded, finely chopped	½ teaspoon salt
	¼ teaspoon pepper

Cook the corn in a small amount of boiling water in a saucepan for 4 minutes or until crisp and tender. Drain and let stand until cool. Combine with the black beans, red pepper, jalapeño pepper, garlic, lime juice, cilantro, salt and pepper in a bowl and mix well. Serve with tortilla chips or as a salad on lettuce leaves.

Note: *If served as a salad, this recipe will yield 4 to 6 servings.*

Mango and Pepper Salsa

Yield: 6 to 10 servings

2 mangos, chopped	1 to 2 jalapeño peppers, seeded, chopped
½ large purple onion, chopped	• Juice of 2 limes
3 to 4 green onions, chopped	½ cup chopped cilantro
1 red bell pepper, chopped	• Salt and pepper to taste
1 yellow bell pepper, chopped	

Combine the mangos, purple onion, green onions, red pepper, yellow pepper, jalapeño peppers, lime juice, cilantro, salt and pepper in a bowl and mix well. Chill, covered, for 8 to 12 hours. Serve with chips or as a salad on lettuce leaves.

Note: *If served as a salad, this recipe will yield 4 to 6 servings.*

Tomatillo Salsa

Yield: 3 cups

5	tomatillos	3	garlic cloves
5	to 8 Roma tomatoes	1/4	bunch cilantro leaves
1/2	onion	1	teaspoon salt
2	jalapeño peppers		

Remove the husks from the tomatillos and rinse. Cut into quarters. Process the tomatillos, Roma tomatoes, onion, jalapeño peppers, garlic cloves, cilantro leaves and salt in a blender or food processor until chunky. Pour into a container with a tight-fitting lid. Store, covered, in the refrigerator for up to a week. Serve with chips or as an accompaniment to fish.

Cranberry Salsa

Yield: 10 to 12 servings

1	(12-ounce) package cranberries, rinsed, drained	1	bunch cilantro
1	cup fresh lime juice	2	small jalapeño peppers, seeded, minced
2	tablespoons shallot quarters	1	tablespoon chopped garlic
1	teaspoon salt	2	cups sugar

Process the cranberries, lime juice, shallots, salt, cilantro, jalapeño peppers, garlic and sugar in a food processor until coarsely chopped. Serve with tortilla chips.

Note: *Can substitute dried cranberries for the fresh cranberries and reduce sugar to taste. Dried cranberries do not have to be soaked before using.*

Wild Mushroom Pâté

Yield: 12 servings

1 teaspoon salt	1/3 cup minced onion
1/4 teaspoon each basil, rosemary, oregano, marjoram and thyme	1/3 cup minced celery
	3 ounces cream cheese, softened
1/4 teaspoon pepper, nutmeg, ground cloves, cayenne pepper and mace	2 eggs
	3/4 cup dry bread crumbs
1 pound assorted wild mushrooms (such as shiitake, oyster and morel), finely chopped	1 teaspoon Worcestershire sauce
	1/4 teaspoon Tabasco sauce
	1 tablespoon Cognac
1/4 cup (1/2 stick) butter, softened	

Mix the salt, herbs and spices in a large bowl. Add the mushrooms, butter, onion, celery, cream cheese, eggs, bread crumbs, Worcestershire sauce, Tabasco sauce and Cognac and mix well. Spoon into a buttered foil-lined 5x9-inch loaf pan. Cover with buttered foil. Bake at 400 degrees for 1 1/2 hours. Cool to room temperature. Invert onto a serving plate and remove the foil. Garnish with red, green and yellow bell pepper rings. Serve with Bristo Brie Cheese Wafers (below) or good quality crackers.

Bristo Brie Cheese Wafers

Yield: 2 to 3 dozen

8 ounces Brie cheese, softened	1/2 teaspoon salt
1/2 cup (1 stick) butter, softened	1 egg
1 1/4 cups flour	1/2 teaspoon water
1 teaspoon dry mustard	1 cup ground English walnuts

Remove the rind from the cheese. Process the cheese and butter in a food processor until smooth. Add the flour, dry mustard and salt and blend lightly. Divide the dough into 2 equal portions. Shape each into logs about 1 1/2 inches in diameter. Brush with a mixture of egg and water. Let stand for a few minutes until dry. Roll in the walnuts. Wrap well and chill in the refrigerator. Cut into 1/4-inch slices and place on an ungreased baking sheet. Bake at 425 degrees for 10 to 15 minutes or until golden brown.

Note: *Dough can be stored in the freezer for 2 weeks and thawed before baking.*

Black Olive Tapenade

Yield: 18 to 24 servings

1	cup kalamata olives	1/2	tablespoon fresh thyme, or
2	tablespoons drained rinsed	1/2	teaspoon dried thyme
	capers	1/2	to 1 teaspoon fresh lemon
1 1/2	tablespoons brandy		juice
1/2	tablespoon extra-virgin	1/2	cup soft bread crumbs
	olive oil	•	Freshly ground pepper
1	small garlic clove, minced		to taste

Process the olives, capers, brandy, olive oil, garlic, thyme and lemon juice in a food processor until puréed. Add the bread crumbs and pulse just until mixed. Season with pepper and additional lemon juice if desired. Store, covered, in the refrigerator for up to 1 week. Serve on toasted French bread rounds.

ROASTED RED PEPPER AND ARTICHOKE TAPENADE

Prepare Roasted Red Pepper and Artichoke Tapenade by draining one 7-ounce jar of roasted red bell peppers and one 6- ounce jar of marinated artichoke hearts. Chop the roasted peppers and artichoke hearts coarsely. Process with 1/2 cup minced fresh parsley, 1/2 cup freshly grated Parmesan cheese and 1 teaspoon fresh lemon juice in a food processor until finely chopped. Season with salt and pepper to taste. Serve with chips or crackers.

Goat Cheese with Basil Pesto

Yield: 12 to 15 servings

1	pound goat cheese, softened	2	cups fresh basil
1	cup (2 sticks) unsalted butter, softened	4	garlic cloves
1	(6-ounce) jar oil-pack sun-dried tomatoes, drained	1/2	teaspoon salt
		1/2	teaspoon pepper
		1/3	cup olive oil

*F*or the goat cheese mixture, process the goat cheese and butter in a food processor until creamy; set aside.

*F*or the sun-dried tomatoes, pat the sun-dried tomatoes dry. Process in a food processor until chopped; set aside.

*F*or the pesto, process the basil, garlic, salt and pepper in a food processor until chopped. Add the olive oil in a fine stream, processing constantly until the mixture is puréed.

*T*o assemble, line an 8-inch springform pan with plastic wrap, leaving an overhang. Layer 1/3 of the goat cheese mixture, 1/2 cup of the pesto, 1/2 of the remaining goat cheese mixture, sun-dried tomatoes, remaining pesto and remaining goat cheese mixture in the prepared pan. Cover with plastic wrap. Chill for 8 to 12 hours.

*T*o serve, uncover and invert onto a serving plate. Serve with table wafers.

Goat Cheese — **Sauvignon Blanc, Pouilly-Fumé, Sancerre**
Gorgonzola cheese — **Soave**
Roquefort cheese — **Sauternes**
Stilton cheese — **Port**
Hard Cheeses — **Nebbiolo, Chianti**
Cheddar Cheese — **Chardonnay**

The following cheeses have virtually no relation to wine: Brie, Camembert, mozzarella, soft cheeses. However, if you think you need wine on the table, a simple young white wine would be the right choice.

---

*P*ESTO

Pesto originated in Genoa (its name comes from the Italian word pestare, which means to pound) and purists still use only Genoese basil to prepare this pesto. The best pesto is made with a mortar and pestle, but an acceptable version can be made in a blender or food processor. Basic pesto is made with only basil, Parmesan cheese, garlic, and olive oil but many variations are possible.

Italian Cheese Terrine

Yield: 20 to 25 servings

8 ounces cream cheese, softened
2 tablespoons (1/4 stick) butter or margarine, softened
1/2 cup grated Parmesan cheese

2 tablespoons commercial pesto
9 (1-ounce) slices Muenster cheese or mozzarella cheese
• Basil Tomato Sauce (below)

Beat the cream cheese and butter at medium speed in a mixer bowl until creamy. Add the Parmesan cheese and pesto and beat until smooth. Line a 5x8-inch loaf pan with plastic wrap, allowing the edges to overhang 6 to 7 inches. Cut 5 slices of the Muenster cheese diagonally into halves. Arrange the cheese triangles slightly overlapping in the prepared pan. Spread 1/2 of the cream cheese mixture over the cheese triangles. Top with 1/2 of the Basil Tomato Sauce. Cut the remaining Muenster cheese into halves crosswise forming rectangles. Continue layering with 1/2 of the cheese rectangles, the remaining cream cheese mixture, remaining Basil Tomato Sauce and remaining cheese rectangles. Fold the plastic wrap over the top and seal securely. Place a heavy object on top to compact the layers. Chill for 8 hours or up to 3 days. Invert the terrine onto a serving platter. Remove the plastic wrap. Garnish with fresh herb sprigs. Serve with crackers or baguette slices.

Basil Tomato Sauce

1 (14-ounce) can whole tomatoes
3/4 cup chopped onion
1 tablespoon minced fresh garlic
2 tablespoons olive oil
2 bay leaves

1/2 teaspoon sugar
1/4 teaspoon basil
1 (7-ounce) jar oil-pack sun-dried tomatoes, drained, chopped

Drain the tomatoes, reserving 1/4 cup juice. Chop the tomatoes. Sauté the onion and garlic in the olive oil in a large skillet over medium heat until tender. Stir in the chopped tomato, reserved juice, bay leaves, sugar and basil. Bring to a boil and reduce the heat. Simmer for 3 to 5 minutes or until thickened, stirring frequently. Remove from the heat. Discard the bay leaves. Stir in the sun-dried tomatoes. Chill, covered, for 2 hours or longer.

Provolone Terrine

Yield: 20 to 25 servings

1/2	cup chopped sun-dried tomatoes	•	Garlic Cream (below)	
1	pound Provolone cheese, thinly sliced	•	Fresh sprigs of basil	
•	Pesto (below)	5	to 6 roasted salted pistachios, shelled	

Drain the sun-dried tomatoes and pat dry. Wet a piece of cheesecloth with water and squeeze dry. Line a 4x8-inch pan with the cheesecloth, leaving an overhang. Cut the provolone cheese slices into halves. Cover the bottom and about 2 1/2 inches up the sides of the prepared pan with about 1/2 of the provolone cheese slices, letting the slices overlap slightly. Divide the remaining provolone cheese slices into 3 equal portions and set aside. Spread 1/2 of the Pesto over the provolone cheese. Cover the Pesto with 1/3 of the remaining provolone cheese, overlapping slightly. Sprinkle with 1/2 of the sun-dried tomatoes. Spread with the Garlic Cream and sprinkle with the remaining sun-dried tomatoes. Layer 1/2 of the remaining provolone cheese, remaining Pesto and remaining provolone cheese over the sun-dried tomatoes. Fold the cloth over the top and press lightly to compact layers. Chill for 2 hours or until firm. Fold back the cloth and invert onto a serving platter. Remove the cloth gently. Arrange sprigs of fresh basil and pistachios over the top. Serve with baguette slices or unsalted crackers.

Pesto

1	cup firmly packed fresh basil leaves	1/2	cup olive oil
1	cup grated Parmesan cheese	2	garlic cloves

Process the basil, Parmesan cheese, olive oil and garlic in a food processor until smooth.

Garlic Cream

8	ounces cream cheese, softened	1/8	teaspoon pepper
1/4	cup (1/2 stick) unsalted butter, softened	1/4	cup roasted salted pistachios, shelled, chopped
1	garlic clove		

Process the cream cheese, butter, garlic and pepper in a food processor until smooth. Stir in the pistachios.

Sun-Dried Tomato Torte

Yield: 35 to 50 servings

4	ounces sun-dried tomatoes packed in oil, drained	1/2	cup fresh basil leaves
24	ounces cream cheese, softened	1	cup pecan pieces
•	Salt to taste	1/2	cup freshly grated Parmesan cheese
2	tablespoons lemon juice	2	teaspoons olive oil
1	teaspoon garlic powder	•	Pepper to taste

Process the sun-dried tomatoes, 8 ounces of the cream cheese and salt in a food processor until smooth. Spread in an 8-inch springform pan lined with plastic wrap. Process 8 ounces of the cream cheese, lemon juice and garlic powder in a food processor until smooth. Spread over the first layer. Process the remaining cream cheese, basil, pecans, Parmesan cheese, olive oil, salt and pepper to taste in a food processor until smooth. Spread over the layers. Chill, covered, for 8 to 10 hours. Invert onto a serving plate and remove the side of the pan.

To garnish, arrange chopped pecans, red bell pepper, green bell pepper, yellow bell pepper, crumbled feta cheese and additional sun-dried tomatoes in concentric circles on the top. Garnish with additional basil leaves. Serve with assorted crackers.

BLOODY MARIA

For Bloody Maria, mix 3 parts Bloody Mary mix and 1 part tequila. Pour over ice in a glass. Garnish with a jalapeño pepper-stuffed olive and a twist of lime.

Mozzarella Crostini

Yield: 3 dozen

1	(16-ounce) loaf unsliced Italian bread	1/2	cup sliced green onions
1/3	cup olive oil	5	to 7 Roma tomatoes, cut into 36 slices
1	garlic clove, minced	1 1/2	cups shredded mozzarella cheese
1/4	teaspoon salt		
1/4	teaspoon pepper		

Cut the bread into thirty-six 1/4- to 1/2-inch slices. Place on a foil-lined baking sheet. Bake at 400 degrees for 5 minutes or until light brown. Combine the olive oil, garlic, salt and pepper in a bowl and mix well. Brush on the bread slices. Sprinkle each with green onions and top with a tomato slice. Sprinkle with cheese. Bake for 5 to 7 minutes or until the cheese melts.

Tex-Mex Caviar

Yield: 6 servings

1	(4-ounce) can chopped black olives	2	garlic cloves
1	(4-ounce) can green chiles	1	tablespoon olive oil
1	medium tomato, chopped	2	tablespoons red wine vinegar
3	green onions, chopped	1	teaspoon white pepper

Combine the olives, green chiles, tomato, green onions, garlic, olive oil, red wine vinegar and white pepper in a bowl and mix well. Chill, covered, until serving time. Remove the garlic and serve with corn chips.

Black-Eyed Pea Dip

Black-eyed peas—fresh, frozen, canned or dried— are eaten everywhere in Texas. They can be gourmet or down-home. Here is a new version of an old-time tradition of serving black-eyed peas on New Year's for "good luck"!
To prepare Black-Eyed Pea Dip, purée two 15-ounce cans black-eyed peas with jalapeño peppers and 2 tablespoons picante sauce in a blender or food processor. Pour into a 1-quart baking dish and cover. Microwave on High for 5 minutes, stirring halfway through. Stir in 1 cup shredded sharp Cheddar cheese. Serve with chips or assorted crackers.

Pepper and Cheese Squares

Yield: 20 servings

6   eggs
1   (5-ounce) can evaporated milk
1   pound Monterey Jack cheese, shredded
1   pound sharp Cheddar cheese, shredded

2   (4-ounce) cans chopped green chiles
3   or 4 finely chopped jalapeño peppers (optional)

Beat the eggs in a bowl using a fork. Add the evaporated milk, Monterey Jack cheese and Cheddar cheese and mix well. Pour 1/2 of the mixture into a buttered 9x13-inch baking dish. Sprinkle with the green chiles and jalapeño peppers. Pour the remaining cheese mixture over the green chiles and peppers. Bake at 350 degrees for 40 minutes. Cool slightly. Cut into 1-inch squares. Garnish with paprika or cayenne pepper.

Fire Crackers

Yield: 40 servings

1   (16-ounce) package frozen phyllo pastry (20 sheets)
2   (12-ounce) jars pickled whole jalapeño peppers, drained

8   ounces Monterey Jack cheese

Thaw the phyllo sheets using the package directions. Cut the stems from the peppers. Cut a slit in the side of each pepper and remove the seeds and membranes. Cut the cheese into pieces to fit inside the peppers. Place the cheese in the peppers. Place the phyllo sheets on a surface sprayed with butter-flavored nonstick cooking spray. Cut into halves across the width of the sheets. Cover the sheets not being used with a damp towel or plastic wrap to prevent drying out. Place 1 phyllo sheet on a surface sprayed with butter nonstick cooking spray. Spray the sheet with butter nonstick cooking spray. Stack another sheet on top of the first and spray with butter nonstick cooking spray. Place 1 pepper on the edge of the short side of the sheets and roll into a tube, twisting and pinching the ends together to seal. Repeat with the remaining phyllo sheets and remaining peppers. Layer in an airtight container with waxed paper separating each layer. Freeze, covered, until ready to bake. Place on a lightly greased baking sheet. Bake at 325 degrees for 15 to 20 minutes or until golden brown.

Tejas Pinwheels

Yield: 10 to 12 servings

1	cup sour cream	1/4	cup chopped green onions
8	ounces cream cheese, softened	1	cup shredded Cheddar cheese
1	(4-ounce) can green chiles, chopped	1	teaspoon garlic powder
1	(4-ounce) can black olives, chopped	•	Chopped jalapeño peppers (optional)
1/4	cup chopped green olives	12	flour tortillas

Beat the sour cream and cream cheese in a mixer bowl until smooth. Add the green chiles, black olives, green olives, green onions, Cheddar cheese, garlic powder and jalapeño peppers and mix well. Microwave the tortillas on High for 45 seconds. Spread the mixture on the tortillas and roll up. Place seamside down on a plate. Chill, covered with plastic wrap, for 1 hour or longer. Remove plastic wrap and cut into 1-inch pieces. Serve with salsa.

Curried Chicken Balls

Yield: 4 dozen

6	ounces cream cheese, softened	3	tablespoons minced green onions
2	tablespoons orange marmalade	3	tablespoons minced celery
2	teaspoons curry powder	1	cup finely chopped toasted macadamia nuts or almonds
3/4	teaspoon salt		
1/4	teaspoon white pepper		
3	cups finely chopped cooked chicken		

Combine the cream cheese, orange marmalade, curry powder, salt and white pepper in a mixer bowl. Beat at medium speed until smooth. Stir in the chicken, green onions and celery. Shape into 1-inch balls and roll in the nuts. Place in an airtight container. Chill, covered for 2 days or freeze for up to 1 month.

Beef and Gorgonzola Meatballs Wrapped in Prosciutto

Yield: 60 servings

2	pounds lean ground round or sirloin	2	teaspoons thyme
1	cup crumbled Gorgonzola cheese or bleu cheese	2	eggs
1/2	cup dry unseasoned bread crumbs	1	tablespoon fresh ground pepper
		1	pound thinly sliced prosciutto, cut into strips

Spray a broiler pan with nonstick cooking spray or line with foil. Combine the ground round, cheese, bread crumbs, thyme, eggs and pepper in a large bowl and mix well. Shape the mixture into 1- or 1 1/2-inch balls. Place each meatball at the end of a strip of prosciutto and roll up; secure with a wooden pick. Place in the prepared pan. Bake at 375 degrees for 15 minutes or until the meatballs are cooked through.

Eggplant in Phyllo Shells

Yield: 40 servings

1	large eggplant, peeled, seeded, finely chopped	5	ounces goat cheese, at room temperature
4	teaspoons olive oil	5	ounces Boursin cheese, at room temperature
4	scallions, finely chopped	1/3	cup frozen orange juice concentrate, thawed
2	teaspoons minced garlic	40	miniature phyllo shells
•	Salt and pepper to taste		
1	large red bell pepper, roasted (page 189)		

Sauté the eggplant in olive oil in a skillet until soft. Add the scallions and garlic. Sauté over low heat for 20 to 30 minutes. Season with salt and pepper. Peel the roasted red pepper. Cut into 1/8- to 1/4-inch strips. Mix the goat cheese, Boursin cheese and orange juice concentrate in a bowl until smooth. Spoon into a pastry bag fitted with a fluted tip. Fill each phyllo shell with the eggplant mixture. Pipe a cheese rosette on top of each. Arrange the red pepper strips over the top.

Note: *Miniature phyllo shells can be found in the frozen food department of your favorite grocery.*

Asparagus "Guacamole"

Yield: 6 to 8 servings

1	pound medium asparagus, rinsed, trimmed	2	tablespoons chopped cilantro
2	tablespoons fresh lime juice	2	tablespoons chopped red bell pepper
2	tablespoons chopped green onions	1/2	tomato, finely chopped
1	(4-ounce) can chopped green chiles	3	dashes of lemon pepper
		•	Dash of Tabasco sauce

Simmer the asparagus in water in a saucepan for 20 minutes or until tender; drain. Process the asparagus and lime juice in a food processor until smooth. Add the green onions, green chiles, cilantro and red pepper. Process until blended. Stir in the tomato, lemon pepper and Tabasco sauce.

Burgundy Mushrooms

Yield: 20 to 24 servings

4	pounds small fresh mushrooms	1 1/2	tablespoons Worcestershire sauce
1	quart burgundy	1	tablespoon MSG (optional)
2	cups boiling water	1	teaspoon garlic powder
4	beef bouillon cubes	1	teaspoon dillseeds
4	chicken bouillon cubes	1	teaspoon ground pepper
2	cups (4 sticks) butter	•	Salt to taste

Combine the mushrooms, burgundy, water, bouillon cubes, butter, Worcestershire sauce, MSG, garlic powder, dillseeds and pepper in a large saucepan. Bring to a slow boil over medium heat and reduce the heat. Simmer, covered, for 5 to 6 hours. Simmer, uncovered, for 3 to 5 hours longer. Season with salt. Serve in a chafing dish with wooden picks.

Say "guacamole" and the first thing that comes to mind is an avocado. Surprise! While this dish offers all the flavor and flair of the Southwest, it is made with asparagus! This results in a delicious and healthy alternative that retains its bright green color and offers all the nutritional value of asparagus with only 1/10 the calories.

Overboard Margaritas

Yield: 6 to 8 servings

1	(12-ounce) can frozen limeade concentrate, thawed	3	tablespoons Triple Sec
1/2	limeade can tequila	3	limeade cans ice cubes

Blend the limeade concentrate, tequila, Triple Sec and ice cubes in a blender until smooth. Serve in glasses with salted rims.

Note: *To salt the rim of a glass, rub a lime section along the glass rim and invert into salt on a plate. Turn the glass until the entire rim is coated with salt.*

Sunrise Mimosas

Yield: 12 to 15 servings

3	cups unsweetened orange juice, chilled	1/2	cup sugar
1/2	cup lemon juice	1/4	cup orange-flavored liqueur
		1	bottle Champagne, chilled

Combine the orange juice, lemon juice, sugar and liqueur in a small punch bowl and stir until the sugar dissolves. Add the Champagne and ice or an ice ring just before serving.

Blushing Bellinis

Yield: 12 to 15 servings

3	(12-ounce) cans peach nectar	1	cup peach schnapps
3	cups white wine	1/2	to 1 cup rum or vodka
2	cups Champagne	1/2	cup confectioners' sugar

Combine the peach nectar, white wine, Champagne, peach schnapps, rum and confectioners' sugar in a large freezer container and stir until the confectioners' sugar is dissolved. Freeze, covered, for 8 to 12 hours. Process in a blender until smooth just before serving.

Slushy Ice Punch

Yield: 30 servings

2	(6-ounce) packages lemon gelatin	1	(46-ounce) can orange drink
6	cups hot water	1	quart apple juice
2	cups sugar	3	tablespoons lemon extract
6	ounces lemon juice	3	tablespoons almond extract
1	(46-ounce) can pineapple juice	2	to 3 quarts ginger ale
		2	to 3 quarts vodka (optional)

Dissolve the gelatin in hot water in a large freezer container. Stir in the sugar, lemon juice, pineapple juice, orange drink, apple juice and flavorings. Freeze, covered, until firm. Remove from the freezer 1 hour before serving and add the ginger ale and vodka.

SCHNAPPS

Schnapps has also been called Holland Gin and it represents those alcoholic beverages produced from grains or potatoes to which different flavorings have been added. Peppermint and peach schnapps are the most familiar, but strawberry, orange, and cinnamon schnapps are also popular. Schnapps is a strong and colorless alcohol that may be enjoyed in a large number of drinks.

By the Bayou

Breads & Brunch

⚓

Armand Bayou
Nature Center

*Armand Bayou Nature Center was created in the early
1970s and named in memory of the environmentalist,
Armand Yramategui. This 2500-acre property
provides visitors with a chance to learn about the
value of our rapidly disappearing natural heritage.
Through education and stewardship programs,
the Center strives to preserve this unique area and the
biological diversity and ecological relationships it contains.
ASSISTANCE LEAGUE® of the Bay Area provides
volunteers and funding for the "Hands on History"
presentations at the Center's Martyn Farm.
Visitors can enjoy the 1890s Martyn Farmhouse,
pictured here, and learn about life on a century-old
Gulf Coast farm and its surrounding ecosystems.*

⚓

A Gathering on the Porch
At Martyn Farm

MARINATED SHRIMP WITH CAPERS, *page 130*
WILD MUSHROOM PÂTÉ WITH BRISTO BRIE CHEESE WAFERS, *page 24*
PROVOLONE TERRINE, *page 28*

SAVIGNON BLANC

CENTER STAGE SALAD, *page 90*
GRILLED PORK TENDERLOIN WITH GARLIC MUSTARD SAUCE, *page 178*
ASPARAGUS VINAIGRETTE, *page 106*
ORZO AND BELL PEPPER SALAD, *page 92*

ZINFANDEL

SUN-DRIED TOMATO BREAD, *page 50*
PESTO SWIRL BREAD, *page 49*

BLANC DE NOIR

ALMOND ANGEL CAKE WITH RASPBERRY SAUCE, *page 209*
SMALL STEAMED CHOCOLATE PUDDINGS, *page 202*

CHAMPAGNE

Bay Oaks Cheese and Scallion Biscuits

Yield: 15 to 20 servings

2 cups flour
1¼ tablespoons baking powder
1 tablespoon sugar
½ teaspoon salt
½ cup (1 stick) butter, cut into pieces
½ teaspoon garlic powder, or 1 garlic clove, minced

⅓ cup (rounded) shredded Cheddar cheese
⅓ cup (rounded) shredded Swiss cheese
⅓ cup finely chopped scallions
¾ to 1 cup buttermilk
• Melted butter

Mix the flour, baking powder, sugar and salt in a large bowl. Cut in ½ cup butter until crumbly. Add the garlic powder, Cheddar cheese, Swiss cheese and scallions and mix lightly with a fork. Make a well in the center. Add the buttermilk gradually, stirring constantly with a fork until moistened; do not overmix. Knead on a lightly floured surface 10 times. Do not over knead the dough. Flatten the dough into an 8-inch circle ¾ inch thick. Cut into 2¼-inch circles. Place on a lightly buttered baking sheet, leaving space between each. Bake at 425 degrees for 12 to 15 minutes or until golden brown. Brush the tops of the biscuits with melted butter. Serve hot.

Executive Chef Bruce Ross of Bay Oaks Country Club was kind enough to share the secret of these Cheese and Scallion Biscuits. These savory treats are one of the many traditions of the country club and a must for our cookbook!

Raisin Scones

Yield: 20 servings

3¹/₄	cups flour	1	cup golden raisins
4	teaspoons cream of tartar	5	tablespoons sugar
2	teaspoons baking soda	1	cup (about) milk
1	teaspoon salt		
6	tablespoons (³/₄ stick) butter or margarine, chilled		

Mix the flour, cream of tartar, baking soda and salt in a large bowl. Cut in the butter until crumbly. Stir in the raisins and sugar. Add enough milk to form a soft sticky dough, stirring constantly. Knead on a lightly floured surface until the dough holds together. Roll into a circle ¹/₂ inch thick. Cut into 2-inch circles. Arrange on a lightly floured baking sheet. Sprinkle the tops lightly with additional flour. Bake at 425 degrees for 10 minutes or until puffed and golden. Serve immediately with butter and jam.

Cinnamon Raisin Twisted Ring

Yield: 6 to 8 servings

1/2 cup chopped pecans	1 teaspoon cinnamon
1/3 cup raisins	1 teaspoon vanilla extract
1/4 cup sifted confectioners' sugar	1 (8-count) package refrigerated
1/4 cup (1/2 stick) butter or margarine, softened	breadsticks
	• Vanilla Glaze (below)

Combine 1/2 of the pecans with the raisins, confectioners' sugar, butter, cinnamon and vanilla in a bowl and mix well. Unroll the breadsticks, pressing the perforations to seal. Spread the raisin mixture over the dough to within 1/2 inch of the edges. Fold in half lengthwise and seal the long edge. Stretch the dough gently into a 24-inch strip and twist slightly. Shape into a circle on an ungreased baking sheet, sealing the ends together. Bake at 350 degrees for 20 to 22 minutes or until golden brown. Cool slightly. Drizzle with Vanilla Glaze. Sprinkle with the remaining pecans.

Vanilla Glaze

1/2 cup confectioners' sugar, sifted	1/4 teaspoon vanilla extract
1 to 2 tablespoons milk	

Combine the confectioners' sugar, milk and vanilla in a bowl and mix until smooth.

Broccoli Corn Bread

Yield: 12 servings

1   (10-ounce) package frozen chopped broccoli, thawed, drained
2   tablespoons chopped onion
3/4   cup small curd cottage cheese

1/2   cup (1 stick) margarine, melted
4   eggs, beaten
1   (8-ounce) package corn bread mix

Combine the broccoli, onion, cottage cheese, margarine and eggs in a bowl and mix well. Stir in the corn bread mix. Pour into a greased 8x10-inch baking pan. Bake at 400 degrees for 20 to 25 minutes or until golden brown.

Note: *May bake in 36 greased miniature muffin cups for 13 to 15 minutes or until golden brown.*

CORN BREAD

This rich and flavorful corn bread is delicious with soup, and you don't even have to prepare a salad or a vegetable to complete the meal. An easy variation is Spinach Corn Bread. Prepare as for Broccoli Corn Bread except substitute one 10-ounce package frozen chopped spinach, thawed and well drained, for the broccoli, increase the onion to 1/2 cup, and add 1/2 teaspoon salt and 1/3 cup buttermilk. This recipe will also yield 2 to 3 dozen miniature muffins.

Fiesta Corn Bread

1 cup cornmeal
1/2 teaspoon baking soda
1 teaspoon salt
2 eggs
1 cup buttermilk
1/3 cup vegetable oil
1 (8-ounce) can cream-style corn

8 ounces sharp Cheddar cheese, shredded
2 garlic cloves, minced
1 small onion, chopped
2 to 3 jalapeño peppers, finely chopped

Mix the cornmeal, baking soda and salt in a bowl. Beat the eggs lightly in a bowl. Stir in the buttermilk. Add to the cornmeal mixture and mix well. Stir in the oil and corn. Mix the cheese, garlic, onion and jalapeño peppers in a bowl. Stir into the batter. Pour into a greased 8x8-inch baking pan. Bake at 375 degrees for 45 to 55 minutes or until brown.

Morning Glory Muffins

Yield: 18 servings

2 cups flour
1 cup sugar
2 teaspoons baking soda
1 teaspoon cinnamon
1 teaspoon nutmeg
1 apple, peeled, grated
1 1/2 cups raisins

1 1/2 cups shredded coconut
1 1/2 cups chopped pecans
1 cup grated carrots
1 cup vegetable oil
3 eggs, beaten
2 teaspoons vanilla extract

Mix the flour, sugar, baking soda, cinnamon and nutmeg in a bowl. Add the apple, raisins, coconut, pecans and carrots and stir until coated. Combine the oil, eggs and vanilla in a bowl and mix well. Add to the apple mixture and stir until moistened; do not overmix. Spoon into greased muffin cups. Bake at 350 degrees for 20 to 25 minutes or until golden brown.

Blue Corn Muffins with Cheddar Cheese and Pine Nuts

Yield: 12 muffins

1	egg	1	teaspoon baking soda
1/2	cup vegetable oil	1	teaspoon baking powder
1/3	cup sugar	3/4	cup shredded white Cheddar cheese
2	teaspoons salt		
3/4	cup buttermilk	2	green onions, finely chopped
1 1/4	cups unbleached flour	1/2	cup pine nuts, toasted
1/2	cup blue cornmeal		

Beat the egg, oil, sugar, salt and buttermilk in a bowl. Mix the flour, cornmeal, baking soda and baking powder in a large bowl. Add the egg mixture and blend just until moistened. Do not overmix. Fold in the cheese, green onions and pine nuts. Fill nonstick muffin cups 2/3 full. Bake at 350 degrees for 30 to 35 minutes or until a wooden pick inserted in the centers come out clean.

PINE NUTS

Pine nuts, also called pignoli, are harvested from pine cones. To toast pine nuts, spread them on a baking sheet and roast in a 350-degree oven for 3 to 5 minutes or until golden brown. Check often because they can burn quickly.

Pumpkin Harvest Muffins

Yield: 24 muffins

3 cups plus 2 tablespoons unbleached flour

3 1/2 teaspoons cinnamon

2 cups sugar

2 tablespoons (1/4 stick) unsalted butter, softened

1/2 cup wheat germ

3/4 teaspoon salt

2 teaspoons baking soda

1/4 teaspoon nutmeg

1 teaspoon cloves

1/4 teaspoon allspice

1 (16-ounce) can pumpkin

3/4 cup vegetable oil

4 eggs, lightly beaten

2 cups grated unpeeled Granny Smith apples

1 cup raisins

Line 24 muffin cups with paper liners or grease the cups. Mix 2 tablespoons of the flour, 2 teaspoons of the cinnamon and 1/2 cup of the sugar in a small bowl. Cut in the butter until crumbly. Mix the remaining 3 cups flour, wheat germ, remaining 1 1/2 cups sugar, salt, baking soda, remaining 1 1/2 teaspoons cinnamon, nutmeg, cloves and allspice in a large bowl. Whisk the pumpkin, oil and eggs in a bowl. Add to the wheat germ mixture and stir until blended. Stir in the apples and raisins. Spoon into the prepared muffin cups. Sprinkle with the butter mixture. Bake at 400 degrees for 20 to 25 minutes or until the tops are golden brown and a wooden pick inserted in the centers comes out clean.

Note: *May spoon into 48 miniature muffin cups and bake for 15 minutes.*

47

Zucchini and Date Wheat Bread

Yield: 2 loaves

3	eggs	1/2	teaspoon baking powder
1	cup vegetable oil	1	teaspoon salt
2	cups sugar	1	tablespoon cinnamon
2	cups grated fresh zucchini	1	cup chopped walnuts
1	tablespoon vanilla extract	1	cup chopped dates
3	cups whole wheat flour	1/2	cup raisins
1	teaspoon baking soda		

Beat the eggs in a mixer bowl until light and fluffy. Add the oil, sugar, zucchini and vanilla and mix until blended. Sift the whole wheat flour, baking soda, baking powder, salt and cinnamon together. Add to the zucchini mixture and blend. Stir in the walnuts, dates and raisins. Pour into 2 greased 4x8-inch or 5x9-inch baking pans. Bake at 325 degrees for 1 hour. Cool in the pans for 15 minutes. Invert onto wire racks to cool completely.

OUT-OF-SIGHT SMOOTHIE

For a delicious, nutritious drink and a good source of calcium, try Out-of-Sight Smoothie. Blend 1 cup plain yogurt, 1/2 cup orange juice, 1/2 cup cranberry juice cocktail, 1 banana, 5 strawberries and 1 cup ice in a blender until the ice is crushed. May add 1/4 block of tofu for extra protein and to make the drink even smoother. Blueberries, pineapple or any other fruit can also be added.

Cheddar Cheese Bread

Yield: 8 to 10 servings

3¹/₃	cups baking mix	2	eggs
2¹/₂	cups shredded Cheddar cheese	1¹/₄	cups milk

Mix the baking mix and cheese in a large bowl. Beat the eggs in a bowl until light and fluffy. Add the milk and beat well. Add to the cheese mixture and mix well. Pour into a greased and floured tube pan. Bake at 350 degrees for 50 minutes. Serve immediately.

Note: *For a spicier variation, add chopped jalapeño peppers to taste and 1 small can corn, drained.*

Pesto Swirl Bread

Yield: 2 loaves

1	(16-ounce) package Hot Roll mix	¹/₂	cup chopped fresh basil, or ¹/₄ cup dried basil leaves
1	cup hot (120 to 130 degrees) water	¹/₂	cup freshly grated Parmesan cheese
2	tablespoons (¹/₄ stick) margarine, softened	1	egg, lightly beaten
1	egg	1	tablespoon coarse salt
¹/₄	cup olive oil	1	tablespoon chopped fresh basil, or 1 teaspoon dried basil
2	garlic cloves, crushed		

Mix the flour and yeast from the roll mix in a large bowl. Add the hot water, margarine and 1 egg and stir until the dough pulls from the side of the bowl. Turn onto a lightly floured surface and shape into a ball. Knead the dough for 5 minutes or until smooth. Cover with a large bowl and let stand for 5 minutes. Divide the dough into halves. Roll each half into a 9x14-inch rectangle. Brush each rectangle with a mixture of the olive oil and garlic. Sprinkle with a mixture of ¹/₂ cup basil and Parmesan cheese. Roll up each rectangle beginning at the long side and pinch each seam to seal. Place the loaves seam side down on a greased baking sheet. Brush lightly with beaten egg. Cover with greased plastic wrap. Let rise for 30 minutes. Remove the plastic wrap. Sprinkle each loaf with a mixture of coarse salt and 1 tablespoon basil. Bake at 350 degrees for 20 to 30 minutes or until golden brown.

Sun-Dried Tomato Bread

Yield: 1 large loaf

2	garlic cloves	3/4	teaspoon rosemary
1/3	cup oil-pack sun-dried tomatoes	3/4	teaspoon pepper
1	bunch scallions	1/3	cup pine nuts, lightly toasted
2 1/2	cups flour	2	tablespoons shortening
2	teaspoons baking powder	2	tablespoons sugar
1 1/4	teaspoons salt	2	eggs
1/2	teaspoon baking soda	1 1/4	cups buttermilk
5	ounces provolone cheese, grated		

Cook the garlic in boiling water to cover in a small saucepan for 15 minutes. Drain the sun-dried tomatoes, reserving 2 tablespoons of the oil. Chop the tomatoes. Cut the scallions into thin slices, including 1 inch of the green portion. Sift the flour, baking powder, salt and baking soda into a large bowl. Add the sun-dried tomatoes, scallions, cheese, rosemary, pepper and pine nuts and toss until combined. Whisk the shortening, reserved oil and sugar in a small bowl until smooth. Drain the garlic and peel. Mash with a fork until smooth. Add to the shortening mixture along with the eggs and buttermilk and mix well. Add to the flour mixture and mix until combined. Pour into a greased 9-inch loaf pan. Bake at 350 degrees for 45 to 50 minutes or until a tester inserted in the center comes out clean. Cool in the pan on a wire rack for 5 minutes. Invert onto the wire rack to cool completely.

Note: *This bread slices best with an electric knife when partially frozen. May store the bread tightly wrapped in the refrigerator for up to 4 days. May bake in 3 greased 3x5-inch loaf pans for 25 to 30 minutes.*

Salsa Bread for the Bread Machine

Yield: 1 (1½-pound) loaf

³/4	cup salsa
¹/3	cup plus 1 tablespoon milk
2	tablespoons (¹/4 stick) butter, softened
3	cups bread flour
2	tablespoons chopped fresh cilantro
2	tablespoons sugar
2	teaspoons bread machine yeast
1½	teaspoons salt

Add the salsa, milk, butter, bread flour, cilantro, sugar, yeast and salt to the bread machine pan in the order recommended by the manufacturer. Set the machine on the basic white bread cycle with medium to normal color setting.

Farmhouse Bread

Yield: 2 loaves

3	envelopes dry yeast
1	cup lukewarm water
1	egg, beaten
6	tablespoons sugar
1	teaspoon salt
6	tablespoons (³/4 stick) butter, melted
1	cup milk
6	cups flour

Dissolve the yeast in the lukewarm water in a small bowl. Combine the egg, sugar, salt, butter and milk in a large mixer bowl and mix well. Stir in the yeast. Add enough flour to form a soft dough. Knead on a lightly floured surface until smooth and elastic or use dough hooks. Let rise, lightly covered, until doubled in bulk. Punch down the dough. Knead on a lightly floured surface. Divide into 2 equal portions. Shape each portion into a loaf and place in 2 greased 5x9-inch loaf pans. Let rise, lightly covered, until doubled in bulk. Bake at 350 degrees for 30 minutes or until light brown and the loaves test done.

CHEDDAR CHEESE CORN SPREAD

Your colorful, zesty Salsa Bread will come to life with this Cheddar Cheese Corn Spread. Mix 3 ounces cream cheese, softened, with 2 tablespoons milk until blended. Add ¹/3 cup shredded Cheddar cheese, ¹/4 cup whole kernel corn, ³/4 teaspoon chili powder and 1 green onion, finely chopped, and mix well. Chill for 1 hour before serving. You can also spread this mixture on flour tortillas, roll up, slice into pinwheels and serve with your favorite salsa.

Country Hot Rolls

Yield: 2 dozen

1	envelope dry yeast	1	teaspoon salt
1/4	cup lukewarm water	1	egg
1/4	cup (1/2 stick) butter	3 1/2	cups flour
1	cup warm milk	•	Butter
3	tablespoons sugar		

Dissolve the yeast in the lukewarm water. Melt 1/4 cup butter in the warm milk in a large mixer bowl. Stir in the sugar and salt. Beat in the egg and yeast. Beat in enough flour gradually to form a soft dough. Place in a buttered bowl, turning to coat the surface. Cover with a pastry cloth. Let rise in a warm place until doubled in bulk. Knead lightly on a lightly floured surface until smooth and elastic, adding additional flour if needed. Shape into 1-inch balls. Place 3 balls in each of 24 greased large muffin cups. Cover with a damp cloth. Let rise for 1 to 2 hours or until doubled in bulk. Bake at 350 degrees for 15 to 20 minutes or until golden brown. Spread the tops with butter and serve hot.

Glazed Orange Rolls

Yield: 2 dozen

6	tablespoons (³/4 stick) butter, softened	3	cups confectioners' sugar
¹/4	cup fresh orange juice	1	recipe Country Hot Rolls dough (page 52)
1	tablespoon orange zest		

*F*or the filling, beat the butter, orange juice and orange zest in a mixer bowl until light and fluffy. Add the confectioners' sugar and beat until smooth.

For Glazed Orange Rolls, prepare the dough. Roll the dough into a 12x15-inch rectangle. Spread ¹/2 of the orange filling over the rectangle. Roll as for a jelly roll. Cut into 24 slices. Place cut side down in greased muffin cups. Let rise, covered, until doubled in bulk. Bake at 400 degrees for 18 to 20 minutes or until golden brown. Spread with the remaining orange filling while hot. Serve immediately.

Note: *Rolls can be cooled on a wire rack covered with a bread cloth and wrapped in foil to serve later. Reheat in a 400-degree oven for 10 to 12 minutes.*

CINNAMON ROLLS

These rolls become delectable Cinnamon Rolls by substituting this filling for the orange filling. For Cinnamon Filling, beat 6 tablespoons butter (³/4 stick), softened, with 3 tablespoons cinnamon and ¹/4 cup water. Beat in 3 cups confectioners' sugar until smooth. Continue as for Glazed Orange Rolls. After baking, store in freezer bags and you will always have a special treat ready for unexpected morning guests.

Crescent Yeast Rolls

Yield: 5 dozen

2	envelopes dry yeast	1	teaspoon salt
1	cup cold water	2	eggs, lightly beaten
1	cup shortening	6	cups flour
1	cup sugar	1/2	cup (1 stick) butter, softened
1	cup boiling water		

Dissolve the yeast in 1 cup cold water for 5 minutes. Combine the shortening, sugar, 1 cup boiling water and salt in a large bowl and mix well. Add the yeast mixture. Do not mix. Add the eggs. Stir in the flour. Let rise, covered, in the refrigerator for 8 to 12 hours. Divide the dough into 3 equal portions. Roll each portion on a lightly floured surface into a circle about 1/4 inch thick. Brush with the butter. Cut each circle into 20 wedges. Roll the wedges up from the wide end. Shape into crescents on ungreased baking sheets. Let rise, covered with a lightweight cloth, in a warm place for 2 to 3 hours. Bake at 400 degrees for 10 to 12 minutes or until golden brown.

Good Morning Oranges

Yield: 8 servings

4	oranges	10	whole cloves
3/4	cup water	•	Zest of 1/2 orange
1	cup sugar	1/2	cup Grand Marnier

Peel the oranges with a sharp knife, removing all white membrane. Cut into 1/2-inch slices and place in an airtight container. Bring the water, sugar, cloves and orange zest to a boil in a saucepan. Boil until the sugar dissolves, stirring frequently. Remove from the heat and cool. Stir in the Grand Marnier. Pour over the oranges. Marinate, covered, in the refrigerator for 8 to 12 hours. Arrange in a bowl and garnish with mint leaves to serve.

Artichoke Bread Pudding

Yield: 8 servings

6	(1/2-inch-thick) slices sourdough bread, trimmed	4	green onions, sliced
1 1/2	cups shredded jalapeño Jack cheese	1	teaspoon dried basil, or 1 tablespoon chopped fresh basil
6	eggs	1/2	teaspoon dried oregano, or 1 1/2 teaspoons fresh oregano
2	egg whites	1/2	teaspoon salt
2 1/2	cups milk	•	Pepper to taste
1	cup sliced mushrooms		
1	(6-ounce) jar marinated artichokes, drained, coarsely chopped		

Place the bread in a greased 9x13-inch baking dish, cutting the bread to fit. Sprinkle with the cheese. Whisk the eggs, egg whites and milk lightly in a medium bowl. Stir in the mushrooms, artichokes, green onions, basil, oregano, salt and pepper. Pour over the cheese. Chill, covered with foil, for 8 to 12 hours. Bake, uncovered, at 325 degrees for 65 to 75 minutes or until the top is puffed and brown.

MINTED BERRIES WITH KIRSCH

To prepare Minted Berries with Kirsch, toss 1 cup raspberries, 1 cup blackberries, 1 cup blueberries and 1 cup sliced strawberries with 1 1/2 tablespoons sugar and 3 tablespoons kirsch. Chill, covered, for 1 hour or longer, stirring occasionally. To serve, spoon into a serving bowl and garnish with mint leaves.

Tortilla-Wrapped Scrambled Eggs with Green Chiles

Yield: 4 servings

2	tablespoons olive oil	•	Salt to taste
1/2	cup chopped onion	1	tablespoon chopped cilantro
2	garlic cloves, minced	1/2	cup rinsed, drained canned
1/4	cup chopped roasted poblano		black beans
	chiles	4	flour tortillas, warmed
1	medium tomato, chopped	1/4	cup sour cream
8	eggs	1/4	cup salsa

Heat the olive oil in a medium skillet. Add the onion. Sauté for 3 minutes or until translucent. Add the garlic. Sauté for 1 minute longer. Stir in the poblano chiles and tomato. Remove from the heat. Beat the eggs in a large bowl until light and fluffy. Season with salt. Return the skillet to the heat and add the beaten eggs. Add the cilantro and black beans. Cook until the eggs are set, stirring constantly to scramble. Spoon into the flour tortillas and top with the sour cream and salsa.

SHELF-STABLE TORTILLAS:

Flour tortillas are a favorite bread item of the shuttle astronauts. Tortillas provide an easy and acceptable solution to the bread crumb and microgravity handling problem, and have been used on most shuttle missions since 1985. However, mold is a problem with commercially packaged tortillas on missions. A shelf-stable tortilla was developed for use on the shuttle with extended mission lengths.

➤

Bacon and Swiss Cheese Strata

Yield: 8 to 12 servings

- Butter
- 12 slices white bread, trimmed
- 1 pound Swiss cheese, grated
- 8 ounces fresh mushrooms, sliced
- 1 to 2 cups crumbled, fried bacon
- 2 cups milk
- 4 eggs
- 1 teaspoon Beau Monde seasoning
- 1 teaspoon Worcestershire sauce
- 2 teaspoons prepared mustard
- Dash of seasoned salt

Spread butter on both sides of the bread. Place in a greased 10x15-inch baking dish. Layer the cheese, mushrooms and bacon over the bread. Combine the milk, eggs, Beau Monde seasoning, Worcestershire sauce, mustard and seasoned salt in a bowl and mix well. Pour over the layers. Chill, covered, for 8 to 12 hours. Remove from the refrigerator 1 hour before baking. Bake, uncovered, at 325 degrees for 1 hour. Let stand for 15 minutes before serving.

'Tato Tacos

Yield: 10 to 12 servings

- 1 pound bulk hot sausage
- 1 (2-pound) package frozen hash brown potatoes
- 1 green bell pepper, chopped
- 1 red bell pepper, chopped
- 1 cup chopped onion
- 3 ribs celery, finely chopped
- 8 eggs, beaten
- 1 pound Cheddar cheese, grated
- Flour tortillas
- Picante sauce

Brown the sausage in a skillet, stirring until crumbly; drain. Add the hash brown potatoes, green pepper, red pepper, onion, celery and eggs and mix well. Pour into a 9x13-inch baking dish sprayed with nonstick cooking spray. Bake at 350 degrees for 45 minutes. Sprinkle with cheese. Bake until the cheese is melted. To serve, place a scoop of the mixture in a warmed tortilla, add some picante sauce and roll up.

The tortillas are stabilized by a combination of modified atmosphere packaging, pH (acidity), and water activity. Mold growth is inhibited by removing the oxygen from the package. This is accomplished by packaging in a high-barrier container in a nitrogen atmosphere with an oxygen scavenger."

(NASA Facts published by NASA at the Lyndon B. Johnson Space Center, July, 1996)

Mexican Brunch Casserole

Yield: 6 to 8 servings

1	pound bulk hot sausage	1/2	cup chopped green onions
6	eggs, beaten	2	slices bread, cubed
2	cups milk	2	cups grated sharp Cheddar
1	teaspoon dry mustard		cheese or Mexican blend
1	teaspoon salt		cheese

Brown the sausage in a skillet, stirring until crumbly; drain. Combine the eggs, milk, dry mustard and salt in a bowl and mix well. Add the sausage, green onions and bread and mix well. Pour into a greased 8x10-inch baking dish. Sprinkle the cheese on top. Chill, covered, for 8 to 12 hours. Let stand at room temperature for 45 minutes. Bake, uncovered, at 350 degrees for 45 to 60 minutes or until set. Serve with flour tortillas, pico de gallo and guacamole.

Tomato Pesto Tart

Yield: 4 or 5 servings

4	ounces pesto	1	tablespoon olive oil
1	(9-inch) tart shell, baked	2	to 3 ounces goat cheese, crumbled
3	tomatoes, thinly sliced	1/4	cup grated Parmesan cheese
10	Greek olives, seeded, chopped		

Spread the pesto in the tart shell. Layer the tomato slices in concentric circles over the pesto. Sprinkle with the olives. Drizzle with olive oil. Sprinkle with the goat cheese and Parmesan cheese. Bake at 425 degrees for 15 to 20 minutes or until the cheese melts.

Southern-Style Sausage and Grits

Yield: 8 to 10 servings

1	pound bulk hot sausage	3	tablespoons butter, melted
3	cups cooked grits	3	cups shredded Cheddar cheese
1 1/2	cups milk	•	Salt and pepper to taste
3	eggs, beaten		

Brown the sausage in a skillet, stirring until crumbly; drain. Combine the sausage, cooked grits, milk and eggs in a large bowl and mix well. Stir in the cheese. Season with salt and pepper. Spoon into a buttered 9x13-inch glass baking dish. Bake at 350 degrees for 1 hour.

Note: *May assemble the night before, chill and bake in the morning. This recipe reheats well in the microwave, too. Cook 3/4 cup uncooked grits in 3 cups of boiling water to obtain 3 cups cooked grits.*

Jack Quiche with Ham and Tomato

Yield: 6 servings

5	eggs	1	(4-ounce) can chopped green chiles, drained
1	tablespoon (¹/₈ stick) butter, melted	¹/₂	cup chopped cooked ham
¹/₄	cup plus 2 teaspoons flour	1	tomato, sliced
¹/₂	teaspoon baking powder		
1	cup cottage cheese		
2	cups shredded Monterey Jack cheese		

Combine the eggs, butter, flour and baking powder in a bowl and mix well. Stir in the cottage cheese, Monterey Jack cheese, green chiles and ham. Spoon into a greased quiche dish. Bake at 400 degrees for 10 minutes. Reduce the oven temperature to 350 degrees. Arrange the tomato slices over the top. Bake for 20 to 25 minutes or until set. Serve warm garnished with sour cream and salsa.

Cream Cheese Biscuits

Yield: 2 dozen

6	ounces cream cheese, softened	2	cups flour
1	cup (2 sticks) butter, softened		

Beat the cream cheese and butter in a mixer bowl until light and fluffy. Add the flour and beat until smooth. Shape into long rolls 2 inches in diameter. Roll each in waxed paper. Chill for 8 to 12 hours or freeze in the freezer. Slice 1¹/₄ inches thick. Arrange on an ungreased baking sheet. Bake at 400 degrees for 10 minutes.

Note: *These biscuits will not rise and look like traditional biscuits.*

Zucchini Nibbles

Yield: 4 to 6 servings

3	cups shredded or chopped zucchini	1/4	teaspoon pepper
1	medium onion, chopped	1/2	cup vegetable oil
4	eggs or equivalent amount of egg substitute	1	cup baking mix
		1	tablespoon chopped parsley
1/4	cup grated Parmesan cheese	1/2	cup shredded Cheddar cheese

Combine the zucchini, onion, eggs, Parmesan cheese, pepper and oil in a large bowl and mix well. Stir in the baking mix, parsley and Cheddar cheese. Spoon into an 8x8-inch baking pan sprayed with nonstick cooking spray. Bake at 350 degrees for 45 to 55 minutes or until the top is golden brown.

German Apple Puffed Pancake

Yield: 6 to 8 servings

1	(8-ounce) package dried apples, or 2 cups sliced peeled apples	1	cup milk
		1	teaspoon sugar
6	tablespoons (3/4 stick) butter or margarine	1/2	teaspoon vanilla extract
		1/4	teaspoon salt
6	eggs or equivalent amount of egg substitute	1	cup flour

Pour enough boiling water over the dried apples to cover in a large bowl. Let stand for 5 to 15 minutes; drain. Place the butter in a 9x13-inch baking pan. Heat at 400 degrees until melted, checking frequently. Process the eggs, milk, sugar, vanilla and salt in a blender until lightly mixed. Add the flour and process until blended. Pour into a large bowl. Stir in the drained dried apples. Pour into the melted butter in the pan. Bake for 20 to 25 minutes or until fluffy and golden brown. Serve immediately with confectioners' sugar and jam.

Note: *Chopped apricots, cherries, dates, figs, pears, raisins or dried currants may be substituted for the dried apples.*

French Toast with Grand Marnier and Berries

Yield: 4 or 5 servings

1	pound French bread	2	cups maple syrup
2	cups orange juice	1/2	cup (1 stick) butter
2	cups half-and-half	3/4	cup blueberries
6	eggs	3/4	cup sliced strawberries
1/2	cup sugar	1	banana, sliced
1 1/2	teaspoons Grand Marnier	1	cup sifted confectioners'
1/2	teaspoon vanilla extract		sugar
1/2	cup (1 stick) butter	1	can whipped cream

For the French toast, cut the bread into 1 1/2-inch slices. Combine the orange juice, half-and-half, eggs, sugar, Grand Marnier and vanilla in a bowl and mix well. Add the bread. Soak for 20 minutes or longer. Sauté the bread in batches in enough butter to coat a large skillet for 4 minutes and turn over. Sauté for 4 minutes longer. Keep the bread slices warm in a 250-degree oven.

For the fruit syrup, combine the maple syrup and 1/2 cup butter in a small saucepan. Heat until the butter is melted. Add the blueberries, strawberries and banana.

To serve, place 2 or 3 pieces of toast on each serving plate. Sprinkle with confectioners' sugar. Pour about 1/3 cup of the fruit syrup over the toast. Top with a dollop of whipped cream.

BURGUNDY SANGRIA WITH STRAWBERRIES

To prepare Burgundy Sangria with Strawberries, stir 1 chilled bottle burgundy, 1/2 cup fresh lemon juice, 1/2 cup orange juice, 1/2 cup sugar and 1/4 cup brandy in a large pitcher until the sugar is dissolved. Cut 1 lemon and 1 orange into slices and stir into the mixture. Chill in the refrigerator. When ready to serve, add 1 chilled 10-ounce bottle club soda. Pour over ice in glasses and garnish with strawberry halves.

Baked French Toast with Orange Zest

Yield: 8 servings

1/4 cup (1/2 stick) unsalted butter	4 eggs, beaten
1/3 cup sugar	2/3 cup orange juice
1/4 teaspoon cinnamon	8 slices white bread
1 teaspoon grated orange zest	• Confectioners' sugar

Place the butter in a 9x13-inch baking pan. Bake at 325 degrees until melted. Sprinkle a mixture of the sugar, cinnamon and orange zest evenly over the butter. Mix the eggs and orange juice in a bowl. Dip the bread slices in the egg mixture. Arrange in a single layer in the butter in the pan. Bake for 15 minutes. Turn over the bread with a spatula. Bake for 10 minutes longer or until golden brown. Sprinkle with confectioners' sugar.

Note: *May use thicker bread such as French bread, but let the bread soak in the egg mixture in the refrigerator for 8 to 12 hours.*

Tex-Mex Waffles

Yield: 8 servings

1/2 cup chopped red bell pepper	1/4 teaspoon salt
1/2 cup chopped green bell pepper	3 eggs
1/2 cup chopped green onions	1 cup plain yogurt
1 teaspoon vegetable oil	1/2 cup milk
1 cup flour	1/3 cup butter or margarine, melted
1 cup yellow cornmeal	• Melted jalapeño pepper jelly
1 tablespoon baking powder	• Shredded Cheddar cheese

Sauté the red pepper, green pepper and green onions in the oil in a medium saucepan for 5 minutes or until tender crisp. Mix the flour, cornmeal, baking powder and salt in a large bowl. Whisk the eggs in a bowl until lightly beaten. Beat in the yogurt, milk and melted butter. Add to the flour mixture and stir until just combined but still lumpy. Fold in the sautéed vegetables. Pour about 1 to 1 1/2 cups batter onto a hot greased waffle iron. Bake until brown using the manufacturer's directions. Repeat with the remaining batter, keeping the baked waffles warm. To serve, top with melted jalapeño jelly and sprinkle with cheese.

Note: *If the batter thickens while standing, add a little milk.*

Apple Sangria

Yield: 20 servings

1	(6-ounce) can frozen orange juice concentrate	1/4	teaspoon cinnamon
1	(6-ounce) can frozen lemonade concentrate	1	quart sparkling water or club soda
1	(6-ounce) can frozen apple juice concentrate	•	Slices of orange, lemon and apple
1	(25-ounce) bottle apple juice or apple cider		

Combine the orange juice concentrate, lemonade concentrate, apple juice concentrate, apple juice and cinnamon in a large pitcher and mix well. Chill until ready to serve. To serve, add the sparkling water and fruit slices and pour over ice in glasses.

Delta Mint Tea

Yield: 1 gallon

7	individual-size tea bags	•	Juice of 7 lemons
12	sprigs of mint	2	cups sugar
•	Peels of 3 lemons	8	cups water
8	cups boiling water		

Steep the tea, mint and lemon peels in 8 cups boiling water in a saucepan for 12 minutes. Stir in the lemon juice and sugar. Strain the mixture into a large pitcher and add 8 cups water.

Setting Sail
Soups & Salads

⚓

South Shore Harbour Marina and Lighthouse

South Shore Harbour has long been a safe haven
for boaters in the Clear Lake area. Before its development
as one of the premier yachting centers along the Gulf Coast,
South Shore was an abandoned clay pit or 'hurricane hole'
used by area boaters who were seeking shelter
during seasonal tropical storms.
The lighthouse at South Shore Harbour, which is registered
on the U.S. Coast Guard charts as a landmark
and aid to navigation, was moved to its present location
from Ports of Call, a once popular NASA Rd. 1 restaurant.
It is a 68-foot steel-frame tower with plywood siding and shows
a rotating white light which is visible for 12 miles.

Ladies Luncheon On Board

PINOT NOIR

Shrimp Bisque

Yield: 10 servings

1	pound medium shrimp	2	tablespoons long grain rice
3	tablespoons butter	2	medium tomatoes, peeled, chopped
2	(14-ounce) cans low-sodium chicken stock	1	teaspoon salt
1	cup dry white wine	1/4	teaspoon cayenne pepper
1/2	cup water	1	bay leaf
2	medium carrots, chopped	1 1/2	cups heavy cream
1	rib celery, chopped	3	tablespoons dry sherry
1	medium onion, chopped		

Peel the shrimp and devein, reserving the shells. Melt 1 tablespoon of the butter in a 5-quart saucepan. Add the reserved shrimp shells. Cook for 5 minutes, stirring frequently. Add the chicken stock, wine and water. Bring to a boil and reduce the heat. Simmer, covered, for 15 minutes. Strain into a small bowl, pressing all the liquid from the shells. Discard the shells.

Melt the remaining 2 tablespoons butter in the same saucepan. Add the shrimp. Cook for 5 minutes or until the shrimp turn pink, stirring occasionally. Remove the shrimp to a small bowl. Add the carrots, celery and onion to the saucepan. Cook for 10 to 12 minutes or until tender, stirring occasionally. Return the strained stock to the saucepan. Add the rice, tomatoes, salt, cayenne pepper and bay leaf. Bring to a boil and reduce the heat. Simmer, covered, for 20 minutes. Remove from the heat and discard the bay leaf. Stir in the shrimp.

Purée the shrimp mixture in small batches in a blender, pouring the puréed mixture into a large bowl after each batch is processed. Return all of the puréed mixture to the saucepan. Add the heavy cream and sherry. Cook over medium heat until heated through; do not boil. Ladle into soup bowls and garnish with chives.

Serving wine with soup is always tricky because you have a liquid with a liquid. Some prefer to eliminate wine with this course, but these are good suggestions.

Clear soups
sherry or madeira

Cream soups
sauvignon blanc, Vouvray

Hearty soups, such as French onion, black bean and minestrone
cabernet sauvignon, zinfandel

Crab and Spinach Bisque

1/2 cup (1 stick) butter	• Dash of thyme
2 cups chopped onions	1/4 cup flour
1/2 cup chopped celery	4 cups heavy cream, heated
1/2 cup chopped green bell pepper	2 (10-ounce) packages frozen
3 tablespoons chopped parsley	chopped spinach, thawed, drained
1 tablespoon Worcestershire sauce	2 cups chicken broth, heated
1 bay leaf	• Salt and pepper to taste
• Dash of basil	2 pounds lump crab meat

Melt the butter in a large saucepan. Add the onions, celery, green pepper, parsley, Worcestershire sauce, bay leaf, basil and thyme. Sauté for 3 to 5 minutes or until cooked through. Add the flour and blend well. Add the heated cream. Simmer for 10 minutes. Purée the spinach and chicken broth in a food processor. Add to the cream mixture. Season with salt and pepper. Add the lump crab meat. Cook until heated through; do not boil. Discard the bay leaf before serving.

Cucumber Avocado Bisque

Yield: 6 to 8 servings

1 medium cucumber, peeled, shredded	1/2 cup heavy cream
1 medium avocado, peeled, pitted	2 tablespoons fresh lemon juice
3 green onions, chopped	• Dash of cayenne pepper
1/2 cup sour cream	• Dash of chopped parsley

Process the cucumber, avocado, green onions, sour cream, heavy cream, lemon juice and cayenne pepper in a food processor for 10 to 15 seconds or until blended. Chill, covered, for 8 to 12 hours to enhance the flavor. Pour into a soup tureen. Sprinkle with parsley. Serve in demitasse cups.

Note: *Serve this soup within 2 days of preparation, since the soup turns brown easily.*

Squash Bisque

Yield: 12 servings

1	cup chopped onion	1	quart homemade chicken broth (page 76)
1/2	cup (1 stick) butter, melted	1	tablespoon salt
2	medium white potatoes, sliced	1/2	teaspoon cayenne pepper, or to taste
2	carrots, sliced	1	cup heavy cream
4	cups sliced yellow squash		

Sauté the onion in the butter in a large saucepan until translucent. Add the vegetables, broth, salt and cayenne pepper. Cook, covered, over low heat for 45 minutes. Purée in batches in a food processor or blender and return to the saucepan. Stir in the cream and adjust the seasonings. Cook until heated through; do not boil. Ladle into soup bowls and garnish with paprika.

Mallorca's Gazpacho Andalucian

Yield: 4 servings

2	cups chopped cucumbers	1/4	cup olive oil
3/4	cup chopped Spanish onion	1/4	cup vegetable oil
2	cups chopped green bell peppers	5	teaspoons white vinegar
3	cups chopped tomatoes	2	garlic cloves
1/4	cup French bread cubes, soaked in water and squeezed dry	1	tablespoon mayonnaise
		•	Salt to taste
		•	Dash of cumin

Reserve 2 tablespoons of each vegetable for garnish. Mix the remaining vegetables, bread, olive oil, vegetable oil, vinegar, garlic, mayonnaise, salt and cumin in a large bowl. Blend in batches in a blender. Strain into a large bowl. Chill, covered, for several hours. Ladle into chilled soup plates. Garnish with the reserved vegetables and toasted bread cubes.

Chef Jaime Duran, his wife Rosario, and their children Jaime Antonio and Martin moved to Houston in the Fall of 1979 from Mallorca, Spain. He studied under Master Chef Bartolome Esteva Jofre in Mallorca and went on to become head chef of the finest hotels on the island. He later worked in England and Scotland before coming to America. After the family moved to Houston, they were terribly homesick so they decided to name the family business "Mallorca" as they knew they would be at work most of the day and thus would always be in Mallorca. Chef Jaime has created dishes in honor of his family and most recently for his beloved Mother Teresa.

—

Cavanagh's Cream of Poblano Soup

Yield: 4 servings

3 (6-inch) corn tortillas, cut into eighths	1/2 teaspoon chopped garlic
2 tablespoons flour	2 tablespoons canola oil
1 teaspoon cumin	2 tablespoons (1/4 stick) butter
1/2 teaspoon chili powder	3 cups chicken stock
1/2 teaspoon salt	1/2 cup half-and-half
1/2 teaspoon pepper	1/2 cup chopped roasted chicken
1/2 cup finely chopped onion	1/2 cup shredded Monterey Jack cheese
1/2 cup finely chopped poblano pepper	

Process the tortillas in a food processor until finely chopped. Add the flour, cumin, chili powder, salt and pepper. Process until the consistency of cornmeal. Sauté the onion, poblano pepper and garlic in canola oil in a stockpot over medium-high heat until the onion is transparent. Stir in the butter until melted. Add the ground tortillas and mix well to form a roux. Cook for 4 to 5 minutes, whisking constantly; do not scorch. Whisk in the chicken stock gradually. Add the half-and-half. Bring to a slow simmer. Simmer for 7 to 10 minutes. Do not boil.

To serve, stir in the chicken. Ladle into soup bowls and top each with cheese. Garnish with additional chopped poblano pepper and additional tortilla strips.

Villa Capri's Potato Soup with Brie

Yield: 8 servings

1	leek bulb	2	cups heavy cream
3	tablespoons unsalted butter	1	cup dry sherry
2	potatoes, peeled, cut into 1/4-inch pieces	7	tablespoons cornstarch
2	cups finely sliced fresh mushrooms	3	green onions, finely sliced
		•	Salt and white pepper to taste
4	cups vegetable broth	•	Croutons with Brie (at right)
		•	Chopped parsley

Cut the leek bulb into halves lengthwise. Cut into 1/4-inch slices. Heat the butter in a large heavy saucepan over medium heat until foamy. Add the potatoes, leek and mushrooms. Sauté for 5 minutes. Add the broth and bring to a boil. Add the cream. Return to a boil and reduce the heat. Add the sherry gradually to the cornstarch in a small bowl, stirring constantly until smooth. Add enough of the cornstarch mixture to the soup to thicken to the desired consistency, stirring constantly.

Return the soup to a boil. Boil for 3 minutes or until the flavor of the cornstarch disappears. Stir in the green onions. Season with salt and white pepper. Ladle into ovenproof bowls and top each serving with a Crouton with Brie, cheese side up. Broil for 30 seconds or until the Brie is melted and has formed a light golden crust. Sprinkle with chopped parsley. Serve at once while very hot.

CROUTONS WITH BRIE

To prepare Croutons with Brie, cut 1/4 of a baguette into eight 1/4-inch-thick slices. Place on a baking sheet. Bake at 300 degrees for 10 minutes or until golden brown. Cut the Brie cheese into 1/4-inch slices and completely cover the croutons with the cheese to prevent the croutons from burning.

Southwest Tomato Soup

Yield: 8 servings

1/2 cup olive oil	1 1/2 teaspoons chopped fresh garlic
1 large yellow onion, julienned	1 (32-ounce) can crushed tomatoes
1 green bell pepper, julienned	1 cup chicken broth
1 poblano pepper, julienned	1 1/2 cups sherry
1 medium jalapeño pepper, julienned	1 bunch fresh cilantro, chopped
1 (4-ounce) can green chiles, julienned	• Salt and cayenne pepper to taste

Heat the olive oil in a 4-quart stockpot over high heat. Add the onion, green pepper, poblano pepper, jalapeño pepper, green chiles and garlic. Sauté for 15 minutes. Reduce the heat to medium. Add the tomatoes, chicken broth and sherry. Increase the heat to high. Bring the mixture to a boil and reduce the heat. Simmer for 45 to 60 minutes. Stir in the cilantro. Season with salt and cayenne pepper.

La Madeleine® French Bakery and Café Tomato Basil Soup

Yield: 8 servings

4	cups chopped, peeled tomatoes	•	Salt to taste
4	cups tomato juice	1/4	teaspoon cracked pepper
12	to 14 fresh basil leaves, plus more for garnish	•	La Madeleine® French Bakery and Café baguette or sourdough loaf
1	cup whipping cream		
1/2	cup (1 stick) sweet unsalted butter, softened		

Combine the tomatoes and juice in a large saucepan. Simmer over medium-low heat for 30 minutes. Remove from the heat and cool slightly. Process with the basil in batches in a blender or food processor until puréed. Return to the saucepan. Add the cream and butter. Cook over low heat until the cream and butter are incorporated, stirring constantly. Season with salt and pepper. Ladle into soup bowls and garnish with additional basil. Serve with the baguette or sourdough loaf.

Peanut Bisque

Yield: 8 servings

1/2	cup chopped celery	1/4	teaspoon salt
1/2	cup chopped onion	1/8	teaspoon white pepper
6	tablespoons (3/4 stick) unsalted butter	1	teaspoon Hungarian paprika
3	tablespoons flour	3	drops of Tabasco sauce
4	cups chicken stock	2 1/2	cups half-and-half
1/2	cup plus 1 tablespoon creamy peanut butter	•	Chopped chives to taste

Sauté the celery and onion in melted butter in a stockpot until tender. Process in a blender until smooth. Return to the stockpot. Stir in the flour. Add the chicken stock gradually, stirring constantly. Bring to a boil. Stir in the peanut butter, salt, white pepper, paprika and Tabasco sauce. Remove from the heat. Stir in the half-and-half. Return to the heat. Heat just to serving temperature; do not boil. Ladle into soup bowls and sprinkle with chives.

Chicken Tortilla Soup

Yield: 8 servings

1/2	cup flour	1	large onion, chopped
1/2	tablespoon pepper	1/2	cup chopped celery
2	teaspoons cumin	1	to 2 green bell peppers, chopped
1 1/2	teaspoons minced garlic	1/4	cup chicken bouillon
1	tablespoon chili powder	8	cups homemade chicken broth (at left)
1	teaspoon thyme	1	to 2 cups chopped cooked chicken
•	Salt to taste	1	to 2 tablespoons minced cilantro
10	to 12 corn tortillas		
1/2	cup (1 stick) butter or margarine		
1	teaspoon olive oil		

Combine the flour, pepper, cumin, garlic, chili powder, thyme and salt in a food processor container. Add the tortillas 1 at a time, processing after each addition until ground. Melt the butter in the olive oil in a large heavy saucepan. Add the onion, celery and green peppers. Sauté until tender. Add the chicken bouillon. Cook until the mixture is blended, stirring frequently. Stir in the ground tortilla mixture. Cook until the roux is thickened, stirring constantly. Add the homemade chicken broth 1 cup at a time, stirring until of the desired consistency. Add chopped chicken. Sprinkle with cilantro. Ladle into soup bowls. Garnish with chopped avocado, sour cream, shredded Cheddar cheese and tortilla chips.

Coastal Crab Chowder

Yield: 6 to 8 servings

1	tablespoon (¹/₈ stick) butter		2	cups chicken stock
2	carrots, chopped		¹/₂	cup dry white wine
2	ribs celery, chopped		1	pound lump crab meat
1	medium onion, chopped		1	cup half-and-half
1	teaspoon dill		2	tablespoons sherry
•	Salt to taste		•	Freshly ground pepper to taste
1	bay leaf		•	Strips of fresh chives
2	tablespoons flour			

Melt the butter in a 6-quart stockpot. Add the carrots, celery, onion, dill, salt and bay leaf. Sauté for 5 minutes. Stir in the flour. Cook for 30 seconds. Stir in the chicken stock and wine. Simmer, covered, over low heat for 15 minutes or until the vegetables are tender. Discard the bay leaf. Process the mixture a small amount at a time in a blender or food processor until chunks are smaller and return to the stockpot. Add the crab meat, half-and-half and sherry. Cook until heated through, stirring constantly. Season with pepper. Ladle into soup bowls and arrange strips of chives across the top.

Seafood Gumbo

Yield: 25 to 30 servings

5	pounds peeled shrimp	2	(15-ounce) cans tomatoes, chopped
•	Salt and black pepper to taste		
•	Cayenne pepper to taste	3/4	to 1 (10-ounce) can tomatoes with green chiles
1 1/2	cups vegetable oil		
3	cups flour	1	(15-ounce) can tomato sauce
4	large onions, chopped	•	Worcestershire sauce to taste
3	large bell peppers, chopped	1	(10-ounce) package frozen okra
1/2	stalk celery, chopped		
6	to 8 garlic cloves, chopped	2	pints oysters
2	links kielbasa sausage	1	pound lump crab meat

Boil the shrimp in enough water to cover seasoned with salt, black pepper and cayenne pepper in a stockpot for 5 minutes. Turn off the heat and let stand, covered, for 5 minutes. Drain the shrimp, reserving the liquid. Combine the vegetable oil and flour in a cast-iron skillet. Cook over medium-low heat until the roux is dark brown, stirring constantly to prevent scorching.

Sauté the onions, bell peppers, celery and garlic in a small amount of vegetable oil or nonstick cooking spray in a skillet until wilted. Boil the sausage in water to cover in a saucepan to remove some of the fat; drain and discard the liquid. Cut the sausage into 1/4-inch slices.

Combine the roux, sautéed vegetables, reserved shrimp liquid, tomatoes, tomatoes with green chiles and tomato sauce in a large stockpot and mix well. Add salt, black pepper and Worcestershire sauce. Bring to a simmer, stirring frequently. Add the okra, sausage, shrimp, oysters and crab meat. Simmer for several hours. Serve with filé (an optional condiment) over cooked medium grain rice.

Note: *For gumbo with less fat, omit the vegetable oil and spread the flour thinly on a baking sheet. Bake in a 300-degree oven for 3 to 5 hours or until the desired degree of brownness, stirring every 20 to 30 minutes to prevent scorching.*

Apricot Melba

Yield: 12 to 18 servings

Apricot Layer
1½ teaspoons unflavored gelatin
⅓ cup cold orange juice
1 (17-ounce) can apricots
1 (3-ounce) package lemon
  gelatin
1 tablespoon lemon juice

Cream Cheese Layer
3 ounces cream cheese, softened
2 tablespoons mayonnaise
2 teaspoons milk
2 tablespoons chopped pecans

Raspberry Layer
1½ teaspoons unflavored gelatin
¼ cup cold water
1 (10-ounce) package frozen
  raspberries, thawed
2 tablespoons lemon juice
1 (3-ounce) package raspberry
  gelatin
1 cup boiling water

Dressing
1 cup mayonnaise
¼ cup whipping cream, whipped

For the apricot layer, soften 1½ teaspoons unflavored gelatin in orange juice in a small bowl. Purée the undrained apricots in a blender. Pour into a saucepan. Bring to a boil. Stir in the lemon gelatin and softened gelatin until dissolved. Stir in 1 tablespoon lemon juice. Pour into a 6-cup gelatin mold or a 9x9-inch pan. Chill until set.

For the cream cheese layer, beat the cream cheese, 2 tablespoons mayonnaise and milk in a mixer bowl until smooth. Stir in the pecans. Spread over the apricot layer. Chill until the top is set.

For the raspberry layer, soften 1½ teaspoons unflavored gelatin in ¼ cup cold water in a small bowl. Drain the raspberries, reserving the juice. Combine the reserved juice with 2 tablespoons lemon juice in a 1-cup measure. Add enough cold water to measure 1 cup. Dissolve the softened gelatin and raspberry gelatin in 1 cup boiling water in a saucepan. Stir in the raspberry juice mixture and raspberries. Let stand until cool. Spoon over the cream cheese layer. Chill until set.

For the dressing and to serve, fold 1 cup mayonnaise into the whipped cream in a bowl. Unmold the gelatin onto a serving dish. Serve with the whipped cream mixture.

Bing Cherry Festive Salad

Yield: 8 servings

1	cup Bing cherry juice	2	(14-ounce) cans Bing cherries,
1/2	cup sweet sherry		drained
3	(3-ounce) packages cherry gelatin	•	Sour Cream Coconut Dressing
1	cup sugar		(below)
3	cups orange juice		

Heat the cherry juice and sherry in a small saucepan. Combine with the gelatin and sugar in a bowl and stir until dissolved. Stir in the orange juice. Chill until cool. Stir in the cherries. Pour into a large ring-mold or 9x13-inch dish. Chill until set. Unmold the gelatin onto a serving plate. Fill the center with Sour Cream Coconut Dressing or serve in a separate dish.

Sour Cream Coconut Dressing

1	cup sour cream	1/2	cup confectioners' sugar
1/2	cup mayonnaise	2	tablespoons Grand Marnier
1	cup shredded coconut		

Combine the sour cream, mayonnaise, coconut and confectioners' sugar in a bowl and mix well. Stir in the Grand Marnier. Chill until serving time.

Blueberry Spinach Salad

Yield: 8 servings

Blueberry Vinaigrette
1   shallot, minced
1/2 pint fresh blueberries
3   tablespoons sugar
1   teaspoon salt
1/3 cup raspberry vinegar
1   cup vegetable oil

Salad
2   bunches leaf spinach, trimmed
1   pint fresh blueberries
2/3 cup crumbled bleu cheese
1/2 cup chopped toasted pecans

For the blueberry vinaigrette, process the shallot, 1/2 pint blueberries, sugar, salt, raspberry vinegar and vegetable oil in a blender until smooth.

For the salad, rinse the spinach and pat dry. Combine with 1 pint blueberries, bleu cheese and pecans in a bowl. Add the blueberry vinaigrette and toss to mix well.

Red, White and Blue Salad

Yield: 8 servings

1   pound spinach, trimmed
1   small bunch green onions, chopped
1/2 cup slivered almonds, toasted
1   pint strawberries
1   cup blueberries
1   cup shredded Monterey Jack cheese
•   Raspberry Vinaigrette (at right)

Rinse the spinach and pat dry. Tear into pieces and place in a salad bowl. Add the green onions and toss to mix well. Sprinkle the top with almonds. Place the strawberries in the center. Surround the strawberries with blueberries. Sprinkle the cheese over the top or arrange around the edge of the bowl. Serve with Raspberry Vinaigrette.

RASPBERRY VINAIGRETTE

For Raspberry Vinaigrette, combine 2/3 cup warm raspberry jelly, 1 tablespoon Creole mustard, 3 tablespoons balsamic vinegar, 3 tablespoons rice vinegar or raspberry vinegar, 1 tablespoon raspberry liqueur or white wine, 1/2 cup olive oil, 1/2 teaspoon salt and 1/2 teaspoon freshly ground pepper in a jar with a tightfitting lid. Cover and shake until blended. Store in the refrigerator.

Texas Winter Salad

Yield: 8 servings

Vinaigrette
1/2 cup malt vinegar
1 cup olive oil
1/2 cup sugar
1/4 cup catsup
• Juice of 1/2 lemon
1 teaspoon celery seeds
1/2 teaspoon salt
1 small onion, grated

Salad
2 pounds spinach, trimmed
2 Texas ruby-red grapefruit, peeled, sectioned
3 small avocados, peeled, sliced
1/2 cup slivered red onions
1/2 cup chopped celery
1/2 cup pecans, toasted

For the vinaigrette, whisk the malt vinegar, olive oil, sugar, catsup, lemon juice, celery seeds and salt in a bowl until blended. Stir in the onion.

For the salad, rinse the spinach and pat dry. Tear into bite-size pieces into a salad bowl. Add the grapefruit, avocados, red onions, celery and pecans and toss to mix well. Add the dressing just before serving and toss to mix well.

Asparagus Salad with Walnuts

Yield: 6 to 8 servings

1 pound fresh asparagus, trimmed
• Salt to taste
3/4 cup walnut pieces
5 tablespoons sugar
3 tablespoons soy sauce
3 tablespoons rice vinegar or distilled cider vinegar

Cook the asparagus in lightly salted water in a saucepan for 7 to 10 minutes or until tender; drain. Cut into bite-size pieces and place in a bowl. Add the walnuts and toss to mix. Combine the sugar, soy sauce and vinegar in a small bowl and mix well. Pour over the asparagus mixture and toss gently. Marinate for several hours or up to 12 hours.

Note: *Toast the walnuts if desired.*

Rocket Coleslaw

Yield: 12 servings

1	head green cabbage, chopped	1	red bell pepper, chopped
1/2	head red cabbage, sliced	•	Rocket Coleslaw Dressing
1/2	small white onion, minced		(below)
1	bunch green onions, chopped		

Combine the green cabbage, red cabbage, white onion, green onions and red pepper in a salad bowl and toss to mix well. Pour Rocket Coleslaw Dressing over the cabbage mixture and toss to mix well.

Rocket Coleslaw Dressing

1 1/2	cups mayonnaise	1 1/2	teaspoons garlic powder
1/4	cup prepared mustard	1	tablespoon sugar
1	tablespoon balsamic vinegar	1	teaspoon salt
1	tablespoon lemon juice	2	teaspoons pepper

Whisk the mayonnaise, mustard, vinegar, lemon juice, garlic powder, sugar, salt and pepper in a bowl.

Fresh Green Bean Salad

Yield: 8 to 10 servings

4 to 5 quarts water	1/2 cup walnuts, toasted
2 pounds fresh green beans, trimmed	1/2 to 3/4 cups crumbled bleu cheese
1 yellow bell pepper, chopped	• Dijon Mustard Dressing (below)
1 red bell pepper, chopped	
1 purple onion, thinly sliced	

Bring 4 to 5 quarts water to a boil in a large saucepan and add the green beans. Cook for 5 to 6 minutes or until bright green and tender-crisp. Drain and place in bowl. Chill, covered, for 8 to 12 hours. Add the yellow pepper, red pepper, purple onion, walnuts and bleu cheese. Add Dijon Mustard Dressing and toss to mix well.

Dijon Mustard Dressing

1/2 cup olive oil	1 tablespoon Dijon mustard
1/2 cup wine vinegar	• Salt and cracked black pepper to taste
2 tablespoons balsamic vinegar	

Combine the olive oil, vinegar, balsamic vinegar, Dijon mustard, salt and pepper in a bowl and whisk until blended.

Deep South Potato Salad

10	medium potatoes	1½	cups mayonnaise
5	hard-cooked eggs, chopped	1	teaspoon balsamic vinegar
½	cup sweet pickle relish	1	tablespoon prepared mustard
½	cup (scant) dill pickle relish	1	tablespoon catsup
1	onion, grated	¼	cup sliced stuffed olives or capers
1	teaspoon salt		(optional)
½	teaspoon pepper		

Boil the unpeeled potatoes in water to cover in a saucepan until tender; drain. Let stand until cool. Peel the potatoes and coarsely chop into a large bowl. Add the eggs, pickle relishes, onion, salt and pepper and mix lightly. Mix the mayonnaise, balsamic vinegar, mustard, catsup and olives in a small bowl. Add to the potato mixture and mix lightly, being careful not to mash the potatoes. Garnish with additional sliced olives. Chill until serving time.

Fiorenza Tomato Salad

6	Roma tomatoes, coarsely chopped	12	Greek olives, pitted
¼	cup capers, rinsed, drained	¼	cup minced green onions
¼	cup chopped fresh Italian parsley	½	teaspoon freshly ground pepper
2	ribs celery, chopped	3	tablespoons red wine vinegar
¼	cup chopped fresh basil	6	tablespoons extra-virgin olive oil
		8	lettuce leaves

Combine the tomatoes, capers, parsley, celery, basil, olives, green onions, pepper, vinegar and olive oil in a bowl and toss to mix well. Marinate, covered, in the refrigerator for 45 minutes or longer. Serve on lettuce leaves.

Grilled Portobello Mushroom Salad

Yield: 8 servings

Marinade and Dressing

1/2	cup balsamic vinegar
3/4	cup olive oil
1	tablespoon minced shallot
1	garlic clove, minced
2	tablespoons minced fresh basil
1	teaspoon sugar
1/2	teaspoon salt
1/2	teaspoon pepper

Salad

2	fresh whole portobello mushrooms
1	head red tip lettuce, torn
1	head Boston lettuce, torn
3	to 4 ounces bleu cheese, crumbled
2	tablespoons chopped fresh parsley
1/2	cup sliced almonds

For the marinade and dressing, combine the balsamic vinegar, olive oil, shallot, garlic, basil, sugar, salt and pepper in a bowl and mix well.

For the salad, clean the mushrooms and remove the stems. Add to the vinegar mixture. Marinate for 20 minutes. Drain the mushrooms, reserving the marinade. Place the mushrooms on a grill rack. Grill over medium heat for 15 minutes, turning once. Return the warm mushrooms to the reserved marinade. Let stand until cool. Drain the mushrooms, reserving the marinade. Cut the mushrooms lengthwise into large strips. Combine the red tip lettuce and Boston lettuce in a salad bowl and toss to mix well. Add the bleu cheese and reserved marinade and toss to coat well. Arrange on 8 salad plates. Arrange the mushrooms strips over the top. Sprinkle with parsley and almonds.

Kaleidoscope Mushroom Salad

Yield: 8 servings

20	ounces sliced mushrooms	1	cup whole kernel corn
•	Basil Vinaigrette (below)	1/2	cup chopped pimentos
8	ounces snow peas	8	large radicchio leaves
1	cup coarsely chopped watercress	8	romaine leaves
		8	Belgian endive leaves
1	cup chopped red onion	4	ounces bleu cheese, crumbled

Marinate the mushrooms in Basil Vinaigrette in a bowl for 30 minutes. Add the snow peas, watercress, onion, corn and pimentos and toss gently.

For each serving, make a cup with radicchio leaves. Arrange the romaine and endive to radiate from the cup. Fill with the mushroom mixture. Sprinkle with bleu cheese.

Basil Vinaigrette

1/3	cup chopped fresh basil	3/4	cup vegetable oil
2	tablespoons Dijon mustard	1/3	cup white wine vinegar
1 1/2	teaspoons seasoned salt	1	tablespoon lemon juice
3/4	teaspoon lemon pepper		

Combine the basil, Dijon mustard, seasoned salt, lemon pepper, vegetable oil, vinegar and lemon juice in a bowl and whisk well.

The salad course can be difficult to pair with a wine mainly because of the presence of vinegar in the dressing. A general rule of thumb is to keep it simple. Serve a light California chardonnay, Mâcon Villages or Sancerre from France.

They are light brown in color and have a smoky pungent flavor. Portobello mushrooms have a shallow saucer-shaped cap. They have a strong meaty flavor and are often used as a meat substitute in vegetarian cooking. Button mushrooms are the familiar all-purpose white mushrooms with which we are all most familiar. They are also called champignons de Paris. Morel mushrooms are various shades of brown. They grow in New England and Michigan and are often found near abandoned orchards. They have a nutty flavor.

Wild Rice Salad

Yield: 10 to 12 servings

2 (6-ounce) jars marinated
   artichokes
1¹/₃ cups olive oil
¹/₂ cup white vinegar
¹/₄ cup grated Parmesan cheese
1   tablespoon sugar
1   teaspoon salt
1   teaspoon celery salt
¹/₂ teaspoon pepper
¹/₂ teaspoon dry mustard
¹/₄ teaspoon paprika

1   garlic clove, minced
1   (6-ounce) package long grain and
    wild rice, cooked
1   (10-ounce) package frozen snap
    peas, thawed
1   red bell pepper, finely chopped
1   bunch green onions, chopped
1   pint cherry tomatoes, cut
    into halves
³/₄ cup pecans, toasted

Drain the artichokes, reserving the marinade. Combine the olive oil, vinegar, reserved artichoke marinade, Parmesan cheese, sugar, salt, celery salt, pepper, dry mustard, paprika and garlic in a jar with a tight-fitting lid. Cover and shake well. Can prepare and store in the refrigerator for 1 week. Let stand until room temperature and shake well before using. Combine the rice, artichokes, snap peas, red pepper, green onions and tomatoes in a bowl and mix well. Add ¹/₂ of the dressing and toss to coat well. Chill, covered, until serving time.

To serve, add a small amount of the remaining dressing and toss to mix well. Sprinkle with pecans.

Garden Salad with Broiled Goat Cheese

Yield: 4 servings

4	slices French bread	1	teaspoon white wine vinegar
6	ounces goat cheese, cut into ¹/₂-inch slices	1	teaspoon dry white wine
•	Olive oil	•	Salt and pepper to taste
1	teaspoon Dijon mustard	3	tablespoons olive oil
		6	cups salad greens

Arrange the bread on a baking sheet. Broil until the bread is toasted on one side. Turn over the bread. Place cheese on each slice of bread and drizzle with olive oil. Broil until the cheese is light brown. Watch carefully. Combine the Dijon mustard, vinegar, wine, salt and pepper in a bowl and mix well. Whisk in 3 tablespoons olive oil 1 tablespoon at a time until thick.

To serve, combine the salad greens and vinaigrette in a bowl and toss lightly to coat. Arrange on salad plates and top with the cheese toast.

ENZO'S BRUSCHETTA WITH ROMAINE

To make Enzo's Bruschetta with Romaine, mix ¹/₄ cup crumbled feta cheese, ¹/₂ cup chopped tomatoes, pinch of chopped white onion, pinch of oregano, pinch of salt and pepper, 4 basil leaves, chopped, 2 teaspoons balsamic vinegar and 2 tablespoons olive oil in a small bowl. Place a romaine leaf on each of four salad plates and top each with a slice of toasted French bread. Spoon the tomato mixture on each bread slice. Drizzle the remaining dressing over each salad.

Center Stage Salad

Yield: 8 servings

2	heads Boston lettuce, torn	3	green onions, finely chopped
6	ounces Roquefort cheese, crumbled	•	Cayenne Pecans (below)
1/2	red onion, thinly sliced	•	Center Stage Vinaigrette (below)

Combine the lettuce, cheese, red onion and green onions in a large salad bowl and toss to mix well. Add Cayenne Pecans and Center Stage Vinaigrette and toss to coat well.

Cayenne Pecans

1/3	cup sugar	1 1/4	teaspoons cinnamon
1/4	cup (1/2 stick) unsalted butter	1/4	to 1/2 teaspoon cayenne pepper
1/4	cup fresh orange juice	1/4	teaspoon ground mace
1 1/2	teaspoons salt	1	pound pecan halves

Heat the sugar, butter, orange juice, salt, cinnamon, cayenne pepper and mace in a heavy skillet over low heat until the butter melts and sugar dissolves. Increase the heat to medium. Add the pecans and toss until coated. Spread in a single layer on a foil-lined baking sheet. Bake at 250 degrees for 1 hour, stirring every 15 minutes. Remove to a large sheet of foil and separate the pecans with a fork. Let stand until cool. Can be stored in an airtight container for up to 5 days. Can be frozen for 1 month, but bring to room temperature before serving.

Center Stage Vinaigrette

1/2	cup olive oil	1/4	teaspoon salt
3	tablespoons raspberry vinegar	1/8	teaspoon white pepper
1	tablespoon minced shallots		

Whisk the olive oil and vinegar in a bowl. Stir in the shallots, salt and white pepper.

Toasted Walnut Spinach Salad

Yield: 4 to 6 servings

1	bunch fresh spinach, trimmed
1	avocado, peeled, sliced
1/2	cup crumbled feta cheese
•	Basil Dressing (below)

1/2	cup walnuts, toasted, coarsely chopped
•	Coarsely ground pepper to taste

Rinse the spinach and pat dry. Tear into medium-size pieces and place in a salad bowl. Arrange avocado over the top. Sprinkle with feta cheese. Chill, covered, until serving time.

To serve, add the Basil Dressing and toss until well coated. Sprinkle with walnuts and pepper.

Basil Dressing

1/4	cup red wine vinegar
2	garlic cloves, minced
3	tablespoons chopped fresh basil leaves

1	tablespoon sugar
1/2	cup olive oil
1/2	teaspoon salt
1/2	teaspoon pepper

Combine the vinegar, garlic, basil and sugar in a bowl and mix well. Add the olive oil gradually, whisking constantly until emulsified. Season with salt and pepper.

Roasting Nuts

Many recipes often call for roasted nuts. There are at least three ways recommended for accomplishing this. The microwave method includes placing a cup of shelled nuts on a paper plate and microwaving for 1 1/2 minutes on High or until hot. The oven method requires spreading the nuts in a single layer on a baking sheet and baking at 350 degrees until just light brown. If using the top of the stove method, melt a small amount of butter or margarine in a skillet. Add the nuts and cook until brown, stirring constantly. Remove from the skillet and drain on paper towels.

Orzo and Bell Pepper Salad

Yield: 4 servings

3/4	cup uncooked orzo	3	tablespoons chopped fresh parsley
2	cups chicken stock		
4 1/2	tablespoons olive oil	1	green onion, chopped
1 1/2	tablespoons red wine vinegar	3	tablespoons drained capers
1	tablespoon Dijon mustard	2	garlic cloves, minced
1	red bell pepper	1/4	cup crumbled feta cheese
1	yellow bell pepper	•	Salt and pepper to taste
3	tablespoons chopped fresh cilantro		

Cook the orzo in the chicken stock in a saucepan for 10 minutes or until tender. Drain if needed and place in a bowl. Mix the olive oil, red wine vinegar and Dijon mustard in a bowl. Add to the orzo immediately and mix well. Place the bell peppers in a non-recycled brown paper bag. Bake at 450 degrees for 10 minutes or until steamed. Remove the bell peppers from the bag. Peel the bell peppers and remove the seeds. Cut into long thin strips. Add the bell peppers, cilantro, parsley, green onion, capers, garlic, feta cheese, salt and pepper to the orzo mixture and toss to mix well. Serve chilled or at room temperature.

Jackson Salad

Yield: 8 servings

1/2	small onion, chopped	2	bunches romaine
1	or 2 garlic cloves, chopped	1	(7-ounce) can hearts of palm, drained, sliced
3	tablespoons cider vinegar		
2	tablespoons spicy brown mustard	1	(8-ounce) can water-pack artichoke hearts, drained, quartered
1/2	teaspoon sugar		
1/2	teaspoon salt		
1/4	teaspoon ground pepper	4	ounces bleu cheese, crumbled
1	cup vegetable oil	8	ounces bacon, cooked, crumbled

Purée the onion, garlic and vinegar in a blender. Spoon into a medium mixer bowl. Add the mustard, sugar, salt and pepper and beat well. Add the vegetable oil in a fine stream, beating constantly until thick. Combine the romaine, hearts of palm, artichoke hearts, bleu cheese and bacon in a bowl and toss to mix well. Add the dressing and toss until coated.

Greek Penne Pasta Salad

Yield: 10 servings

1 pound penne, cooked	1/2 cup chopped orange bell pepper
1/3 cup balsamic vinegar	1/2 medium red onion, chopped
4 ounces prosciutto, chopped	8 ounces Greek black olives, pitted, chopped
1 (6-ounce) jar marinated artichoke hearts, drained, chopped	8 ounces feta cheese, crumbled
1 cup coarsely chopped spinach	3/4 cup pine nuts, toasted
1/2 cup chopped red bell pepper	1 (6-ounce) bottle lemon pepper salad dressing or Italian salad dressing
1/2 cup chopped yellow bell pepper	
1/2 cup chopped green bell pepper	

Drain the hot pasta. Add the balsamic vinegar and toss to coat well. Combine the pasta, prosciutto, artichoke hearts, spinach, bell peppers, red onion, black olives and feta cheese in a large bowl and toss to mix well. Sprinkle with the pine nuts. Add the salad dressing and toss to mix well. Chill, covered, in the refrigerator until serving time.

Layered Spinach Tortellini Salad

Yield: 8 (1-cup) servings

9 ounces uncooked refrigerated cheese tortellini	3/4 cup sliced green onions
2 cups shredded red cabbage	1 (16-ounce) bottle ranch salad dressing
6 cups torn spinach leaves	8 slices bacon, cooked, crumbled
1 cup cherry tomato halves	

Cook the pasta using the package directions. Drain and rinse with cold water. Let stand until cool. Layer the cabbage, spinach, pasta, tomatoes and green onions in a large clear glass bowl. Pour the salad dressing evenly over the top. Sprinkle with the bacon. Chill, covered, for 8 to 12 hours.

Chicken, Coconut and Pecan Salad with Citrus Vinaigrette

Yield: 8 servings

6	boneless skinless chicken breasts	1	cup shredded coconut
1¹/₂	cups orange juice	¹/₄	cup chopped pecans
1¹/₂	cups pineapple juice	¹/₄	cup finely chopped green onions
¹/₂	cup soy sauce	¹/₄	cup finely chopped fresh parsley
¹/₄	cup sesame oil		
3	teaspoons ginger		

Place the chicken in a single layer in a container. Combine the orange juice, pineapple juice, soy sauce, sesame oil and ginger in a bowl and mix well. Reserve 1¹/₂ cups of the marinade. Pour the remaining marinade over the chicken. Marinate, covered, in the refrigerator for 8 to 12 hours. Drain the chicken, discarding the marinade. Grill the chicken for 4 minutes on each side or until cooked through. Chop the chicken and place in a large bowl. Place the coconut and pecans on a baking sheet. Bake at 350 degrees for 15 minutes or until golden brown, stirring occasionally. Add toasted coconut and pecans, reserved marinade, green onions and parsley to the chicken and toss to mix well. Serve in a pineapple wedge and garnish with pineapple slices.

Selected in 1992 as one of North America's Outstanding Chefs in America's 2000, J. B. Holstein, CWC, graduated from a Bay Area high school and Delgado College in New Orleans. He studied under Ann Willan, Director of La Varenne at the Greenbrier®, White Sulphur Springs, West Virginia and was selected to study with Madeleine Kaman at the Beringer Vineyards in St. Helena, California. Winner of awards for innovative recipes, he has worked locally at the Space Center Houston's restaurant, and Rice Epicurean, San Felipe. Chef J. B. is currently working in the Orlando, Florida area. We are delighted that J. B. chose to share this recipe creation with us.

Chicken Salad with a Twist

Yield: 4 to 6 servings

6	ounces rotini or fusilli	1	cup chopped cucumbers
2	cups chopped cooked chicken	1	cup chopped celery
1/2	cup Italian salad dressing	1	medium red onion or Texas 1015
1/2	cup mayonnaise		sweet white onion
1	teaspoon pepper	3/4	cup sliced black olives
3	tablespoons lemon juice	•	Salt to taste
1	teaspoon dry mustard		

Cook the pasta using the package directions; drain. Add the chicken and Italian salad dressing and mix well. Let stand until cool. Combine the mayonnaise, pepper, lemon juice and dry mustard in a bowl and blend well. Stir in the cucumbers, celery, onion and olives. Add to the cooled pasta mixture and mix well. Season with salt. Chill, covered, for 2 hours or longer to blend the flavors.

Mexican Chicken Salad

Yield: 12 servings

11	or 12 chicken breasts	1	tablespoon cumin
•	Juice of 1 lemon	1	teaspoon salt
3/4	cup mayonnaise	1/2	teaspoon pepper
3/4	cup sour cream	1	cup chopped red bell pepper
3/4	cup chopped green onions	1	cup chopped peeled jicama
3	(4-ounce) cans chopped green chiles, drained	•	Chili powder to taste

Place the chicken breasts in a large roasting pan. Sprinkle with lemon juice. Bake, covered, at 350 degrees for 30 to 40 minutes or until the chicken is cooked through. Do not overcook. Remove from the oven and cool chicken in the covered pan. Skin the chicken, discarding the skin and bones. Cut into bite-size pieces. Combine the chicken, mayonnaise, sour cream, green onions, green chiles, cumin, salt and pepper in a large bowl and mix well. Chill, covered, for 2 to 12 hours. Stir in the red pepper and jicama just before serving. Sprinkle with chili powder. Garnish with a sprig of cilantro.

Note: *Can also be served in a pita pocket with avocado slices.*

JICAMA

Our neighbor to the south introduced Texas cooks to the mild flavor of jicama. This edible, tuberous root is a native of Mexico, Central America, and South America. Its crisp texture and juicy taste add a delightful crunch to salads. Jicama can also be sprinkled with juice and eaten as a snack.

Smoked Chicken and Green Apple Salad

Yield: 4 to 6 servings

1	cup pecans	2	green apples, chopped
1	garlic clove, minced	1	red or yellow bell pepper, julienned
1	tablespoon Dijon mustard		
1	tablespoon white wine vinegar	12	ounces smoked chicken or turkey, cubed
1	to 2 tablespoons dried summer savory	1	small purple onion, thinly sliced
1/4	cup plus 2 tablespoons olive oil		

Sprinkle the pecans in a single layer on a baking sheet. Bake at 400 degrees for 4 minutes or until toasted. Cool and break into pieces. Combine the garlic, Dijon mustard, white wine vinegar and summer savory in a bowl and mix well. Whisk in the olive oil gradually. Combine the apples, red pepper, chicken and onion in a bowl and toss to mix well. Whisk the dressing and pour over the chicken mixture. Toss to mix well. Sprinkle with pecans.

Crab Meat Topping Over Tomatoes and Asparagus

Yield: 6 servings

1 cup mayonnaise	2 hard-cooked eggs, chopped
1/4 cup lemon juice	1 tablespoon chopped onion
1 teaspoon prepared mustard	18 tomato slices
1 teaspoon salt	6 lettuce leaves
1/4 teaspoon pepper	• Salt to taste
1 (12-ounce) package frozen crab meat, thawed, flaked	1 (14-ounce) can asparagus spears, drained
1 cup grated carrots	• Paprika to taste

Mix the mayonnaise, lemon juice, mustard, salt and pepper in a bowl. Combine the crab meat, carrots, eggs and onion in a bowl and mix well. Add the mayonnaise mixture and toss lightly. Chill, covered, until serving time. Arrange 3 tomato slices on each lettuce leaf on a salad plate. Sprinkle with salt. Place the asparagus spears on the tomatoes. Top with the crab meat mixture and sprinkle with paprika.

Note: *Can substitute two 6- or 7-ounce cans crab meat for the frozen crab meat. Fresh asparagus can be substituted for the canned asparagus.*

Landry's Spicy Shrimp Salad

Yield: 6 servings

1 1/2 pounds cooked, shelled shrimp, cut into bite-size pieces	1 teaspoon chili powder
3/4 cup chopped celery	1/4 teaspoon cayenne pepper
3/4 cup chopped green onions	• Salt and black pepper to taste
1 tablespoon chopped fresh cilantro	1 cup mayonnaise
2 teaspoons cumin	1 tablespoon Worcestershire sauce
1 teaspoon white pepper	2 teaspoons Cajun hot sauce
	1 teaspoon Dijon mustard

Combine the shrimp, celery, green onions, cilantro, cumin, white pepper, chili powder, cayenne pepper, salt and black pepper in a bowl and toss to mix well. Combine the mayonnaise, Worcestershire sauce, hot sauce and Dijon mustard in a medium bowl and whisk until blended. Add to the shrimp mixture and toss to mix well.

Green Salad with Shrimp and Avocado

Yield: 8 to 10 servings

2	to 3 avocados		1	teaspoon peppercorns
2	pounds large shrimp, cooked, peeled		1/4	teaspoon cayenne pepper
2	cups salad oil		1	to 2 teaspoons salt
1	cup cottage cheese		1	bunch spinach
1/2	medium onion, chopped		1	head romaine
5	ounces white vinegar		1	head iceberg lettuce
•	Juice of 1 lemon		1	pound bacon, cooked, crumbled (optional)
1	garlic clove			

Peel the avocados and cut into slices. Place in a large bowl and add the shrimp. Process the oil, cottage cheese, onion, white vinegar, lemon juice, garlic, peppercorns, cayenne pepper and salt in a blender. Pour over the shrimp mixture and mix gently. Chill, covered, until serving time. Rinse the spinach, romaine and iceberg lettuce thoroughly and shake well. Wrap in a dampened kitchen towel until serving time.

To serve, tear the crisp spinach, romaine and iceberg lettuce into bite-size pieces. Add to the chilled shrimp mixture and toss lightly. Sprinkle with the bacon.

CHUTNEY DRESSING

To prepare Chutney Dressing, combine 1/4 cup white wine or balsamic vinegar, 1/4 cup olive oil, 3 tablespoons chutney, 1 tablespoon honey, 1/4 teaspoon salt, 1 teaspoon dry mustard and curry powder to taste in a bowl and mix well. Serve over a salad of romaine, drained mandarin oranges, thin red onion slices, sliced black olives and toasted almonds.

Skirting the Shore
Side Dishes

⚓

Houston Yacht Club

In 1897, after a summer filled with boating excursions,
sailing parties and regattas, a group of yachtsmen organized
what is today the oldest yacht club in Texas,
the Houston Yacht Club. The club was chartered by the
State of Texas in June 1905. After several locations along
Buffalo Bayou and the Houston Ship Channel,
the Houston Yacht Club finally made its home in Shoreacres
on Galveston Bay in 1926. A Spanish mission-style clubhouse
was built the following year. During World War II,
the clubhouse was occupied by the United States Coast Guard
which used it as a training facility and members' motorboats
were used to patrol the ship channel, a vital oil port.
HYC's rich tradition of hosting national
and international regattas thrives and the club continues
to make yachting history from its docks on Galveston Bay.

Beach House Cookout

Black Bean and Corn Salsa, *page 22*
Sliced Fresh Cantaloupe and Assorted Fruit

Creole Barbecued Pork Loin, *page 175*
Herb-Marinated Grilled Vegetables, *page 116*
Creamy Macaroni and Cheese Gratin, *page 118*
Farmhouse Bread, *page 51*

Tri-Chocolate Chip Cookies, *page 217*
Peanut Butter Fudge Cookies, *page 218*

Texas Sun Tea, *page 119*

Asparagus with Maltaise Sauce

Yield: 6 to 8 servings

2¹/2 pounds asparagus	¹/4 cup (¹/2 stick) butter, melted
1 tablespoon water	• Maltaise Sauce (below)

Trim the asparagus. Place in a microwave-safe dish with the water. Microwave on High for 10 to 15 minutes or until tender; drain. Place in a serving dish. Drizzle with the melted butter. Serve with Maltaise Sauce.

Maltaise Sauce

3 egg yolks	• Salt to taste
2 tablespoons lemon juice	• Dash of Tabasco sauce
2 tablespoons boiling water	3 tablespoons orange juice
¹/2 cup (1 stick) butter, melted	2 teaspoons grated orange zest

Place the egg yolks and lemon juice in a double boiler. Heat over hot water until thickened, whisking constantly with a wire whisk. Add the boiling water 1 tablespoonful at a time, beating constantly. Add the butter gradually, beating constantly. Season with salt and Tabasco sauce. Continue to heat until thickened, beating constantly. Beat in the orange juice 1 tablespoon at a time. Beat in the orange zest.

This sauce was originally flavored with blood oranges from Malta. Regular orange juice and 2 to 3 drops of red food coloring has the same effect.

Asparagus Vinaigrette

Yield: 20 servings

Asparagus
- Salt to taste
- 3 pounds 1/4-inch-thick small asparagus

Vinaigrette
- 1 cup vegetable oil
- 1/4 cup egg substitute
- 3 tablespoons sour cream
- 3 tablespoons chopped fresh tarragon
- 1 tablespoon Dijon mustard
- 1 tablespoon tarragon vinegar or white wine vinegar

For the asparagus, bring lightly salted water to a boil in a large saucepan. Add the asparagus. Cook for 3 to 5 minutes or until tender-crisp; drain. Plunge asparagus into ice water. Let stand until cool; drain. Place asparagus in a bowl. Chill, covered, until serving time.

For the vinaigrette, whisk the vegetable oil gradually into the egg substitute in a bowl until thick and creamy. Whisk in the sour cream, tarragon, Dijon mustard and tarragon vinegar. Chill, covered, in the refrigerator.

To serve, mound the asparagus on a serving platter. Drizzle the vinaigrette over the top.

Far East Broccoli

Yield: 6 servings

- 3 (10-ounce) packages frozen broccoli spears, or 6 cups fresh broccoli
- 3 tablespoons rice vinegar
- 3 tablespoons Chinese sesame oil
- 1 tablespoon soy sauce
- 1 tablespoon prepared mustard

Steam the broccoli in a steamer using the manufacturer's directions until tender-crisp; drain. Combine the rice vinegar, Chinese sesame oil, soy sauce and mustard in a salad bowl and mix well. Add the broccoli and toss until coated.

Spicy Black Beans and Tomatoes

Yield: 8 servings

1	teaspoon olive oil	2	(15-ounce) cans black beans,
3	garlic cloves, minced		rinsed, drained
2	(14-ounce) cans tomatoes, drained,	1/2	teaspoon ground red pepper
	chopped	1	teaspoon minced fresh cilantro

Coat a large nonstick skillet with nonstick cooking spray. Add the olive oil. Heat over medium-high heat until hot. Add the garlic. Sauté until tender. Add the tomatoes and reduce the heat. Cook, uncovered, for 10 minutes or until slightly thickened. Stir in the black beans, red pepper and cilantro. Cook, covered, for 15 minutes. Garnish with additional fresh cilantro.

Broiled Whole Portobello Mushrooms

Yield: 2 to 4 servings

3	tablespoons olive oil	2	to 4 portobello mushrooms
1/3	cup balsamic vinegar	1/2	cup shredded Monterey Jack
•	Pinch of sugar		cheese, Swiss cheese or mozzarella
1/2	teaspoon minced garlic		cheese

Whisk the olive oil, vinegar, sugar and garlic in a bowl until mixed. Add the whole mushrooms. Marinate for 1 hour. Drain the mushrooms, reserving the marinade. Place the mushrooms in a broiler pan. Spoon the marinade on top of each mushroom. Sprinkle the cheese on top of each. Broil for 5 to 10 minutes or until the cheese begins to bubble. Serve immediately.

Note: *May sauté the mushrooms in the olive oil mixture for 1 minute on each side instead of marinating in the olive oil mixture.*

Mexican Corn

Yield: 4 to 6 servings

1/4	cup (1/2 stick) butter or margarine, melted	1/4	cup chopped onion
2	cups fresh corn kernels	1	teaspoon salt
1/4	cup chopped red bell pepper	1/2	teaspoon pepper
1/4	cup chopped green bell pepper	1	cup chopped fresh tomatoes

Melt the butter in a skillet. Add the corn, red pepper, green pepper, onion, salt and pepper. Cook, covered, over medium heat for 7 to 8 minutes, stirring occasionally. Add the tomatoes. Cook for 2 to 3 minutes or until the tomatoes are heated through.

Shoe Peg Corn with Green Chiles

Yield: 8 servings

1/4	cup (1/2 stick) margarine	2	(4-ounce) cans diced green chiles, drained
8	ounces cream cheese	•	Salt and pepper to taste
1/4	cup milk	•	Tabasco sauce to taste
2	(12-ounce) cans white Shoe Peg corn, drained	•	Paprika to taste

Heat the margarine, cream cheese and milk in a saucepan until creamy, stirring constantly. Add the corn, green chiles, salt, pepper and Tabasco sauce and mix well. Spoon into a 1 1/2-quart baking dish sprayed with nonstick cooking spray. Sprinkle with paprika. Bake at 350 degrees for 30 minutes.

Removing Corn Silks

Have you ever had problems removing the strands of corn silk from the ear of corn? Simply dampen a paper towel or terry cloth and brush it downward on the corn kernels. A shoehorn provides an ideal utensil for removing kernels from the cob when you wish to prepare fresh creamed corn. Its shape fits the cob naturally.

Cajun Green Beans

Yield: 14 to 16 servings

1	(36-ounce) package frozen cut green beans	1/2	cup chopped peppered bacon
2	tablespoons Creole seasoning	1/4	cup (or more) chopped onion
1/4	teaspoon red pepper flakes	1/4	cup chopped celery
1/4	cup (or more) chopped red bell pepper	2	tablespoons chopped green bell pepper
		3/4	cup (1 1/2 sticks) butter

Place the green beans in a large baking dish. Sprinkle with Creole seasoning, red pepper flakes, red pepper, bacon, onion, celery and green pepper. Dot with the butter. Bake at 375 degrees for 30 minutes or until the green beans are tender and bright green in color, stirring every 10 minutes.

Note: *May freeze, covered, until ready to bake.*

Green Beans with Roquefort Cheese and Walnuts

Yield: 4 servings

1	pound tender fresh green beans	4	ounces crumbled Roquefort cheese
4	slices (1/4-inch-wide) thick peppered bacon	1 1/2	cups walnuts, toasted (see page 91)
		•	Freshly ground pepper to taste

Bring water to a boil in a saucepan and add the green beans. Reduce the heat. Simmer for 3 minutes or until tender-crisp; drain. Rinse under cold water and drain again. Cook the bacon in a skillet for 5 to 7 minutes or until crisp and crumbly. Remove to paper towels to drain. Add the green beans to the skillet. Cook over medium heat for 2 minutes or until heated through. Add the Roquefort cheese. Cook for 30 seconds or until the Roquefort cheese begins to melt, tossing constantly. Sprinkle with the walnuts and pepper. Serve immediately.

Twice-Baked Potato Casserole

Yield: 8 to 10 servings

3	pounds large Yukon gold potatoes or russet potatoes (about 6), scrubbed	1	teaspoon freshly ground pepper
6	large garlic cloves	1	bunch green onions, trimmed, sliced
2 1/2	cups low-fat cottage cheese	3/4	cup shredded extra-sharp Cheddar cheese
1 1/2	cups sour cream	1/2	teaspoon paprika
1	tablespoon salt		

Place the potatoes and unpeeled garlic in a large saucepan and cover with cold water. Bring to a simmer over medium heat. Reduce the heat to low. Cook for 15 to 20 minutes or until the potatoes are tender; drain. Let stand for 20 minutes or until cool enough to handle. Peel the potatoes and grate into a large bowl. Squeeze the garlic cloves from the skins into a food processor container. Add the cottage cheese. Process until smooth. Add the sour cream, salt and pepper. Process until just combined. Add the cottage cheese mixture and green onions to the grated potatoes and mix well. Spoon into a 2-quart baking dish sprayed with nonstick cooking spray. Sprinkle with Cheddar cheese and paprika. Bake at 350 degrees for 30 to 40 minutes or until golden brown.

Note: *The recipe can be prepared and stored, covered, in the refrigerator for up to 2 days. Bake as above until golden brown.*

Red Potatoes with Artichokes and Feta Cheese

Yield: 6 servings

2	pounds small red potatoes, quartered	2	garlic cloves, minced
2	(14-ounce) cans artichoke hearts, drained, cut into halves	1/2	teaspoon salt
		1/2	teaspoon pepper
		1	tablespoon olive oil
2	tablespoons chopped fresh thyme	4	ounces feta cheese, crumbled

Combine the potatoes, artichoke hearts, thyme, garlic, salt, pepper and olive oil in a large bowl and toss to mix well. Spoon into an oiled 9x13-inch baking dish. Bake at 425 degrees for 55 minutes. Spoon into a serving dish. Add the feta cheese and toss to mix well.

Sweet Potato Balls

Yield: 6 to 8 servings

1	(23-ounce) can sweet potatoes, drained	12	large marshmallows
1/2	cup (1 stick) butter, melted	1	cup chopped pecans
•	Dash of cinnamon	1/2	to 1 cup flaked coconut

Cook the sweet potatoes in a saucepan until heated through. Mash the sweet potatoes. Add the butter and cinnamon and mix well. Let cool slightly. Cover each marshmallow with 1 large heaping tablespoon sweet potato mixture, shaping to form a ball. Roll each ball in a mixture of the pecans and coconut. Arrange in a buttered 9x13-inch baking dish. Bake at 350 degrees for 10 minutes.

Buy garlic heads that are firm with no green sprouts. Keep garlic at room temperature and use within one month. Fresh garlic is milder in taste and grows stronger as it grows stale. Whole garlic cloves have the mildest flavor—the flavor becomes stronger the more they are minced or crushed. Do not burn garlic— it is bitter. Roasted garlic is sweeter in taste. An easy way to peel garlic is to microwave the cloves on High for 15 to 30 seconds. Squeeze each clove at its end until the garlic pops from its skin.

Baked Florentine Casserole

Yield: 6 servings

2 (10-ounce) packages frozen chopped spinach
6 ounces cream cheese, softened
1 (10-ounce) can cream of mushroom soup
1 (2-ounce) can French-fried onions
• Dash of salt and pepper
1/4 cup (1/2 stick) butter
1 cup crushed butter crackers

Cook the spinach using the package directions and drain. Combine the cream cheese and soup in a saucepan. Heat until the cream cheese is melted, stirring constantly. Stir in the spinach and French-fried onions. Season with salt and pepper. Pour into a buttered 9x11-inch baking dish. Melt the butter in a small saucepan. Stir in the crackers. Sprinkle on top of the spinach mixture. Bake at 350 degrees for 25 to 30 minutes or until bubbly.

Spinach Gratin with Eggs

Yield: 4 servings

1 pound spinach leaves, trimmed
2 tablespoons clarified butter
1 teaspoon garlic purée
1 cup heavy cream
1 1/2 tablespoons unsalted butter, softened
• Salt and pepper to taste
4 hard-cooked eggs, sliced
1/4 cup grated Parmesan cheese

Rinse the spinach in cold water and place in a strainer. Pat the leaves partially dry, leaving some moisture on the leaves. Heat the clarified butter in a nonreactive sauté pan. Add the spinach. Sauté until the spinach is wilted. Add the garlic. Sauté until the spinach is cooked through. Add the cream. Cook until thickened, stirring constantly. Stir in the butter. Season with salt and pepper. Spoon into a buttered 9-inch round baking dish. Arrange the hard-cooked egg slices around the edge. Sprinkle with Parmesan cheese and pepper. Bake at 400 degrees for 15 to 20 minutes or until bubbly.

Note: *To clarify butter, heat the butter in a saucepan until melted. Remove the impurities from the melted butter by allowing the sediment to settle, then pouring off the clear yellow liquid.*

Phyllo Spinach Pie

Yield: 8 servings

3	(10-ounce) packages frozen chopped spinach, thawed	•	Salt and pepper to taste
1	medium onion, chopped	3	eggs, lightly beaten
3/4	cup olive oil	8	ounces feta cheese, crumbled
1	tablespoon oregano	12	to 14 phyllo sheets
		1/2	cup (1 stick) butter, melted

Drain the spinach and remove as much water as possible. Simmer the onion in the olive oil in a skillet until golden brown. Stir in the spinach, oregano, salt and pepper. Cook until most of the liquid is evaporated. Turn off the heat. Add a mixture of the eggs and feta cheese and stir to mix. Layer 6 or 7 phyllo sheets on a greased baking sheet, brushing each sheet with butter and keeping the remaining phyllo sheets covered with a damp towel. Spread the spinach mixture over the phyllo layers. Layer the remaining phyllo sheets over the spinach, brushing each sheet with butter. Bake at 375 degrees for 25 minutes or until golden brown.

BLOODY MARYS WITH A KICK

To prepare Bloody Marys with a Kick, combine 2 quarts tomato juice, 1/4 cup Worcestershire sauce, 6 tablespoons chopped horseradish, 2 tablespoons chopped fresh garlic, 2 tablespoons lemon juice, 2 tablespoons lime juice, 2 tablespoons dried dill, 1 teaspoon ground white pepper, 1 teaspoon celery salt, 1 teaspoon garlic salt, 1/2 teaspoon cayenne pepper and salt to taste in a large pitcher and mix well. Adjust the seasonings and chill in the refrigerator. Add 1 1/2 ounces vodka to each 8-ounce serving. Garnish with dilled green beans and lime wedges.

Herbed Squash Casserole

Yield: 6 to 8 servings

3	pounds yellow squash, chopped	8	ounces sour cream
1/2	cup (1 stick) butter	•	Salt and pepper to taste
1	large yellow onion, chopped	1	(8-ounce) package herb bread
2	medium carrots, grated		stuffing
2	(10-ounce) cans cream of chicken soup		

Cook the squash in a small amount of water in a saucepan until tender; drain. Spoon the squash into a bowl. Melt the butter in the saucepan. Add the onion and carrots. Sauté until tender and remove from the heat. Add the squash and mash. Stir in the soup and sour cream. Season with salt and pepper. Add half the herb stuffing and mix well. Sprinkle some of the remaining herb stuffing in a buttered baking dish. Add the squash mixture. Top with the remaining herb stuffing. Bake at 350 degrees for 30 minutes or until bubbly.

Squash and Tomato Toss

Yield: 6 servings

2	medium zucchini, sliced	2	tablespoons (1/4 stick) butter
2	medium yellow squash, sliced	1	cup mushrooms
•	Salt to taste	2	medium tomatoes, chopped
1/2	cup chopped onion	1	cup shredded Cheddar cheese
2	jalapeño peppers, seeded, sliced		

Cook the zucchini and yellow squash in a small amount of salted water in a saucepan for 7 minutes; drain. Sauté the onion and jalapeño peppers in the butter in a skillet. Add the mushrooms. Sauté until tender. Stir in the squash mixture. Season with salt. Spoon into a 7x11-inch baking dish. Sprinkle with the tomatoes and cheese. Bake at 350 degrees for 15 to 20 minutes or until heated through.

Artichoke Royale

Yield: 4 servings

1 (8-ounce) package frozen artichoke hearts
2 tablespoons (¼ stick) butter
2 tablespoons flour
3 ounces cream cheese, softened
⅔ cup milk
⅓ cup water
1 chicken bouillon cube, crushed
1 bunch green onions, finely chopped
⅔ cup grated Parmesan cheese
• Freshly ground pepper to taste

Thaw the artichoke hearts, discarding the liquid. Arrange in a single layer in a shallow 1½-quart baking dish. Melt the butter in a small saucepan. Blend in the flour. Cook until golden brown, stirring constantly. Remove from the heat. Blend in the cream cheese. Add the milk and water gradually, stirring constantly. Stir in the bouillon. Bring to a boil, stirring frequently. Remove from the heat. Stir in the green onions. Spoon evenly over the artichoke hearts, covering completely. Sprinkle evenly with the Parmesan cheese. Sprinkle lightly with pepper. Bake, uncovered, at 325 degrees for 1½ hours or until the top is brown. Serve hot.

Note: *May substitute 1 teaspoon powdered chicken base for the chicken bouillon cube.*

ISLAND ICED TEA

For Island Iced Tea, heat 1 cup brewed tea, ⅓ cup apricot nectar and ⅓ cup unsweetened pineapple juice in a small saucepan over medium-high heat for 1 to 2 minutes or until heated through. Remove from the heat and stir in 2 tablespoons dark rum if desired. Pour into a small pitcher if desired and chill in the refrigerator. Place 3 ice cubes in each of two 8-ounce glasses. Pour half the tea mixture into each glass and garnish with lime or lemon slices.

Marinated Artichokes with Rice

Yield: 4 servings

2	(8-ounce) packages chicken-flavored rice	1	bunch green onions with tops, chopped
2	(6-ounce) jars marinated artichoke hearts	1/3	cup mayonnaise

Cook the chicken-flavored rice using the package directions. Drain the artichoke hearts, reserving 1/2 cup of the marinade. Chop the artichokes. Combine the rice, artichokes, green onions, reserved marinade and mayonnaise in a bowl and mix well. Serve hot or cold.

Herb-Marinated Grilled Vegetables

Yield: 6 to 8 servings

3/4	cup olive oil	1/2	teaspoon salt
1/4	cup red wine vinegar	1/2	teaspoon fresh ground pepper
1	tablespoon minced garlic	2	pounds assorted bite-size
1	teaspoon chopped fresh rosemary		vegetable pieces such as bell
1	teaspoon chopped fresh thyme		peppers, zucchini, eggplant, onion
1	teaspoon chopped fresh basil		and mushrooms
1	teaspoon chopped fresh oregano		

Whisk the olive oil, vinegar, garlic, herbs, salt and pepper in a small bowl. Arrange the vegetables in a shallow dish or plastic container. Pour the marinade over the vegetables. Marinate, covered, in the refrigerator for 2 hours. Drain the vegetables, reserving the marinade. Place the vegetables in a grill basket. Grill 6 inches from the hot coals for 6 to 8 minutes or until tender, basting with the reserved marinade.

Note: *Grilling times will vary according to the vegetables that are used. The vegetables may also be broiled. May use 1/2 teaspoon dried herbs instead of the fresh herbs.*

Grits Soufflé with Caramelized Onions

Yield: 6 servings

4 cups milk	3 cups shredded smoked Gouda or Cheddar cheese
1 cup quick-cooking grits	3 eggs, beaten
1/2 cup (1 stick) butter	• Caramelized Onions (below)
1/2 teaspoon salt	
1/8 teaspoon cayenne pepper	

Bring the milk to a boil in a large saucepan. Stir in the grits and reduce the heat. Cook for 4 minutes or until thickened, stirring constantly. Remove from the heat. Stir in the butter, salt, cayenne pepper and cheese. Beat in the eggs with a wire whisk. Pour into a buttered 2¹/₂-quart soufflé or baking dish. Bake at 350 degrees for 1 hour or until puffed and golden brown.

To serve, spoon the Caramelized Onions over the hot grits. Serve immediately.

Caramelized Onions

1/4 cup olive oil	2 tablespoons sugar
5 large Texas 1015 onions or Vidalia onions, thinly sliced	

Heat the olive oil in a skillet. Add the onions. Sauté for 12 to 15 minutes or until golden brown, shaking the skillet constantly. Sprinkle with the sugar. Sauté until the onions are golden brown and crisp. Remove to paper towels to drain.

Creamy Macaroni and Cheese Gratin

Yield: 6 to 8 servings

1/2 cup (1 stick) butter	4 cups shredded mild Cheddar cheese or Velveeta cheese cubes
1/4 cup plus 2 tablespoons flour	
1/2 teaspoon cayenne pepper	1 pound elbow macaroni, cooked
1/2 teaspoon salt	3/4 cup heavy cream
1/2 teaspoon white pepper	1/2 cup fresh bread crumbs
2 egg yolks	1 tablespoon (1/8 stick) butter, melted
3 1/4 cups hot milk	

Melt 1/2 cup butter in a medium saucepan over low heat. Stir in the flour. Cook for 4 minutes to form a light roux, stirring constantly. Add the cayenne pepper, salt and white pepper. Whisk the egg yolks into the hot milk. Stir into the roux gradually. Cook until thickened, stirring constantly. Reduce the heat to low. Stir in 2 cups of the cheese. Cook until the cheese melts. Pour over the hot cooked macaroni in a large bowl and mix well. Sprinkle 1/2 cup of the remaining cheese in a buttered 8x11-inch baking dish. Layer 1/2 of the macaroni mixture, 1/2 cup of the remaining cheese, remaining macaroni mixture and remaining cheese in the prepared dish. Pour the cream over the layers. Sprinkle a mixture of the bread crumbs and 1 tablespoon melted butter over the top. Place in a larger pan of hot water. Bake at 350 degrees for 30 minutes or until golden brown. Let stand for 10 minutes before serving.

Red Beans and Rice

Yield: 6 servings

1	pound dried red beans	3	bay leaves
1	pound smoked meaty ham hock	1	teaspoon white pepper
2	cups chopped onions	1	teaspoon thyme
2	cups chopped celery	1	teaspoon garlic powder
2	cups chopped green bell peppers	1	teaspoon oregano
1/4	cup chopped fresh parsley	1/2	teaspoon salt
1	(8-ounce) can tomato sauce	1/2	teaspoon black pepper
1	cup diced stewed tomatoes	1	pound andouille sausage, cut into 1/2-inch pieces
		•	Hot cooked rice

Sort and rinse the red beans. Place in a stockpot. Cover with 2 inches water and let soak for 8 to 12 hours. Add enough water to barely cover the beans. Add the ham hock, onions, celery, green peppers, parsley, tomato sauce, stewed tomatoes, bay leaves, white pepper, thyme, garlic powder, oregano, salt and black pepper. Bring to a boil over high heat and reduce the heat. Simmer, covered, for 2 hours, adding additional water if needed. Remove the ham hock. Add the sausage. Cook, uncovered, over low heat for 40 minutes, stirring occasionally. Remove and discard the bay leaves. Spoon over hot cooked rice. Serve with Cajun hot sauce.

TEXAS SUN TEA

In our state, iced tea is not just a summertime drink; it's a way of life. You sit, sip, and enjoy the cool, refreshing, thirst-quenching year-round drink, preferably in a porch swing. Follow these easy directions for your own Texas Sun Tea. Fill a gallon jar with cold water. Place 3 family-size tea bags in the water, with the tags hanging outside the lid. Place in the sun for 3 to 4 hours. Chill in the refrigerator. Remove the tea bags when of the desired strength. Sweeten if desired and serve over ice. Garnish with lemon slices and mint leaves.

Risotto with Fresh Basil and Mozzarella Cheese

Yield: 4 servings

3	quarts water	2	tablespoons shredded fresh basil or chopped fresh parsley
1	tablespoon salt		
1½	cups uncooked arborio rice	1¼	cups shredded mozzarella cheese
6	tablespoons (¾ stick) butter, chopped	⅔	cup freshly grated Parmesan cheese

Bring the water to a boil in a large saucepan. Add the salt. Add the rice and mix with a wooden spoon. Cover the saucepan. Bring to a steady boil. Cook for 15 to 20 minutes or until the rice is tender but al dente, stirring occasionally with a wooden spoon. Drain and spoon the rice into a warm serving bowl. Add the butter and stir until melted. Stir in the basil. Add the mozzarella cheese and mix quickly and thoroughly. Add the Parmesan cheese and stir 2 to 3 times. Serve immediately.

Arborio Rice

The arborio grain grows only in the sun-soaked valley of the River Po in northern Italy, where climate and soil content create the ideal conditions for this plump succulent rice to thrive. Unlike long grain rice, arborio rice cooks to a smooth creaminess but still retains a good bite to the grain–what the Italians call al dente. This is why it is highly prized in the preparation of the authentic Risotto.

Seaworthy

Seafood

Kemah Waterfront

Once a gambling mecca, the Kemah Waterfront
has become an inviting tourist destination along upper
Galveston Bay. The area has attracted entrepreneurs
who have developed beautiful marinas and art galleries,
amusement parks, attractive waterfront hotels and
restaurants for which Philippine and Vietnamese fishermen
provide freshly caught seafood. As a center for shrimping,
the sight of the shrimp boats tied to the docks recalls the long
and colorful history of these small fishing communities.

⚓

Bay Area Extravaganza

South-of-the-Border Crab Meat Spread with Chips, *page 125*
Burgundy Mushrooms, *page 34*
Mozzarella Crostini, *page 30*

Gaido's Baked Oysters Ponzini, *page 142*

Toasted Walnut Spinach Salad, *page 91*
Fusilli with Roasted Tomatoes, Asparagus and Shrimp, *page 151*

French Baguette

Margarita Mousse Dessert, *page 224*

Chablis Muscadet or Chardonnay

Grilled Salmon Roll with Capers and Cucumbers

Yield: 12 to 14 servings

24 ounces cream cheese, softened	1 tablespoon chopped fresh dill
1 tablespoon prepared horseradish	1 teaspoon Nature's seasoning
1 tablespoon lemon juice	1½ pounds salmon fillets
1 tablespoon Worcestershire sauce	• Salt and lemon pepper to taste

Line a 10x15-inch baking sheet with plastic wrap. Combine the cream cheese, horseradish, lemon juice, Worcestershire sauce, dill and Nature's seasoning in a bowl and beat well. Spread evenly in the prepared pan into a rectangle ¼ inch thick. Chill in the refrigerator. Season the salmon with salt and lemon pepper and place on a grill rack. Grill until the salmon flakes easily with a fork. Chill in the refrigerator.

Flake the salmon into small pieces. Layer the salmon over the cream cheese mixture. Roll gently as for a jelly roll, beginning at the long edge and using the plastic wrap to assist in rolling up. Place on a serving tray. Garnish with fresh dill and thinly sliced lemons. Serve on pumpernickel bread with condiments of chopped purple onion, capers and chopped cucumbers.

SOUTH-OF-THE-BORDER CRAB MEAT SPREAD

To prepare South-of-the-Border Crab Meat Spread, blend 16 ounces cream cheese, softened, and 1 cup picante sauce in a bowl. Fold in 1 pound of crab meat. Spoon into a 9- or 10-inch pie plate. Sprinkle with 6 ounces of slivered almonds. Bake at 350 degrees for 15 to 20 minutes or until bubbly and the almonds are golden brown. Serve with tortilla chips or crackers.

Black Caviar Pie

Yield: 15 to 20 servings

6	hard-cooked eggs, finely chopped	8	ounces cream cheese, softened
3	tablespoons mayonnaise	2/3	cup sour cream
1	large sweet onion, finely chopped	1	(3-ounce) jar black lumpfish caviar

Combine the hard-cooked eggs and mayonnaise in a bowl and mix well. Spread in a greased 8-inch springform pan. Sprinkle with the onion. Beat the cream cheese and sour cream in a mixer bowl until smooth. Drop by spoonfuls over the onion layer and spread with a knife until the top is completely covered and smooth. Chill, covered with plastic wrap, for 3 to 12 hours.

To serve, uncover and spread the caviar over the top. Run a knife around the side to loosen. Remove the side of the pan. Garnish with thin lemon wedges arranged in a pinwheel fashion in the center and fresh sprigs of parsley. Serve with toast points or crisp unsalted crackers.

Perry's Stuffed Clams

Yield: 24 servings

2	dozen small hard-shell clams, scrubbed	2	tablespoons finely chopped fresh parsley
2	tablespoons water	1/4	teaspoon chopped fresh oregano leaves
1/4	cup (1/2 stick) butter or margarine, softened	3	tablespoons soft bread crumbs
1	large garlic clove, minced		

Place the clams and water in a large heavy saucepan. Simmer, covered, over medium heat for 5 to 10 minutes or until the clams open. Remove from the heat and let stand until cool enough to handle. Remove the clams from the shells, reserving 1/2 of the shells. Combine the butter, garlic, parsley, oregano and bread crumbs in a small bowl and mix well. Place 1 clam in each reserved shell. Spread with 1 teaspoon of the butter mixture. Arrange in a shallow baking pan. Broil 4 inches from the heat source for 3 to 4 minutes or until light brown. Serve with lemon wedges.

Note: *Can make ahead by covering and refrigerating until ready to broil.*

Perry's Italian Kitchen offers Old World Sicilian dishes including veal, seafood, and specialty salads. Family recipes add a creative flair and bring new tastes to the table. The sister restaurant, Perry's Grille & Steakhouse, has provided Clear Lake with casual elegance accompanied by mouthwatering steaks and fine wines.

Gulf Coast Shrimp Terrine

Yield: 12 to 15 servings

1	envelope unflavored gelatin	1	teaspoon salt
1/2	cup cold water	1	teaspoon prepared mustard
16	ounces cream cheese, softened	1	teaspoon sugar
1/2	cup mayonnaise	1	teaspoon Worcestershire sauce
1/2	cup catsup	1/2	teaspoon Tabasco sauce
2	tablespoons grated onion	2	cups minced shrimp

Soften the gelatin in the cold water in a bowl. Beat the cream cheese and mayonnaise in a bowl until smooth. Heat the catsup, onion, salt, mustard, sugar, Worcestershire sauce and Tabasco sauce in a saucepan; do not boil. Add the gelatin mixture and stir until dissolved. Add the cream cheese mixture and mix well. Fold in the shrimp. Pour into a 1-quart fish mold lined with plastic wrap or sprayed with nonstick cooking spray. Chill until set. Unmold onto a serving platter. Garnish as desired. Serve with melba toast, crackers or cucumber slices.

Spicy Shrimp with Green Sauce

Yield: 8 servings

2¹/₂ pounds shrimp	1¹/₂ teaspoons celery seeds
1 teaspoon salt	2 bay leaves, crumbled
1 tablespoon mustard seeds	¹/₄ cup olive oil
1 tablespoon peppercorns	• Juice of 1 lemon
1 tablespoon thyme	¹/₂ cup dry white wine
³/₄ teaspoon red pepper flakes	• Green Sauce (below)
³/₄ teaspoon cayenne pepper	

Toss the unpeeled shrimp with salt, mustard seeds, peppercorns, thyme, red pepper flakes, cayenne pepper, celery seeds and bay leaves in a bowl. Pour enough of the olive oil in a large skillet to cover the bottom. Add the shrimp. Sauté over medium-high heat. Add the lemon juice and white wine. Sauté for 6 to 7 minutes or until the shrimp turn pink. Chill in the refrigerator.

To serve, peel the shrimp, leaving the tails intact. Place the shrimp on a serving plate. Serve the Green Sauce in a small serving bowl. Garnish with lemon slices and parsley.

Green Sauce

1 pound tomatillos	2 teaspoons mustard seeds, toasted
¹/₄ cup rice wine vinegar	
1 tablespoon (or more) lime juice	1 tablespoon green Tabasco sauce
1 tablespoon minced garlic	1 tablespoon grated horseradish
1¹/₂ teaspoons sugar	

Remove the husks from the tomatillos and rinse well. Cut the tomatillos into quarters and place in a food processor container. Add the rice wine vinegar, lime juice, garlic, sugar, mustard seeds, green Tabasco sauce and horseradish and process until finely chopped.

Tomatillos

Tomatillos are a fruit that belong to the tomato family. They are also known as Mexican green tomatoes or husk tomatoes due to their parchmentlike covering. Tomatillos are a favorite in Mexican or Latin American foods such as enchiladas, salsas, tacos, or guacamole. Choose ones that are firm to the touch and have a dry, tight-fitting husk. Remove the outer covering and rinse inside fruit before cooking. When tomatillos are left uncooked and added to salads, the dish will have a more acidic tang. To store, place unhusked tomatillos in a paper bag and keep in the refrigerator.

Marinated Shrimp with Capers

Yield: 8 to 10 servings

1	(3-ounce) package shrimp boil	2½	tablespoons undrained capers
8	bay leaves	1	cup vegetable oil
½	cup chopped celery tops	1	cup apple cider vinegar
2½	teaspoons celery seeds	1	teaspoon salt
2½	to 3 pounds shrimp, peeled	•	Few dashes of Tabasco sauce
2	cups thinly sliced small onion rings		

Fill a large stockpot with water. Add the shrimp boil, bay leaves, celery tops and celery seeds. Bring to a boil. Add the shrimp. Boil until the shrimp turn pink. Remove the shrimp from the water, letting the celery seeds cling to the shrimp. Alternate layers of the onion rings, shrimp and capers in a container with a tightfitting lid. Mix the vegetable oil, apple cider vinegar, salt and Tabasco sauce in a bowl and pour over the layers. Marinate, covered, for 2 to 4 days.

Pinsec (Fried Won Tons)

Yield: 60 won tons

2 eggs

8 ounces uncooked shrimp, peeled, chopped

4 ounces ground pork

1/2 cup fresh crab meat

1/2 cup finely chopped water chestnuts

1/4 cup finely chopped green onions

2 garlic cloves, minced

1 tablespoon minced ginger

• Salt and pepper to taste

60 won ton wrappers

1 cup vegetable oil

1 (8-ounce) jar plum sauce

Beat the eggs in a bowl until frothy. Reserve 1/4 of the eggs. Add the shrimp, pork, crab meat, water chestnuts, green onions, garlic, ginger, salt and pepper to the remaining eggs and mix well. Drop 1 teaspoonful of the shrimp mixture onto each won ton wrapper. Fold to form a triangle, brushing the edges with the reserved beaten eggs to seal. Fry in batches in hot oil in a skillet for 1 to 2 minutes or until golden brown. Drain on paper towels. Serve with plum sauce.

Mascarpone Seafood Cheesecake

Yield: 12 to 16 servings

1/2	cup (1 stick) butter, melted	1/4	cup finely minced green onions
40	saltine crackers	8	ounces shrimp, peeled, sautéed,
16	ounces cream cheese, softened		chopped
2	(17-ounce) containers mascarpone	7	ounces lump crab meat
	cheese	•	Salt and pepper to taste
6	eggs	•	Pine Nut Cream Sauce with
2	tablespoons flour		Shrimp and Lump Crab Meat
1/4	cup finely minced chives		(below)

Coat the bottom of a 10-inch springform pan lightly with some of the butter. Process the crackers in a food processor until crumbly. Add enough of the remaining butter gradually, processing constantly until the mixture begins to hold together. Press in the prepared pan. Beat the cream cheese and marscarpone cheese lightly in a mixer bowl using a paddle or flat whip. Add the eggs and flour and mix well. Fold in the chives, green onions, shrimp and crab meat using a spatula. Season with salt and pepper. Spoon in the prepared pan. Bake at 350 degrees for 1 hour or until light golden brown and the middle is of a pudding consistency. Let cool slightly. Remove the side of the pan. Cut into wedges and serve with Pine Nut Cream Sauce with Shrimp and Lump Crab Meat.

Pine Nut Cream Sauce with Shrimp and Lump Crab Meat

2	tablespoons (1/4 stick) butter	1/3	cup white wine
2	tablespoons flour	1/2	cup heavy cream
1 1/2	cups fresh chopped basil	1/3	cup chicken stock
1/3	cup freshly grated Parmesan	1/3	cup pine nuts
	cheese	12	boiled shrimp, peeled, cut into
1/2	teaspoon finely chopped garlic		thirds
•	Pinch of salt and pepper	3/4	cup lump crab meat
1	tablespoon fresh lemon juice		

Melt the butter in a large saucepan. Stir in the flour. Add the basil, Parmesan cheese, garlic, salt, pepper, lemon juice, white wine, cream, chicken stock and pine nuts. Simmer over medium heat until thickened, stirring constantly. Fold in the shrimp and crab meat.

Note: *This sauce is also good served over pasta.*

Villa Capri's Fish Fillets with Pecan Crunch Coating

Yield: 4 servings

2   tablespoons Dijon mustard
2   tablespoons (¼ stick) butter,
     melted
¼   cup honey
¼   cup fresh bread crumbs
¼   cup chopped fresh parsley, or
     2 teaspoons dried parsley

¼   cup finely chopped pecans or
     walnuts
4   (4- to 6-ounce) fish fillets
•   Salt and pepper to taste

Combine the Dijon mustard, butter and honey in a bowl and mix well. Mix the bread crumbs, parsley and pecans in a bowl. Season the fillets with salt and pepper. Place on a lightly greased baking sheet. Brush with the mustard mixture. Sprinkle with the bread crumb mixture and pat to adhere to the surface. Bake at 450 degrees for 10 minutes per inch of thickness or until the fish flakes easily with a fork. Serve with lemon wedges.

Because of the variety of the fish available in the Bay Area, this creative dish by Frankie Camera is a hit. Camera is from Capri, and his restaurants, Frenchies and Villa Capri, specialize in Italian dishes. He and his brother Giusseppi, and brother-in-law Mario, are master chefs of international cuisine.

All King's Day Catfish

Yield: 4 servings

4	(5- to 8-ounce) catfish fillets	1/4	cup chopped green onions
•	Salt to taste	1/4	cup chopped red bell pepper
•	Cayenne pepper to taste	1/4	cup chopped purple bell pepper
1/2	cup flour	1	teaspoon chopped garlic
1/4	cup vegetable oil	1/4	cup chicken stock or bouillon
6	tablespoons (3/4 stick) unsalted butter	4	ounces sliced mushrooms
		3	tablespoons chopped fresh parsley

Season the fish with salt and cayenne pepper. Dredge the fish in the flour and shake off the excess. Heat the vegetable oil in a large skillet over medium heat. Add the fish. Sauté for 5 to 6 minutes or until brown. Remove to a hot plate. Melt 4 tablespoons of the butter in a small skillet over medium-high heat. Add the green onions, red bell pepper, purple bell pepper and garlic. Cook for 3 minutes, moving the skillet back and forth instead of stirring. Add the stock, mushrooms and remaining 2 tablespoons butter. Cook until the butter is incorporated, moving the skillet back and forth. Season with salt and cayenne pepper. Place the hot fish on individual serving plates and spoon the sauce evenly over the top of each. Sprinkle with the parsley.

Pignoli-Crusted Salmon

Yield: 4 servings

4	(6-ounce) salmon fillets	2	tablespoons fresh lemon juice
2	tablespoons Dijon mustard	1/4	cup heavy cream
1/2	cup bread crumbs	1/4	cup (1/2 stick) butter, chopped
1/2	cup pignoli or pine nuts	1/8	teaspoon salt
1	teaspoon vegetable oil	1/8	teaspoon pepper
1	tablespoon (1/8 stick) butter		

Brush the fish with Dijon mustard. Sprinkle a mixture of the bread crumbs and pignoli on 1 side of fish and pat to adhere to the surface. Heat the vegetable oil and 1 tablespoon butter in an ovenproof skillet over medium heat until foamy. Add the fish crumb side down. Cook for 3 to 5 minutes or until golden brown. Turn over the fish. Bake at 350 degrees for 7 to 10 minutes or until the fish flakes easily. Heat the lemon juice in a saucepan until reduced to 1 teaspoon. Add the cream. Boil for 3 minutes or until slightly thickened, stirring constantly. Add 1/4 cup butter, whisking until melted. Season with salt and pepper. Spoon over the fish.

Chilled Salmon Steaks with Lemon Dill Sauce

Yield: 6 servings

1 1/2 cups water	2 bay leaves
1/4 cup lemon juice	6 (1 1/2-inch-thick) salmon steaks
1 medium onion, sliced	
10 whole black peppercorns	• Lemon Dill Sauce (at right)
3 sprigs of parsley	

Combine the water, lemon juice, onion, peppercorns, parsley and bay leaves in a saucepan. Bring to a boil. Add the fish. Poach for 8 to 12 minutes or until the fish flakes easily. Drain the fish and place in an airtight container. Chill, covered, for 2 hours.

To serve, place the fish on a serving platter. Spoon the Lemon Dill Sauce over the top. Garnish with dill and lemon wedges.

LEMON DILL SAUCE

For Lemon Dill Sauce, combine 3/4 cup mayonnaise, 3 tablespoons buttermilk, 2 tablespoons chopped fresh dill or 1/2 teaspoon dried dill, 1 tablespoon snipped fresh chives, 1/2 teaspoon lemon zest and 2 teaspoons lemon juice in a bowl and mix well. Chill, covered, for 1 hour.

Smoked Salmon and Spinach Roulade

Yield: 24 servings

1	(10-ounce) package frozen spinach, thawed, squeezed dry
1/2	cup chopped fresh parsley
1/3	cup flour
1/4	cup low-fat sour cream
•	Dash of hot red pepper sauce
•	Salt and freshly ground pepper to taste
2	large egg yolks
6	large egg whites, stiffly beaten
6	ounces low-fat cream cheese
3/4	cup low-fat cottage cheese
1	tablespoon fresh lemon juice
8	ounces salmon fillet, smoked
1/4	cup snipped fresh chives
3	tablespoons drained capers
1	tablespoon prepared horseradish (optional)

Coat an 11x17-inch baking sheet with nonstick cooking spray. Line the baking sheet with parchment paper or waxed paper and spray with nonstick cooking spray. Purée the spinach, parsley, flour, sour cream and red pepper sauce in a food processor until smooth. Season with salt and pepper. Add the egg yolks and pulse until mixed. Spoon into a bowl. Fold 1/3 of the stiffly beaten egg whites into the spinach mixture using a rubber spatula; fold the spinach mixture into the remaining egg whites. Spread in the prepared pan.

Bake at 375 degrees for 20 minutes or until the top springs back when lightly touched. Cool in the pan on a wire rack for 5 minutes. Invert onto a towel and remove the parchment paper. Cover with another towel. Purée the cream cheese and cottage cheese in a food processor until smooth. Sprinkle the spinach cake with lemon juice and spread with 1/2 of the cream cheese mixture, leaving a 1/4-inch border around the edges. Layer the smoked salmon and remaining cream cheese mixture over the top. Sprinkle with the chives, capers and horseradish. Season with pepper. Roll up starting at the long edge as for a jelly roll, using the towel to lift and assist in rolling. Wrap in plastic wrap and chill for at least 4 hours. Cut into 24 slices with a serrated knife.

Sesame-Crusted Chilean Sea Bass with Watermelon Salsa

Yield: 2 servings

1	cup cornstarch	2	(6- to 8-ounce) sea bass fillets
1/4	cup black sesame seeds	•	Olive oil for sautéing
1/4	cup white sesame seeds	•	Watermelon Salsa (at right)
•	Salt and pepper to taste	•	Fresh cumin

Mix the cornstarch, black sesame seeds, white sesame seeds, salt and pepper in a shallow dish. Add the fish and dredge until coated on both sides. Heat the olive oil in a sauté pan. Add the fish. Cook for 4 to 6 minutes on each side or until the fish flakes easily. Remove to a warm serving dish. Top with Watermelon Salsa and sprinkle with cumin.

Broiled Flounder with Parmesan Topping

Yield: 4 to 6 servings

4	to 6 flounder fillets	3	tablespoons light mayonnaise
•	Lemon juice to taste	3	tablespoons chopped green onion tops
1/2	cup grated Parmesan cheese		
1/4	cup (1/2 stick) butter, softened	•	Dash of hot sauce

Brush the fish with lemon juice to taste and place on a lightly greased rack in a broiler pan. Broil 4 inches from the heat source for 6 to 8 minutes. Combine the Parmesan cheese, butter, mayonnaise, green onion tops and hot sauce in a bowl and mix well. Spread over the fish. Broil for 2 to 3 minutes longer or until the fish flakes easily. Serve with lemon wedges.

Watermelon Salsa

Watermelon Salsa, a creation by Bay Brewery, was a First Place Winner in the Specialty Salsa at the Texas Hill Country Food and Wine Festival. To prepare, combine 4 cups diced seeded watermelon, 2 cups diced seedless yellow tomatoes, 1 seedless serrano pepper, minced, 1/4 cup chopped flat-leaf parsley and 1/4 cup chopped Bermuda onion in a bowl and mix well. Stir in 1/4 cup fresh orange juice, 1/4 teaspoon cardamom, 1/4 teaspoon cinnamon and salt and pepper to taste. Chill, covered, for 1 hour.

Red Snapper Puttanesca

Yield: 4 servings

4	red snapper fillets	2	tablespoons drained capers
1	tablespoon lemon juice	2	tablespoons minced anchovies
1/4	teaspoon pepper	1/4	cup chopped fresh basil
2	teaspoons olive oil	1	tablespoon chopped fresh oregano
1	onion, chopped	1	bay leaf
3	garlic cloves, minced	1/4	cup chopped fresh parsley
3	large tomatoes, peeled, chopped		
8	niçoise or kalamata olives, pitted, sliced		

Place the fish in a shallow baking dish. Sprinkle with lemon juice and pepper. Heat the olive oil in a large nonstick skillet over medium heat. Add the onion and garlic. Sauté for 2 minutes. Add the tomatoes, olives, capers, anchovies, basil, oregano and bay leaf. Bring to a boil and reduce the heat to low. Simmer for 5 minutes. Pour over the fish. Sprinkle with parsley. Bake at 350 degrees for 30 minutes or until the fish flakes easily. Discard the bay leaf. Serve with lemon wedges and sprigs of fresh parsley.

Deviled Crab

Yield: 4 servings

1	medium green bell pepper, chopped	1/4	cup (1/2 stick) butter
2	ribs celery, chopped	1	pound fresh crab meat
1	small onion, chopped	1	cup cracker crumbs
1	(2-ounce) jar pimento, chopped	•	Salt and pepper to taste
		•	Dash of Tabasco sauce

Sauté the green pepper, celery, onion and pimento in the butter in a skillet. Add the crab meat and cracker crumbs and mix well. Season with salt, pepper and Tabasco sauce. Spoon into crab shells or a nonstick baking dish. Broil until brown.

Southern Favorite Crab Cakes

Yield: 4 or 5 servings

2/3 cup mayonnaise	2 tablespoons finely chopped green onions
1 tablespoon lemon juice	1 pint fresh lump crab meat
1/4 teaspoon red pepper	1 cup dry bread crumbs
1 tablespoon Old Bay seasoning	2 tablespoons (1/4 stick) butter
1/4 teaspoon dry mustard	• Cool Dill Sauce (at right)
1 (2-ounce) jar pimento, chopped, drained	• Hot Dill Butter Sauce (at right)

Combine the mayonnaise, lemon juice, red pepper, Old Bay seasoning, dry mustard, pimento and green onions in a bowl and mix well. Fold in the crab meat and 1/2 cup of the bread crumbs. Shape into 3-inch patties 1/2 inch thick. Roll in the remaining bread crumbs. Melt the butter in a skillet. Add the patties. Cook for 3 minutes on each side or until golden brown, turning once.

To serve, spoon a small amount of Cool Dill Sauce or Hot Dill Butter Sauce over each crab cake.

DILL SAUCES

For Cool Dill Sauce, process 1 cup mayonnaise, 1/2 cup sour cream, 2 to 3 tablespoons lemon juice and 1 tablespoon chopped fresh dill in a food processor until smooth.

For Hot Dill Butter Sauce, heat 1/2 cup (1 stick) butter, 3 tablespoons chopped fresh dill, 2 tablespoons lemon juice, 1 teaspoon minced garlic and 1 teaspoon minced green onions in a saucepan until the butter melts. Simmer for 3 minutes.

Crab Crepes Florentine

Yield: 12 to 15 crepes

CREPES

To make Crepes, process 1½ cups flour, 1 teaspoon sugar, ½ teaspoon salt, 1½ cups milk, 3 eggs and 1 teaspoon melted butter in a blender until smooth. Let stand at room temperature for 1 hour. Brush a 7-inch crepe pan or skillet with a little butter and heat the pan. Add about 1½ teaspoons of the batter, tilting the pan to evenly distribute. Bake until golden brown on each side, turning once. Repeat with the remaining batter. Crepes can be stored in an airtight container with waxed paper between each layer in the refrigerator or freezer.

1	(6- to 8-ounce) package frozen crab meat, or 1 (7-ounce) can King crab meat	5	tablespoons flour
		2	cups milk
		1	cup heavy cream
1	(10-ounce) package chopped frozen spinach	3/4	teaspoon salt
1/4	cup finely chopped onion	1/8	teaspoon black pepper
8	ounces mushrooms, finely chopped	1/8	teaspoon red pepper
		1/4	teaspoon nutmeg
7	tablespoons butter	1½	cups shredded Swiss cheese
		1/3	cup grated Parmesan cheese
		12	to 15 crepes (at left)

Thaw the frozen crab meat; drain. Cut the crab meat into bite-size pieces. Cook the spinach using package directions; drain. Press the spinach between paper towels to extract all the liquid. Sauté the onion and mushrooms in 2 tablespoons of the butter in a skillet. Add the crab meat and spinach.

Melt the remaining 5 tablespoons butter in a 1-quart saucepan. Blend in the flour. Add the milk and cream. Cook until smooth and thickened, stirring constantly. Season with salt, black pepper, red pepper and nutmeg. Add 1/2 cup of the sauce to the crab meat mixture and mix well. Stir the Swiss cheese into the remaining sauce.

Spread the crab meat mixture down the center of each crepe and roll up. Spoon a thin layer of the sauce in a large buttered baking dish. Arrange the crepe roll-ups in a single layer in the prepared dish. Spoon the remaining sauce over the crepe roll-ups and sprinkle with Parmesan cheese. Bake, covered, at 350 degrees for 20 minutes. Bake, uncovered, for 15 to 20 minutes longer or until golden brown and bubbly.

Peppy Clam Shells

Yield: 3 or 4 servings

1/2 cup finely chopped onion	1/4 teaspoon salt
1/2 cup finely chopped celery	• Dash of pepper
1/4 cup finely chopped green bell pepper	• Dash of Worcestershire sauce
1/4 cup (1/2 stick) butter	• Dash of hot sauce
2 tablespoons flour	1/2 cup crushed butter crackers
1 tablespoon grated Parmesan cheese	1 (7-ounce) can minced clams
	1 tablespoon (1/8 stick) butter, melted

Sauté the onion, celery and green pepper in 1/4 cup butter in a skillet until tender. Stir in the flour, Parmesan cheese, salt, pepper, Worcestershire sauce and hot sauce. Add 1/4 cup of the cracker crumbs and mix well. Stir in the undrained clams. Cook until bubbly, stirring constantly. Spoon into 3 or 4 large baking shells. Mix the remaining cracker crumbs and 1 tablespoon butter in a bowl. Spoon onto the clam mixture in each shell. Bake at 350 degrees for 15 minutes. Garnish with cherry tomatoes and parsley.

Crawfish Fettuccini

Yield: 4 to 6 servings

1 pound crawfish tails, peeled	1 teaspoon chopped jalapeño peppers
1 cup chopped onions	
1/2 cup chopped green bell pepper	1/4 teaspoon garlic powder
1/2 cup (1 stick) butter	1/2 teaspoon salt
1/4 cup flour	1/4 teaspoon black pepper
1 1/2 cups milk	1/4 teaspoon red pepper
1 tablespoon chopped fresh parsley	8 ounces fettuccini, cooked
8 ounces Velveeta cheese	• Grated Parmesan cheese

Rinse the crawfish tails and pat dry. Sauté the onions and green pepper in the butter in a skillet until tender. Add the flour and milk. Cook for 10 minutes, stirring frequently. Add the parsley and crawfish. Cook, covered, for 15 minutes. Add the Velveeta cheese, jalapeño peppers, garlic powder, salt, black pepper and red pepper. Simmer for 15 minutes, stirring constantly. Layer the pasta in a nonstick 9x13-inch or 2-quart baking dish. Pour the crawfish mixture over the pasta. Sprinkle with Parmesan cheese. Bake at 350 degrees for 15 to 20 minutes or until bubbly.

Gaido's Baked Oysters Ponzini

Yield: 4 to 5 dozen

1	large yellow onion, finely chopped	1/2	teaspoon salt
1	cup chicken stock	1/4	teaspoon nutmeg
1 1/4	pounds mushrooms, finely chopped	1	pound Swiss cheese, sliced
1 2/3	cups heavy cream	2 1/2	cups grated Parmesan cheese
1/2	cup dry white wine	4	or 5 egg yolks
1	teaspoon cayenne pepper	4	to 5 cups rock salt
		4	to 5 dozen oysters on the half shell

Sauté the onion in a nonstick skillet until brown. Combine the chicken stock, onion, mushrooms, cream, wine, cayenne pepper, salt and nutmeg in a stockpot. Bring almost to a boil. Turn off the heat. Add the Swiss cheese 1 slice at a time, stirring constantly after each addition until melted. Stir in the Parmesan cheese. Add the egg yolks and mix well. Cook over low heat until thickened, stirring constantly. Spread the rock salt in a large baking pan 1/4 to 1/2 inch deep. Nestle the oysters in the rock salt. Pour 2 tablespoons of the sauce on top of each oyster. Bake at 350 degrees for 15 minutes or until the edges of the oysters curl.

Note: *May prepare the sauce 1 to 2 days ahead of using.*

Artichoke Shrimp Casserole

Yield: 4 to 6 servings

4½ tablespoons butter
4½ tablespoons flour
¾ cup milk
¾ cup heavy cream
• Salt and pepper to taste
¼ cup sherry
1 tablespoon Worcestershire sauce

4 ounces fresh mushrooms
2 tablespoons butter
1 (14-ounce) can artichoke hearts, drained
1 pound shrimp, cooked, peeled
¼ cup grated Parmesan cheese
• Paprika to taste

Melt 4½ tablespoons butter in a saucepan. Stir in the flour. Add the milk and cream. Cook until thickened, stirring constantly. Remove from the heat. Season with salt and pepper. Stir in the sherry and Worcestershire sauce. Sauté the mushrooms in 2 tablespoons butter in a skillet for 6 minutes. Arrange the artichoke hearts in a buttered 2-quart baking dish. Sprinkle with the shrimp. Layer the mushrooms over the shrimp. Pour the sauce over the layers. Sprinkle with Parmesan cheese and paprika. Bake at 350 degrees for 25 to 30 minutes or until bubbly.

Shrimp Aioli

Yield: 10 servings

2¹/₂	to 3 pounds shrimp	2	recipes Aioli Sauce (below)
¹/₄	cup (¹/₂ stick) butter	1	tablespoon chopped parsley
¹/₂	cup olive oil		for garnish
•	Juice of 1 lemon, strained		

Peel the shrimp and butterfly. Chill, covered, in the refrigerator. Melt the butter in the olive oil in an ovenproof skillet over medium heat. Add the shrimp. Sauté for 8 to 10 minutes or until the shrimp turn pink. Sprinkle with the lemon juice and stir. Bake at 325 degrees for 1 minute. Do not overcook. Prepare the plates with Aioli Sauce (at left). Serve immediately.

Aioli Sauce

8	to 10 garlic cloves, peeled	1	teaspoon Dijon mustard
2	egg yolks, at room temperature	³/₄	cup peanut oil, at room temperature
•	Salt and white pepper to taste	³/₄	cup olive oil, at room temperature
•	Juice of 1 lemon, strained		

Purée the garlic in a food processor. Add the eggs and blend. Add the salt, white pepper, lemon juice, Dijon mustard and process until a smooth paste forms. Add the peanut oil and olive oil gradually, processing constantly until thick and firm. Spoon into an airtight container. Chill, covered, until ready to use.

Note: *When doubling the recipe for Aioli Sauce, make only 1 batch at a time.*

To serve Shrimp Aioli, place the Aioli sauce in a pastry bag or plastic squeeze bottle. Make a rectangle 2 inches wide and 3 inches long on each serving plate. Line the shrimp up in the rectangle like soldiers. Sprinkle with 1 tablespoon finely chopped parsley.

Captain's Barbecued Shrimp

Yield: 8 servings

4	garlic cloves, minced	2	teaspoons salt
3/4	cup chopped green onions	2	teaspoons paprika
1/2	cup chopped fresh parsley	1	to 2 teaspoons red pepper flakes
2	cups tomato sauce	1	teaspoon black pepper
1 1/4	cups honey	3	bay leaves
1	cup olive oil	1 1/2	teaspoons thyme
1/2	cup lime juice	1/2	teaspoon Tabasco sauce
1/4	cup Worcestershire sauce	4	pounds large or jumbo shrimp

Mix the garlic, green onions, parsley, tomato sauce, honey, olive oil, lime juice, Worcestershire sauce, salt, paprika, red pepper flakes, black pepper, bay leaves, thyme and Tabasco sauce in a large bowl. Adjust the seasonings to taste. Rinse the shrimp. Slit the unpeeled shrimp between the legs. Add to the marinade. Marinate, covered, in the refrigerator for 2 to 12 hours. Drain the shrimp and place in a grill basket. Grill until the shrimp turn pink.

Baked Shrimp with Succulent Sauce

Yield: 10 servings

1	cup (2 sticks) butter, melted	2	teaspoons Tabasco sauce
1	cup (2 sticks) margarine, melted	1	teaspoon rosemary
		2	teaspoons salt
6	tablespoons Worcestershire sauce	3	garlic cloves, minced
		5	to 6 pounds unpeeled shrimp
•	Juice of 2 lemons	2	lemons, sliced
1/4	cup pepper		

Combine the butter, margarine, Worcestershire sauce, lemon juice, pepper, Tabasco sauce, rosemary, salt and garlic in a bowl and mix well. Pour 1/2 cup of the sauce into a 12x13-inch baking pan. Layer the shrimp and lemon slices in the prepared pan. Pour the remaining sauce over the layers. Bake at 400 degrees for 15 to 20 minutes or until the shrimp turn pink, stirring 1 or 2 times.

A fun and delicious meal! Serve with baguettes of hot French bread, a generous amount of napkins, a bowl for the shrimp shells, and big plastic bibs. Guests should open the hot shrimp with their fingers and dip the bread into the sauce.

Grilled Jumbo Shrimp with Prosciutto and Basil

Yield: 6 servings

1	cup dry white wine	24	peeled fresh jumbo shrimp with tails
1	cup olive oil		
1/4	cup fresh lemon juice	24	large basil leaves
2	tablespoons Dijon mustard	24	thin prosciutto slices, trimmed
1/2	cup chopped fresh basil		
•	Freshly cracked peppercorns to taste		

Combine the wine, olive oil, lemon juice, Dijon mustard, 1/2 cup chopped basil and peppercorns in a bowl and mix well. Pour over the shrimp in a shallow dish. Marinate, covered, in the refrigerator for 3 hours or longer, turning occasionally. Drain the shrimp, reserving the marinade. Bring the reserved marinade to a boil in a saucepan. Boil for 2 to 3 minutes. Wrap the middle of each shrimp with a basil leaf and then a slice of prosciutto. Thread 4 shrimp lengthwise beginning at the head on a metal skewer. Place the shrimp on a wire rack. Grill over hot mesquite coals for several minutes or until the shrimp turn pink, basting with the cooked marinade. Serve immediately.

Villa Capri's Shrimp Curry

Yield: 4 servings

1/2	cup (1 stick) butter or margarine	2	cups half-and-half
3	tablespoons flour	3	cups cooked peeled shrimp
2	tablespoons curry powder, or to taste	•	Chutney (page 149)
		•	Orange Rice (page 149)

Melt the butter in a skillet over medium-high heat. Add the flour and curry powder a small amount at a time, stirring constantly. Add the half-and-half gradually, stirring constantly. Reduce the heat to medium. Cook for 3 to 5 minutes or until thickened, stirring constantly. Add the shrimp and stir until the shrimp are coated with the sauce. Cook until the shrimp are heated through.

To serve, place Chutney and other condiments such as shredded coconut, chopped roasted peanuts, mandarin orange slices and sliced green onions in separate small sauce dishes. Serve the curry with the condiments and Orange Rice.

Villa Capri hosted a special "Tastes of the World" dinner for an international group from NASA and this is one of the dishes. Curry dishes are traditionally served with chutney and assorted condiments. To enjoy the full essence of any curry dish, add a dab of a different condiment with each mouthful. The Orange Rice was also served with the Shrimp Curry. There are many different curry powders on the market. Always add the curry powder a small amount at a time, tasting after each addition and adjusting the amount to your taste.

Chutney

Yield: 4 servings

1	quart apple cider vinegar	12	ounces raisins
3	onions, finely chopped	2	tablespoons white mustard seeds
1	pound unpeeled apples, finely chopped	1	tablespoon ground ginger
		2	cups packed dark brown sugar

Bring the vinegar to a boil in a saucepan. Boil for 3 minutes. Let stand until cool. Add the onions, apples, raisins, mustard seeds, ginger and brown sugar. Bring to a boil and reduce the heat. Simmer for 25 to 30 minutes or until thickened, stirring frequently. Let stand until cool. Place in an airtight container. Store for several weeks in the refrigerator or for several months in the freezer.

Note: *Can be served with pork, roast beef or lamb.*

Orange Rice

Yield: 4 servings

2	cups water	1	teaspoon salt
1	tablespoon grated orange zest	1	cup long grain rice
1/2	cup orange juice		

Bring the water, orange zest, orange juice and salt to a boil in a saucepan. Stir in the rice. Return to a boil and reduce the heat, stirring constantly. Cook, covered, for 20 to 25 minutes or until the rice is tender and the liquid is absorbed. Fluff with a fork before spooning into a serving dish.

Shellfish
chablis, California chardonnay, muscadet or sauvignon blanc

Whitefish
chardonnay, Alsace riesling, Puligny-Montrachet or Chassagne-Montrachet

Salmon
pinot noir, sauvignon blanc, Pouilly Fumé and red burgundy

Tuna
sauvignon blanc, Viognier, white burgundy or chardonnay

Rigatoni with Shrimp and Feta Cheese

Yield: 4 servings

5	tablespoons olive oil	2	cups chopped peeled Roma tomatoes
1¼	pounds large shrimp, peeled		
¼	teaspoon red pepper flakes	⅓	cup chopped fresh basil
6	ounces feta cheese, crumbled	1	teaspoon dried oregano
1	small garlic clove	•	Salt and pepper to taste
½	cup dry white wine	12	ounces rigatoni

Heat 3 tablespoons of the olive oil in a skillet. Add the shrimp. Sauté until the shrimp turn pink. Stir in the red pepper flakes. Spoon into a baking dish. Sprinkle with feta cheese. Add the remaining olive oil to the skillet. Add the garlic and sauté briefly. Add the wine. Cook for 2 minutes over high heat. Stir in the tomatoes, basil, oregano, salt and pepper. Simmer for 10 minutes. Spoon over the shrimp. Bake, covered, at 400 degrees for 10 minutes. Cook the pasta in a saucepan using the package directions until al dente; drain. Add the shrimp mixture and toss to coat. Serve immediately.

Fusilli with Roasted Tomatoes, Asparagus and Shrimp

Yield: 4 or 5 servings

12	plum tomatoes, cut into quarters lengthwise	12	ounces fusilli or rotini
2	teaspoons extra-virgin olive oil	2	teaspoons extra-virgin olive oil
•	Freshly ground pepper to taste	2	teaspoons fresh lemon juice
1	small garlic bulb	1	tablespoon chopped fresh oregano, or 1 teaspoon dried oregano
1	pound thin asparagus, trimmed, cut into 2-inch pieces	1	tablespoon chopped fresh thyme, or 1 teaspoon dried thyme
1	pound large shrimp, peeled	•	Salt to taste

Toss the tomatoes with 2 teaspoons olive oil in a large roasting pan. Sprinkle with pepper. Cut 1/2 inch from the top of the garlic bulb and discard. Remove any loose peel from the garlic bulb. Wrap in foil and add to the roasting pan. Place the pan on the lowest oven rack. Bake at 450 degrees for 20 minutes or until the tomatoes are wrinkled and beginning to brown. Sprinkle the asparagus and shrimp over the tomatoes. Bake for 10 minutes or until the shrimp turn pink and the asparagus is tender. Remove the garlic from the pan. Cover the pan to keep warm. Unwrap the garlic and let stand until cool. Separate the garlic cloves. Squeeze the garlic pulp into a bowl and mash to form a paste.

Cook the pasta in boiling water in a saucepan for 8 minutes or until al dente. Drain the pasta and return to the saucepan. Add 2 teaspoons olive oil, mashed garlic, lemon juice, oregano, thyme, salt and pepper and toss to coat evenly. Add to the roasting pan and toss gently to combine, scraping up the brown bits from the bottom of the pan. Serve immediately.

Martini Shrimp

Yield: 4 servings

1/4 cup olive oil	1/8 teaspoon cayenne pepper
2 pounds shrimp, peeled	1/2 cup drained sun-dried tomato
1 tablespoon minced shallots	strips
2 large garlic cloves, minced	1 cup heavy cream
1/4 cup dry white vermouth	1/2 teaspoon salt
1/4 cup vodka or gin	• White pepper to taste

Heat the olive oil in a large heavy sauté pan. Add the shrimp. Sauté for 2 to 3 minutes or until the shrimp turn pink. Remove the shrimp to a warm platter. Add the shallots and garlic to the pan. Sauté for 3 minutes. Add the vermouth, vodka, cayenne pepper and sun-dried tomatoes. Cook over high heat for 5 to 10 minutes or until the liquid is reduced and syrupy. Add the cream, salt and white pepper. Cook for 5 minutes or until thickened. Return the shrimp to the pan. Cook for 1 minute or until heated through.

Show-Off Shrimp

Yield: 12 servings

1/2	cup (1 stick) butter or margarine	1	(16-ounce) can mushrooms, drained
1/2	cup flour	3	pounds shrimp, cooked, peeled
1	cup chicken broth	8	ounces vermicelli, cooked, drained
1	cup heavy cream		
1	cup shredded Swiss cheese	•	Grated Parmesan cheese
1/4	cup sherry	•	Slivered almonds
1/8	teaspoon white pepper		

Melt the butter in a small saucepan. Add the flour. Cook for 2 minutes, stirring constantly. Stir in the chicken broth and cream. Cook over low heat until thickened, stirring constantly. Add the Swiss cheese, sherry and white pepper. Cook until the cheese melts, stirring constantly. Stir in the mushrooms and remove from the heat. Stir in the shrimp. Add the pasta and toss to coat. Spoon into a greased 9x13-inch baking dish. Sprinkle with Parmesan cheese and almonds. Broil for 5 to 7 minutes or until light brown. Serve immediately.

Cooking with Wine

Follow these tips when cooking with wine: Simmer wine to burn off the alcohol and bring out the fruit flavor, except when using wine with a high sugar content, such as Late Harvest Riesling. When deglazing a pan, add the wine and cook over low heat to reduce slowly to avoid a bitter flavor. To compensate for the pronounced acidity that develops when wine is reduced, add fresh or dried fruit. Use quality wine; it has a more concentrated flavor, so use less. Avoid anything sold as cooking wine. Save leftover wines for cooking. Cork the bottles and store in the refrigerator for up to 1 week.

Risotto with Grilled Shrimp

Yield: 3 servings

5	cups chicken stock	1	cup frozen peas
2	tablespoons (1/4 stick) unsalted butter	1	teaspoon grated lemon zest
1	tablespoon olive oil	1	tablespoon (1/8 stick) unsalted butter
1/3	cup finely minced onion	1/3	cup grated Parmesan cheese
1	garlic clove, minced	1	tablespoon fresh lemon juice
1 1/2	cups arborio rice	•	Salt and pepper to taste
1/2	cup dry white wine	•	Grilled Shrimp (at left)

Bring the chicken stock to a simmer in a saucepan. Heat 2 tablespoons butter and olive oil in a heavy Dutch oven over medium heat. Add the onion and garlic. Sauté for 1 to 2 minutes or until softened. Add the rice. Cook for 1 minute, stirring to coat. Add the wine. Cook until the wine is completely absorbed, stirring constantly.

Reserve 1/4 cup of the simmering stock. Add the remaining simmering stock 1/2 cup at a time to the rice mixture, cooking until the stock is almost absorbed after each addition and stirring frequently. Add the reserved stock, peas and lemon zest. Cook for 5 minutes or until the peas are tender, stirring constantly. Add 1 tablespoon butter, Parmesan cheese and lemon juice. Stir in salt and pepper to taste. Spoon immediately onto serving plates. Top with Grilled Shrimp. Serve immediately.

GRILLED SHRIMP

For Grilled Shrimp, rinse and peel 12 ounces shrimp. Coat with a mixture of olive oil, salt and garlic pepper. Thread onto metal skewers and place on a grill rack. Grill for 2 minutes and turn over the shrimp. Grill for 2 minutes longer. Remove from the skewers to serve.

Shrimp Creole

Yield: 2 servings

1/3	cup shortening	1	cup water
1/4	cup flour	1	(8-ounce) can tomato sauce
1	pound shrimp, peeled	1 1/2	teaspoons salt
1	garlic clove, minced	1/8	teaspoon cayenne pepper, or
1/2	cup chopped onion		to taste
1/2	cup chopped green bell pepper	2	bay leaves
2	tablespoons minced fresh parsley		

Melt the shortening in a skillet over high heat. Add the flour. Cook until the flour is light brown, stirring constantly. Reduce the heat. Add the shrimp. Cook for 3 minutes or until the shrimp turn pink. Add the garlic, onion, green pepper and parsley. Cook for 2 minutes. Increase the heat. Add the water gradually, stirring constantly. Add the tomato sauce, salt, cayenne pepper and bay leaves. Bring to a boil and reduce the heat. Simmer, covered, for 20 to 30 minutes or until of the desired consistency. Remove the bay leaves before serving. Serve over hot cooked rice with a green salad and garlic bread.

Shrimp Ratatouille

Yield: 6 to 8 servings

3	yellow squash, cut into 1/4-inch slices	1	green bell pepper, chopped
3	medium zucchini, cut into 1/4-inch slices	1/2	cup olive oil
1	medium eggplant, peeled, sliced	1	(28-ounce) can diced tomatoes
2	teaspoons salt	2	pinches cayenne pepper
2	garlic cloves, crushed	1/2	(8-ounce) package feta cheese, crumbled (optional)
1	large onion, chopped	1 1/2	pounds cooked shrimp, peeled

Sprinkle the squash, zucchini and eggplant with salt. Let stand for 3 minutes; rinse and drain. Sauté the garlic, onion and green pepper in 1/4 cup of the olive oil in a skillet. Spoon into a large stockpot. Sauté the squash, zucchini and eggplant in the remaining olive oil in the skillet. Add to the stockpot. Stir in the tomatoes and cayenne pepper. Simmer for 3 minutes or until tender. Stir in the feta cheese and shrimp just before serving.

Embark!
Entrées

University of Houston-Clear Lake

Located on 524 heavily wooded acres between Armand
Bayou Nature Center and the National Aeronautics
and Space Administration's Johnson Space Center,
the University of Houston-Clear Lake provides both the
peace of a natural setting and the opportunities of
a high-technology, metropolitan community.
The university was authorized by the 1971
Legislature as an upper-level undergraduate and
graduate institution. More than 7,000 students attend day
and evening classes in the arts, sciences and professions.
While not an official dock, the university is the
educational anchor of our community.

⚓

Graduation Dinner

GRILLED SALMON ROLL WITH CAPERS AND CUCUMBERS, *page 125*
MANGO AND PEPPER SALSA WITH CHIPS, *page 22*
EGGPLANT IN PHYLLO SHELLS, *page 33*

PINOT NOIR

KALEIDOSCOPE MUSHROOM SALAD, *page 87*

MARINATED BEEF TENDERLOIN WITH TARRAGON BURGUNDY WINE SAUCE, *page 161*
RED POTATOES WITH ARTICHOKES AND FETA CHEESE, *page 111*
ASPARAGUS WITH MALTAISE SAUCE, *page 105*

BAY OAKS CHEESE AND SCALLION BISCUITS, *page 41*

CABERNET SAUVIGNON

GRAND MARNIER SOUFFLÉ, *page 205*

CHAMPAGNE

Marinated Beef Tenderloin with Tarragon Burgundy Wine Sauce

Yield: 8 to 10 servings

1	(5-pound) beef tenderloin, trimmed	3	tablespoons dried parsley flakes
1¹/₂	cups burgundy	3	tablespoons paprika
1	cup tarragon vinegar	1	tablespoon plus 1¹/₂
³/₄	cup olive oil		teaspoons Beau Monde
³/₄	cup soy sauce		seasoning

Place the beef in a large baking dish. Combine the wine, vinegar, olive oil, soy sauce, parsley flakes, paprika and Beau Monde seasoning in a bowl and mix well. Pour over the beef, turning to coat both sides. Marinate, covered, in the refrigerator for 3 hours, turning over the beef after 1¹/₂ hours. Uncover and place on the bottom oven rack; do not drain. Broil for 20 minutes. Turn over the beef. Broil for 20 minutes longer. Bake, covered, at 350 degrees for 10 to 15 minutes or until done to taste. Cut the beef into slices and serve with the sauce.

NO-FUSS BARBECUED POT ROAST

For No-Fuss Barbecued Pot Roast, place one 5-pound chuck roast in a large Dutch oven. Add one undrained 32-ounce jar whole dill pickles and one 12-ounce jar chili sauce. Bake at 275 degrees for 8 hours or until cooked through. Cut the pickles into slices and serve with the roast. Any leftover roast can be shredded for barbecue sandwiches.

161

Prime Rib
merlot

Steak
cabernet sauvignon or red bordeaux

Rack of Lamb
cabernet sauvignon or red bordeaux

Tenderloin of Beef with Bleu Cheese

Yield: 6 to 8 servings

1/4	cup (1/2 stick) butter or margarine
1	teaspoon minced fresh garlic
1/2	teaspoon coarsely ground pepper
1	(2- to 3-pound) beef tenderloin, trimmed, tied
2	tablespoons (1/4 stick) butter or margarine
1	(4-ounce) package bleu cheese, crumbled
1	cup beef broth
1/4	cup madeira
2	cups sliced fresh mushrooms
1/2	cup chopped pecans, toasted
1/2	cup pine nuts or sliced almonds, toasted
1/3	cup 1/4-inch sliced green onions

Melt 1/4 cup butter in a 10-inch skillet until sizzling. Stir in the garlic and pepper. Place the beef in the skillet. Cook over medium-high heat for 7 to 9 minutes or until brown on all sides. Drain the beef, reserving the juices in the skillet. Place the beef in a foil-lined 9x13-inch baking pan. Bake at 400 degrees for 35 to 50 minutes or until a meat thermometer registers 140 degrees for rare, 160 degrees for medium or 170 degrees for well done.

Melt 2 tablespoons butter in the pan juices in the skillet, stirring to deglaze the skillet. Stir in the bleu cheese. Cook over medium heat for 4 to 5 minutes or until the bleu cheese is melted, stirring occasionally. Stir in the beef broth and wine. Add the mushrooms. Cook for 4 to 5 minutes or until the mushrooms are tender. Stir in the pecans, pine nuts and green onions.

To serve, carve the beef and serve with the sauce.

Steak with Peppercorn Sauce

Yield: 4 to 6 servings

1 to 2 tablespoons crushed peppercorns	1 tablespoon vegetable oil
1 tablespoon (1/8 stick) butter, softened	1/4 cup dry red wine
1/2 teaspoon garlic powder	2 tablespoons Cognac
1 (2-pound) beef top sirloin steak, cut 1 inch thick	1/2 cup heavy cream
	2 tablespoons chopped fresh parsley
	• Salt to taste

Mix the crushed peppercorns, butter and garlic powder in a bowl. Spread evenly on both sides of the steak. Heat the vegetable oil in a skillet over medium-high heat. Add the steak. Cook for 7 minutes for rare, 8 minutes for medium-rare or 9 minutes for medium, turning over the steak to brown evenly on each side. Remove the steak to a serving platter to keep warm. Add the wine and Cognac to the skillet. Cook over high heat for 1 minute, stirring to deglaze the skillet. Reduce the heat. Add the cream and parsley. Cook for 1 to 2 minutes or until thickened, stirring constantly. Season with salt to taste.

To serve, cut the steak cross grain into thin slices. Pour the sauce over the steak. Garnish with additional parsley.

Note: *May substitute filet mignon for the top sirloin steak.*

Medallions of Beef Tenderloin

Yield: 10 to 12 servings

5¹⁄₂	pounds beef tenderloin	1	small jar Creole or spicy brown mustard
¹⁄₄	cup olive oil	•	Béarnaise Sauce (below)
2	tablespoons cracked black peppercorns	•	Bordelaise Sauce (page 165)
1	tablespoon cracked green peppercorns	•	Choron Sauce (page 165)
1	tablespoon garlic powder	•	Brown Sauce (page 165)

Rub the beef with olive oil, black peppercorns, green peppercorns, garlic powder and Creole mustard. Cook in a large skillet until light brown. Place on a rack in a roasting pan. Bake at 325 degrees for 40 to 55 minutes or to the desired degree of doneness.

To serve, cut the beef into medallions and place on serving plates. Serve with Béarnaise Sauce, Bordelaise Sauce, Choron Sauce or Brown Sauce or a combination of each.

Béarnaise Sauce

Yield: ³⁄₄ cup

3	tablespoons white wine	¹⁄₂	cup (1 stick) butter
1	tablespoon dried tarragon leaves	3	egg yolks
1	teaspoon lemon juice	1	teaspoon chopped fresh tarragon

Combine the wine, dried tarragon and lemon juice in a small saucepan. Cook over high heat until the mixture is reduced to 2 tablespoons; strain. Melt the butter in a saucepan. Bring almost to the boiling point. Process the egg yolks in a blender or food processor until blended. Add the butter in a thin stream, processing constantly. Add the reduced wine mixture, processing constantly just until blended. Stir in the fresh tarragon and pour into a serving bowl.

Bordelaise Sauce

Yield: 2 cups

1 tablespoon (1/8 stick) butter
2 tablespoons finely minced shallots
1/3 cup brandy
1 cup dry red wine
1 1/2 cups Brown Sauce (at right)

- Juice of 1/2 lemon
- Salt and pepper to taste
- Dash of Tabasco sauce
1 cup sliced mushrooms
1/4 cup (1/2 stick) butter, softened

Melt 1 tablespoon butter in a saucepan. Add the shallots. Sauté until transparent. Add the brandy and wine. Cook until the mixture is reduced by 1/2. Add the Brown Sauce, lemon juice, salt, pepper and Tabasco sauce. Sauté the mushrooms in 2 tablespoons of the remaining butter. Add to the sauce. Simmer for 5 minutes. Remove from the heat. Stir in the remaining 2 tablespoons butter and keep warm.

CHORON SAUCE

To make Choron Sauce, stir 1 tablespoon tomato paste into the Béarnaise Sauce (page 164). Serve immediately. Choron Sauce is very good on beef or seafood.

BROWN SAUCE

To prepare Brown Sauce, blend 2 tablespoons clarified butter into 1/4 cup flour in a saucepan until smooth. Add 2 cups veal or beef stock gradually, stirring constantly until smooth. Simmer until thickened, stirring constantly.

Grilled Filets Mignons with Stilton Sauce

Yield: 4 servings

4	(6- to 8-ounce) filets mignons	3	tablespoons butter, softened
•	Seasoned salt to taste	•	Stilton Sauce (below)
•	Ground pepper to taste		

Season beef with seasoned salt and pepper. Rub with the butter. Place on a grill rack. Grill over hot coals until done to taste. Serve immediately with Stilton Sauce and hot cooked rice or noodles.

Stilton Sauce

3/4	cup madeira	1/2	cup (1 stick) butter, softened
2	tablespoons minced shallots	6	ounces Stilton, Gorgonzola
1	garlic clove, minced		or Roquefort cheese,
1	cup heavy cream		crumbled, softened
1/2	cup demi-glace or brown stock	•	Seasoned salt to taste
		•	Cayenne pepper to taste

Combine the wine, shallots and garlic in a small saucepan. Cook over medium-high heat until the mixture is reduced to about 2 tablespoons. Add the cream and demi-glace. Cook over high heat until the mixture is reduced to about 1 cup. Beat the butter and Stilton cheese in a bowl until smooth. Add a small amount at a time to the saucepan, whisking constantly. Simmer for 3 minutes, stirring constantly. Strain into a serving bowl. Season with seasoned salt and cayenne pepper.

Roquefort Filets Mignons with Brandy

Yield: 4 servings

3	tablespoons butter	1	tablespoon chopped fresh
4	(6-ounce) filets mignons, cut 1		rosemary, or 1 1/2 teaspoons dried
	inch thick		rosemary
•	Salt and pepper to taste	1	to 2 cups crumbled Roquefort
2	cups beef broth		cheese
3/4	cup brandy		

Melt the butter in a medium heavy skillet or electric skillet on medium-high heat. Season the beef with salt and pepper and add to the skillet. Cook for 4 minutes per side for medium-rare or to the desired degree of doneness. Remove the beef to a warm serving plate and cover with foil. Add the beef broth, brandy and rosemary to the skillet. Bring to a boil. Boil for 10 to 12 minutes or until the sauce is reduced to 1 cup, stirring to deglaze the skillet. Spoon over the beef. Top each serving with Roquefort cheese.

Peppered Beef

Yield: 6 servings

1	(8- to 9-pound) eye-of-round	•	Cracked black pepper
	beef roast		

Cover the roast completely with pepper. Place in a baking or broiler pan. Bake, loosely covered with a tent of foil, at 500 degrees for 5 minutes per pound for rare, 10 to 12 minutes per pound for medium-well done or to the desired degree of doneness. Turn off the oven; do not open the oven door. Let stand in the oven for 2 hours. Remove from the oven and let stand until cool. Cut into thin slices to serve.

Note: *For a spicier version, cover the roast with 1 teaspoon salt, 1 teaspoon black pepper and 1 teaspoon red pepper.*

Flank Steak with Caper Sauce

Yield: 4 servings

1	(1½-pound) flank steak, scored	⅓	cup dry vermouth
1	tablespoon (⅛ stick) butter	1	tablespoon Dijon mustard
1	tablespoon olive oil	¼	teaspoon Worcestershire sauce
3	tablespoons butter	2	tablespoons drained capers

Cover the steak with plastic wrap and pound until flattened. Melt 1 tablespoon butter with the olive oil in a 12-inch skillet. Add the steak. Cook for 5 to 6 minutes or until brown on both sides, turning once. The steak should be pink in the middle. Remove the steak to a carving board and cover with foil to keep warm. Melt 3 tablespoons butter in the pan drippings in the skillet. Whisk in the vermouth, Dijon mustard, Worcestershire sauce and capers. Remove from the heat and keep warm.

To serve, cut the steak cross grain into slices. Spoon the sauce over the sliced steak.

Veal Verrette

Yield: 10 servings

2	cups flour	1	cup pearl onions
2	cups bread crumbs	5	tablespoons butter
•	Salt and black pepper to taste	•	Sherry to taste
20	(4-ounce) veal cutlets	•	White pepper to taste
2	tablespoons olive oil	•	Garlic powder to taste
2	cups sliced mushrooms	•	Cayenne pepper to taste
2	cups chopped artichoke hearts		

Mix the flour, bread crumbs, salt and black pepper together. Pound the veal until thin. Dredge in the flour mixture. Sauté in 2 tablespoons olive oil in a skillet. Sauté the mushrooms, artichokes and pearl onions in 5 tablespoons butter in a skillet until tender. Add the sherry and season with salt, white pepper, garlic powder and cayenne pepper.

To serve, place the veal on a serving plate and spoon the mushroom mixture over the top.

A native of Galveston, Texas, Jesse Verrette moved to Miami, Florida, and became a chef at the age of nineteen. He trained while in the U. S. Army and is presently the chef at South Shore Harbour Country Club in League City.

Meat Roll with Mozzarella Cheese and Mushrooms

Yield: 6 to 8 servings

1	(16-ounce) package hot roll mix	1	teaspoon basil
1	pound ground beef	•	Salt and pepper to taste
1	pound mild sausage	1	(4-ounce) can sliced mushrooms, drained
1	medium onion, chopped	16	ounces mozzarella cheese, shredded
1	teaspoon garlic powder		
1	teaspoon oregano		

Prepare the roll mix using the package directions. Let the dough rise until doubled in bulk. Brown the ground beef and sausage with the onion in a skillet, stirring until the ground beef and sausage are crumbly; drain well. Sprinkle with garlic powder, oregano, basil, salt and pepper. Add the mushrooms and mix well. Roll the dough into an 11x15-inch rectangle. Spread the ground beef mixture over the rectangle, leaving a 1-inch border. Sprinkle with the cheese. Roll up the dough beginning at the long side and pinch the seam to seal. Place seam side down on a baking sheet; cut a few slits in the top to vent. Bake at 350 degrees for 15 to 20 minutes or until golden brown. Cool for 10 minutes. Cut into slices to serve.

GAME NIGHT
BUFFET

Deep-Dish Taco Pie

Yield: 4 to 6 servings

1 (14-ounce) package tortilla chips
1 pound lean ground beef
1/2 cup picante sauce
1 (4-ounce) can mild green chiles, chopped
1 tablespoon chili powder
3/4 teaspoon salt
1/4 teaspoon cayenne pepper (optional)
1 medium avocado, peeled, chopped

1 large fresh tomato, chopped
2 tablespoons freshly squeezed lime juice
2 tablespoons chopped fresh cilantro or parsley
1 tablespoon chopped onion
1/4 teaspoon black pepper
1 cup shredded Monterey Jack cheese
2 cups shredded lettuce

Crush enough of the tortilla chips in a plastic bag to measure 4 cups. Reserve the remaining chips for garnish. Line a greased 10-inch deep-dish pie plate with the crushed chips. Combine the ground beef, picante sauce, green chiles, chili powder, 1/2 teaspoon of the salt and cayenne pepper in a large bowl and mix well. Place in the prepared pie plate, patting to cover the chips. Bake, uncovered, at 375 degrees for 20 to 25 minutes or until cooked through. Combine the avocado, tomato, lime juice, cilantro, onion, remaining 1/4 teaspoon salt and black pepper in a bowl and toss gently to mix.

To serve, sprinkle the cheese over the hot ground beef mixture. Arrange the lettuce around the outside edge. Spoon the avocado mixture in the center. Place the reserved chips around the outside edge.

HOMEMADE STOCK

To prepare Homemade Stock, bake 4 pounds beef, veal or lamb bones, 2 large unpeeled onions, quartered, 4 unpeeled carrots, cut into pieces, 1 bunch parsley, chopped, 1 bunch thyme, 3 bay leaves, 4 cloves, 10 peppercorns and 4 unpeeled garlic cloves at 425 degrees for 30 minutes or until brown, stirring often. Add 2 cups wine. Simmer for 15 minutes. Add to a stockpot with 4 to 6 quarts of water. Simmer for about 3 hours. Broth is ready to use at this point, but will be richer if cooked for 2 to 3 hours longer, adding additional water if needed. Strain the broth. Cool. Store in the refrigerator for 3 to 4 days or freeze for up to 3 months.

Lamb Spinach Roulade

Yield: 10 servings

12	ounces mushrooms, chopped	1/8	teaspoon pepper
3	green onions, minced	1	(4 1/2-pound) leg of lamb, butterflied, deboned
6	tablespoons (3/4 stick) margarine	•	Salt and pepper to taste
8	slices wheat bread	1	cup water or Homemade Stock (at left)
2	(10-ounce) packages frozen spinach, thawed, squeezed dry	2	tablespoons dry red wine
3	ounces feta cheese	1	teaspoon instant beef bouillon
1/2	teaspoon salt	1/4	teaspoon salt

Sauté the mushrooms and green onions in the margarine in a 10-inch skillet until tender. Remove from the heat. Tear the bread into pieces and place in the mushroom mixture. Add the spinach, feta cheese, 1/2 teaspoon salt and 1/8 teaspoon pepper and toss to mix.

Sprinkle the inside of the leg of lamb with salt and pepper to taste. Spread with the spinach stuffing. Roll up and tie with string. Place lean side down on a rack in a roasting pan. Insert a meat thermometer into the thickest portion. Bake at 325 degrees for about 2 1/2 hours (30 to 35 minutes per pound) or until the thermometer registers 160 degrees. Place on a warm large platter. Let stand for 15 minutes. Remove the rack from the roasting pan. Skim the pan juices. Add the water, wine, bouillon granules and 1/4 teaspoon salt. Bring just to a boil over medium-high heat, stirring to deglaze the roasting pan. Pour into a serving bowl.

To serve, remove the string from the lamb. Cut into slices. Serve with the sauce.

Marinated Butterflied Leg of Lamb

Yield: 6 to 8 servings

1	(6- to 7-pound) leg of lamb, butterflied, trimmed	•	Juice of 1 lemon
1	medium onion, chopped	2	tablespoons Dijon mustard
3	garlic cloves, minced	1	teaspoon salt
3/4	cup olive oil	1	teaspoon basil
1/2	cup dry white wine	1	teaspoon oregano
1/4	cup chopped parsley	1	bay leaf, crushed

Place the lamb in a glass dish. Combine the onion, garlic, olive oil, wine, parsley, lemon juice, Dijon mustard, salt, basil, oregano and bay leaf in a bowl and mix well. Pour over the lamb. Marinate, covered, in the refrigerator for 4 to 12 hours. Insert 2 long skewers at right angles through the lamb to form an "x" or place in a wire grill basket. Place on the grill rack. Grill over medium heat for 30 to 40 minutes or until a meat thermometer registers 140 degrees for rare or 150 degrees for medium-rare, turning every 15 minutes. Remove from the grill and let rest for 5 to 10 minutes before slicing.

Note: *The skewers or basket make it easier to turn the lamb and keep it from curling during grilling.*

Lamb Chop Stilton

Yield: 4 servings

8	(1-inch-thick) lamb chops	8	(1/8-inch-thick) slices Stilton cheese
6	to 8 teaspoons Dijon mustard		

Brush each lamb chop with about 1/2 teaspoon Dijon mustard. Place on a rack in a broiler pan. Broil for 6 minutes. Turn over each lamb chop and brush with the remaining Dijon mustard. Broil for 5 minutes. Top each lamb chop with a slice of cheese. Broil for 1 minute or until the cheese melts.

Rack of Lamb with Herb Crust

Yield: 2 or 3 servings

1	rack of baby lamb (about 7 chops)	2	tablespoons Dijon mustard
1	cup fresh white bread crumbs	2	tablespoons olive oil
1/2	cup finely chopped flat-leaf parsley or chervil	1	teaspoon coarse kosher salt
1	garlic clove, minced	•	Freshly ground pepper to taste

Let the lamb stand at room temperature for 30 to 45 minutes. Trim the lamb, leaving the rib bones as long as possible and 1/4 inch of fat on the outside of the rack. Cut neat crisscrosses in the fat using a sharp knife. Place on a rack in a roasting pan. Bake at 400 degrees for 15 to 20 minutes. Remove the lamb from the oven and reduce the oven temperature to 375 degrees. Combine the bread crumbs, parsley, garlic, Dijon mustard, olive oil, kosher salt and pepper in a small bowl. Pat the crumb mixture on top of the rack of lamb and on the bony side to form a crust. Return to the oven. Bake for 10 to 15 minutes or until brown.

Creole Barbecued Pork Loin

Yield: 4 to 6 servings

1 (3- to 4-pound) boneless pork loin roast
• Creole Seasoning (below)
1 cup (2 sticks) butter

3 to 5 garlic cloves, minced, or to taste
• Juice of 1 lemon

Place the pork in a glass dish. Rub with some of the Creole Seasoning. Marinate, covered, in the refrigerator for 4 hours. Melt the butter in a small saucepan. Add the garlic, lemon juice and 2 1/2 teaspoons of the Creole Seasoning. Place the pork on a grill rack. Sear the pork on all sides over high heat. Reduce the heat to medium or place the pork on a higher grill rack. Grill for 45 to 60 minutes or until a meat thermometer registers 145 to 150 degrees when inserted into the thickest portion, basting with some of the butter mixture every 10 to 15 minutes. Place the remaining butter mixture in a roasting pan. Add the pork. Increase the grill heat to high. Place the pan on the grill rack. Grill for 5 minutes, turning the pork.

To serve, cut the pork into slices and serve with any remaining pan drippings.

Creole Seasoning

2 1/2 tablespoons paprika
2 tablespoons salt
2 tablespoons garlic powder
1 tablespoon black pepper

1 tablespoon onion powder
1 tablespoon cayenne pepper
1 tablespoon oregano
1 tablespoon thyme

Combine paprika, salt, garlic powder, black pepper, onion powder, cayenne pepper, oregano and thyme in a bowl and mix well. Store in an airtight container.

Crown Roast of Pork with Apple Stuffing

Yield: 10 to 12 servings

1 (6- to 7-pound) crown roast of pork (about 12 ribs)	• Apple Stuffing (below)
• Salt and pepper to taste	• Roasted Potatoes, Carrots and Leeks (page 177)

Season the pork with salt and pepper. Fill the center of the roast with Apple Stuffing. Place the roast on a rack in a shallow roasting pan. Cover the rib bones and stuffing with foil to prevent overbrowning during baking. Bake at 350 degrees for about 35 minutes per pound or until a meat thermometer registers 170 degrees when inserted between the ribs. Remove the foil 30 to 60 minutes before the end of the baking time to brown the ribs and the stuffing. Remove the pork to a serving platter. Garnish with fresh parsley and spiced crab apples. Carve the pork from the top down between the ribs, allowing 1 rib per serving. Serve with Apple Stuffing and Roasted Potatoes, Carrots and Leeks.

Apple Stuffing

1	cup chopped onion	1/4	cup chopped parsley
1	cup chopped celery	1/3	cup apple juice
3	medium apples, cored, chopped	1/2	teaspoon salt
6	cups 1/2-inch bread cubes	1/2	teaspoon cinnamon
3/4	cup (1 1/2 sticks) butter, melted	1/2	teaspoon poultry seasoning

Combine the onion, celery, apples, bread cubes, butter, parsley, apple juice, salt, cinnamon and poultry seasoning in a large bowl and mix well. Use to stuff Crown Roast of Pork. Can also serve as a side dish by spooning the remaining stuffing into a greased baking dish and baking at 350 degrees for 30 minutes.

Roasted Potatoes, Carrots and Leeks

Yield: 10 to 12 servings

3	medium leeks (about 2 pounds)	2	tablespoons olive oil
1	(16-ounce) package baby carrots	3	garlic cloves, minced
2	pounds new potatoes	1/4	teaspoon salt
		1/4	teaspoon pepper

Trim the leeks, leaving about 4 inches of dark leaves and removing the tough outer leaves. Cut the leeks diagonally into 1-inch slices and rinse well. Place the leeks, carrots and potatoes in a 10x15-inch baking pan lined with foil. Drizzle a mixture of the olive oil, garlic, salt and pepper over the vegetables and stir gently to coat. Bake at 350 degrees for 1 1/2 hours or until the vegetables are tender, stirring occasionally.

HEARTY HARVEST DINNER

Apricot Melba
page 79

Crown Roast of Pork with Apple Stuffing and Roasted Potatoes, Carrots and Leeks
pages 176-177

Phyllo Spinach Pie
page 113

Country Hot Rolls
page 52

Holiday Cherry Pies
page 223

Japanese Fruitcake Pie
page 223

Gewürztraminer or Red Burgundy

Grilled Pork Tenderloin with Garlic Mustard Sauce

Yield: 6 to 8 servings

1½ cups soy sauce	¼ cup bourbon
3 tablespoons dark molasses	3 pounds pork tenderloin
½ cup packed brown sugar	• Garlic Mustard Sauce (below)

Combine the soy sauce, molasses, brown sugar and bourbon in a bowl and mix well. Place the pork in a glass dish. Pour the soy sauce mixture over the pork. Marinate, covered, in the refrigerator for 8 to 12 hours. Bring the pork to room temperature. Drain the pork, reserving the marinade. Bring the reserved marinade to a boil in a saucepan. Boil for 2 minutes. Place the pork on a grill rack. Sear on all sides, basting with the reserved marinade. Grill, covered, for 20 to 30 minutes or until the pork is cooked through. Do not overcook. Remove to a serving platter. Let stand for 1 to 2 minutes. Carve diagonally into ½-inch slices. Serve with Garlic Mustard Sauce.

Garlic Mustard Sauce

¾ cup white wine vinegar	2 eggs, at room temperature
2 tablespoons dry mustard	¾ cup sugar
2 garlic cloves, pressed	

Combine the vinegar, dry mustard and garlic in a glass bowl. Let stand at room temperature for 8 to 12 hours. Beat the eggs in a mixer bowl until frothy. Add the sugar 1 tablespoon at a time, beating well after each addition. Combine with the vinegar mixture in a double boiler. Cook over simmering water for 5 minutes or until thick enough to coat a spoon.

Wine choices for veal and pork will change with preparation methods. The lighter preparation would take a chardonnay. A heavier preparation needs a chianti or barbera. Roast veal or pork works well with cabernet sauvignon, medium-bodied bordeaux or zinfandel.

Polynesian Pork Roast

Yield: 10 to 12 servings

2	tablespoons dry mustard	1/2	cup soy sauce
2	teaspoons thyme	2	garlic cloves, minced
1	(4- to 5-pound) pork loin roast, boned, rolled and tied	1	teaspoon ginger
1/2	cup sherry	•	Currant Sauce (below)

Rub a mixture of the dry mustard and thyme all over the pork. Place in a sealable plastic food storage bag in a shallow dish. Mix the sherry, soy sauce, garlic and ginger in a bowl. Pour over the pork in the bag and seal the bag. Marinate in the refrigerator for 8 to 12 hours, turning occasionally. Remove the pork from the marinade. Place the pork on a rack in a shallow roasting pan. Bake or grill, uncovered, at 325 degrees for 2 to 3 hours or until a meat thermometer registers 165 degrees when inserted into the thickest portion.

To serve, carve the pork into slices and ladle the Currant Sauce over each serving.

Currant Sauce

1	(10-ounce) jar currant jelly	1	tablespoon sherry
1	tablespoon soy sauce		

Dissolve the jelly in a small saucepan over medium heat, stirring occasionally. Add the soy sauce and sherry and mix well.

Southwestern Pork Tenderloin

Yield: 4 servings

1	(2- to 3-pound) pork tenderloin	1	teaspoon grated orange zest
2	garlic cloves	1/2	cup orange juice
2	teaspoons minced fresh thyme	•	Orange and Black Bean Salsa (below)

Place the pork in a shallow dish. Mix the garlic, thyme, orange zest and orange juice in a bowl. Pour over the pork. Marinate, covered, in the refrigerator for 2 hours or longer. Drain the pork, discarding the marinade. Place the pork on a rack in a roasting pan. Bake at 400 degrees for 40 minutes or until a meat thermometer registers 160 degrees when inserted into the thickest portion.

To serve, cut the pork into slices. Spoon Orange and Black Bean Salsa over each serving.

Orange and Black Bean Salsa

2	oranges, peeled, chopped	2	tablespoons chopped fresh cilantro
1	cup rinsed drained black beans	•	Chopped jalapeño peppers to taste
1	red bell pepper, chopped		
2	tablespoons red wine vinegar		

Combine the oranges, black beans, red pepper, red wine vinegar, cilantro and jalapeño peppers in a bowl and mix well. Chill until serving time.

BOURBON-ROASTED PORK TENDERLOIN

For Bourbon-Roasted Pork Tenderloin, marinate 3 pounds pork tenderloin in a mixture of 1/3 cup soy sauce, 1/3 cup bourbon, 3 tablespoons brown sugar and 2 garlic cloves, pressed, for several hours to overnight. Drain, reserving the marinade. Boil the reserved marinade in a saucepan for 2 minutes. Place the pork on a rack in a roasting pan. Bake at 325 degrees for 1 hour or until the pork is cooked through, basting frequently with the cooked reserved marinade.

Applejack Pork Chops

Yield: 8 servings

8   tablespoons (1 stick) butter
3   unpeeled Granny Smith apples, cut into 1/3-inch slices
3   unpeeled Red Delicious apples, cut into 1/3-inch slices
2   teaspoons sugar
8   (1-inch-thick) pork chops

•   Lemon pepper to taste
1   cup chopped white onion
1/2   teaspoon thyme
1/3   cup Applejack or Calvados
1   cup heavy cream
1/3   cup apple cider

Melt 3 tablespoons of the butter in a large skillet. Add the apples and sugar. Sauté until golden brown. Remove from the heat. Season the pork chops with lemon pepper. Cook the pork chops in 2 tablespoons melted butter in a skillet for 3 minutes on each side or until brown and cooked through. Remove the pork chops to a warm plate. Melt remaining 3 tablespoons butter in the drippings in the skillet. Add the onion and thyme. Sauté until the onion is transparent. Add the Applejack. Cook until the liquid is reduced to a glaze. Stir in the cream and cider. Season with lemon pepper. Cook until thickened, stirring constantly.

To serve, arrange the pork chops and apples on a serving platter. Serve with the sauce.

Note: *Can substitute a 3-pound pork tenderloin for the pork chops, seasoning with lemon pepper and adding 1 cup chicken broth. Bake at 350 degrees until a meat thermometer registers 160 to 170 degrees when inserted in the thickest portion. Prepare the apples and sauce as above.*

Chicken and Pork Adobo

Yield: 6 servings

1½ pounds chicken pieces	¾ cup white vinegar
1½ pounds pork loin, cut into large chunks	1 tablespoon peppercorns
	2 bay leaves
12 to 14 garlic cloves	1 tablespoon vegetable oil
½ cup soy sauce	

Place the chicken and pork in a medium saucepan with garlic, soy sauce, vinegar and peppercorns. Marinate for 2 hours. Remove the chicken from the saucepan. Add the bay leaves to the saucepan. Cook the pork in the marinade over low heat for 30 minutes. Return the chicken to the saucepan. Cook for 30 minutes or until the chicken and pork are cooked through. Remove the garlic to hot vegetable oil in a skillet. Sauté until brown. Add the pork and chicken. Sauté until brown. Add the marinade, discarding the bay leaves. Simmer for 10 minutes. Serve with hot steamed white rice.

A rich, marinated stew of chicken and pork, this is one of the most popular dishes in the Philippines. The method of cooking is a preservation process due to the use of vinegar. The finished dish will keep for up to 2 days without refrigeration with the taste improving every day, but today's cooks will probably prefer to refrigerate the stew.

Opelousas Baked Chicken

Yield: 8 servings

4	chicken halves	1	cup water
•	Creole seasoning	1	(1-ounce) jar paprika
1	cup vegetable oil	1	teaspoon chili powder

Season the chicken generously with Creole seasoning. Rub the seasoning on each side. Place in a baking pan. Pour a mixture of the vegetable oil and water over the chicken. Bake at 275 degrees until the chicken is hot. Sprinkle with the paprika and chili powder. Continue baking for 3 to 5 hours or until the chicken is cooked through and dark brown, basting every 30 minutes.

Chicken with Wine and Herbs

Yield: 4 servings

1	tablespoon flour	1/4	teaspoon rosemary
1/4	teaspoon garlic salt	1/4	teaspoon basil
1/4	teaspoon paprika	1/2	cup white zinfandel
4	large boneless skinless chicken breasts	1 1/2	teaspoons cornstarch
		1	tablespoon water
2	tablespoons olive oil	1/2	cup sour cream

Mix the flour, garlic salt and paprika in a shallow dish. Dredge the chicken in the flour mixture. Brown both sides of the chicken in hot olive oil in a skillet. Sprinkle with the rosemary and basil. Add the wine. Simmer, covered, for 25 minutes or until the chicken is cooked through. Remove the chicken to a serving platter. Remove and discard any excess oil from the skillet. Mix the cornstarch and water in a small cup. Add to the drippings in the skillet. Cook until thickened, stirring constantly. Stir in the sour cream. Spoon over the chicken.

Pesto-Stuffed Chicken Rolls

Yield: 6 servings

6	large boneless skinless chicken breasts	1/4	cup commercial pesto
1/4	teaspoon salt	1/2	cup finely chopped red bell pepper
3/4	teaspoon pepper	3/4	cup cornflake crumbs
4	ounces cream cheese, softened	1/2	teaspoon paprika

Place the chicken between 2 sheets of plastic wrap. Pound 1/4 inch thick with a meat mallet or flatten with a rolling pin. Sprinkle with salt and pepper. Combine the cream cheese, pesto and red pepper in a bowl and mix well. Spread 2 tablespoons of the cream cheese mixture over each chicken breast. Roll up lengthwise and secure with wooden picks. Dredge in a mixture of cornflake crumbs and paprika. Place in a 7x11-inch baking dish coated with nonstick cooking spray. Bake at 350 degrees for 35 minutes or until cooked through.

To serve, let stand for 10 minutes and remove the wooden picks. Cut into 1-inch slices with an electric knife. Garnish with sprigs of fresh basil.

Note: *Can prepare the chicken rolls a day ahead of time and store in the refrigerator. Return to room temperature and bake when ready to serve.*

Layered Chicken Asparagus

Yield: 12 servings

6	whole chicken breasts, cooked	2	teaspoons Worcestershire sauce
1	medium onion, chopped		
1/2	cup (1 stick) butter	1/4	teaspoon Tabasco sauce
1	(10-ounce) can cream of chicken soup	1	teaspoon salt
		1/2	teaspoon pepper
1	(8-ounce) can mushrooms	1	teaspoon MSG (optional)
1	(5-ounce) can evaporated milk	2	tablespoons chopped pimento
		2	(11-ounce) cans asparagus tips, drained
1	cup shredded sharp Cheddar cheese	1/2	cup slivered almonds

Chop the chicken into bite-size pieces, discarding the skin and bone. Sauté the onion in the butter in a large skillet until translucent. Add the chicken soup, undrained mushrooms, evaporated milk, cheese, Worcestershire sauce, Tabasco sauce, salt, pepper, MSG and pimento. Cook until the cheese melts, stirring occasionally. Layer the chicken, asparagus and sauce 1/2 at a time in a nonstick 9x13-inch baking dish. Sprinkle with the almonds. Bake, uncovered, at 350 degrees for 1 hour or until bubbly. Do not add additional liquid while baking.

Chicken and Goat Cheese Roulade with Roasted Red Pepper Wine Sauce

Yield: 4 servings

1	tablespoon minced, oil-pack sun-dried tomatoes	1	teaspoon olive oil
4	ounces goat cheese	4	boneless skinless chicken breasts
1	tablespoon chopped fresh basil leaves	1	egg white, beaten
½	teaspoon chopped fresh thyme leaves	½	cup cracker crumbs
		½	teaspoon crushed dried basil
		•	Roasted Red Pepper Wine Sauce (below)

Drain the oil from the sun-dried tomatoes and pat dry. Combine the cheese, 1 tablespoon basil, thyme, sun-dried tomatoes and olive oil in a medium bowl. Divide into 4 equal portions. Shape each portion into a log. Place the chicken breasts between 2 sheets of plastic wrap. Pound ¼ inch thick with a meat mallet. Place a cheese log on each chicken breast. Roll up and secure with a wooden pick. Dip in the beaten egg white; coat with a mixture of cracker crumbs and ½ teaspoon basil. Place seam side down in a nonstick baking dish. Bake, covered, at 350 degrees for 30 minutes. Uncover and spray the chicken with olive oil nonstick cooking spray. Increase the oven temperature to 450 degrees. Bake for 10 minutes or until the chicken is cooked through.

To serve, cut each roll into 4 slices on a serving plate. Spoon Roasted Red Pepper Wine Sauce over the top.

Roasted Red Pepper Wine Sauce

2	red bell peppers, roasted, peeled, seeded	1	teaspoon balsamic vinegar
2	garlic cloves, minced	1	teaspoon olive oil
⅓	cup dry white wine	•	Salt and white pepper to taste
		¼	cup heavy cream

Process the red peppers, garlic, wine, vinegar, olive oil, salt and white pepper in a food processor or blender until smooth. Pour into a saucepan. Add the cream. Simmer for 10 minutes, stirring frequently.

Note: *For how to roast peppers, see page 189.*

Stuffed Chicken with Spinach Ricotta

Yield: 6 servings

5	to 6 ounces fresh spinach	•	Nutmeg to taste
8	ounces ricotta cheese	1	tablespoon Dijon mustard
2	to 3 garlic cloves, pressed	6	chicken breasts
1	small onion, finely chopped	1/4	cup white wine or lemon
•	Salt and pepper to taste		juice

Rinse the spinach and pat dry. Chop the spinach into fine pieces. Combine the spinach, cheese, garlic, onion, salt, pepper and nutmeg in a bowl and mix well. Let stand for a few minutes. Rub Dijon mustard on the skin of the chicken. Raise the skin on each chicken breast gently and stuff with the cheese mixture. Place in a 9x13-inch baking pan. Bake at 325 degrees for 50 minutes. Drizzle with the wine. Bake for 10 minutes or until the chicken is cooked through, basting frequently. Remove to a serving plate. Let stand for 10 minutes before serving.

Roasted Chicken
a young bordeaux or cabernet sauvignon

Fried Chicken
chardonnay, rose of cabernet sauvignon, upper level beaujolais

Barbecued Chicken
merlot, zinfandel, cabernet

Traditional Thanksgiving Turkey
gewürztraminer for a white wine; pinot noir or French burgundy for a red wine

Chicken à la Scampi

Yield: 4 or 5 servings

1   bunch green onions, chopped
1   teaspoon minced garlic
1/4   cup (1/2 stick) butter
1/4   cup olive oil
•   Juice of 1 lemon, strained
2   pounds boneless skinless chicken
    breasts, cut into 1/2-inch pieces

1   teaspoon salt
1/2   teaspoon pepper
2   large tomatoes, coarsely chopped
1/4   cup chopped fresh parsley
1   (12-ounce) package fettuccini,
    cooked

Sauté the green onions and garlic in butter and olive oil in a skillet until tender. Add the lemon juice, chicken, salt and pepper. Cook for 8 to 10 minutes or until the chicken is cooked through, stirring constantly. Add the tomatoes and parsley. Cook, covered, for 5 to 6 minutes or until the tomatoes are heated through. Serve over the hot buttered fettuccini.

Chicken and White Bean Chili

Yield: 10 to 12 servings

1	red bell pepper, roasted (at right)	2	(14-ounce) cans chicken broth
2	poblano peppers, roasted (at right)	2	(14-ounce) cans whole kernel white corn
1½	pounds chicken breasts, cut into 1-inch pieces	3	(16-ounce) cans cannellini
2	tablespoons olive oil	2	teaspoons cumin
1	large onion, chopped	2	pinches ground cloves
2	shallots, chopped	¾	cup chopped fresh cilantro
6	garlic cloves, minced	•	Green Tabasco sauce to taste

Peel the roasted peppers and chop. Brown the chicken in the olive oil in a skillet. Stir in the onion, shallots and garlic. Cook until the vegetables are light brown. Add the chicken broth, corn and undrained beans and stir gently. Add the cumin, cloves, cilantro and green Tabasco sauce. Cook for 10 to 15 minutes or until the chicken is cooked through. Add the chopped peppers. Cook for 5 minutes. Serve with corn bread muffins and green onions.

ROASTING PEPPERS

Roasting peppers is usually accomplished in one of two ways. Peppers may be held with tongs over a gas flame, turning the peppers as they become blackened and charred. To blacken peppers under a broiler, the peppers should be cut into halves and seeded. Place on a baking sheet with the skin side up and flattened. Broil 3 to 4 inches from the heat source for 10 minutes or until the skins are blackened and charred. Place in a plastic or paper food storage bag and seal. Let stand for 15 minutes. Peel the peppers and chop when the peppers are cool enough to handle.

Chicken with Apple and Brandy Cream Sauce

Yield: 4 servings

4	boneless skinless chicken breasts	1/4	cup brandy
•	Salt and pepper to taste	3	Golden Delicious apples or
•	Flour		Granny Smith apples, peeled,
3	tablespoons butter		sliced
1/2	cup Calvados	1	cup heavy cream

Season the chicken with salt and pepper. Dredge in flour until coated. Melt the butter in a skillet. Add the chicken. Cook for 4 minutes on each side or until brown and cooked through. Remove to a warm platter. Drain the skillet, reserving 1 tablespoon of the pan drippings. Add the Calvados, brandy and apples to the reserved drippings in the skillet. Simmer over medium heat for 7 minutes or until the apples are tender and the liquid is syrupy. Remove the apples using a slotted spoon and place with the chicken. Add the cream to the skillet. Bring to a boil. Cook until thickened, stirring constantly. Return the chicken and apples to the skillet. Cook for 2 minutes or until heated through.

To serve, arrange the chicken on a serving platter. Spoon the apples and sauce over the chicken.

Chicken Dijon

Yield: 6 to 8 servings

6	to 8 boneless skinless chicken breasts	1/4	cup Dijon mustard
		2	(14-ounce) cans chicken broth
•	Salt and pepper to taste	2	garlic cloves, chopped
1/4	cup (1/2 stick) margarine	1	cup chopped onion
2	tablespoons flour	1/4	cup parsley

Sprinkle the chicken with salt and pepper. Melt the margarine in a large skillet. Add the chicken. Cook until the chicken is brown on all sides. Stir the flour into the pan drippings. Mix the Dijon mustard, chicken broth, garlic, onion and parsley in a bowl. Pour over the chicken. Simmer for 30 to 40 minutes or until the chicken is tender and cooked through, turning occasionally. Remove the chicken to a serving platter. Continue simmering the sauce until slightly thickened, stirring to deglaze the skillet. Spoon over the chicken. Serve with hot cooked rice or noodles.

Marinated Curried Cornish Game Hens with Sauce Veronique

Yield: 2 or 3 servings

2   Cornish game hens,
     cut into halves
1   tablespoon canola oil

1   tablespoon honey
1   teaspoon curry powder
•   Sauce Veronique (at right)

Place the hens in a shallow dish. Mix the canola oil, honey and curry powder in a bowl. Pour over the hens. Marinate, covered, in the refrigerator for 2 hours. Place in a 9x13-inch glass baking dish sprayed with nonstick cooking spray. Bake, covered, at 350 degrees for 45 minutes. Bake, uncovered, for 10 minutes longer or until cooked through. Serve the Sauce Veronique to accompany the hens.

Sauce Veronique

For Sauce Veronique, mix 1/2 cup mayonnaise and 2 tablespoons milk in a bowl. Stir in green grape halves and curry powder to taste.

Tomato Zucchini Lasagna with Roasted Red Pepper Sauce

Yield: 6 servings

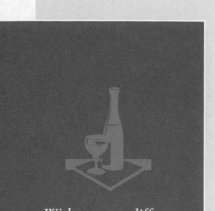

1/4 cup olive oil	1/8 teaspoon black pepper
1 cup chopped onion	6 cups (1/4-inch-thick) sliced zucchini
3 garlic cloves, minced	
4 large red bell peppers, roasted, peeled (page 189)	6 medium tomatoes, sliced 1/4 inch thick
3/4 cup fresh bread crumbs	9 lasagna noodles, cooked
1 tablespoon balsamic vinegar	1/2 cup chopped fresh basil
1/4 teaspoon salt	• Freshly grated Parmesan cheese
1/8 teaspoon ground red pepper	

Heat 2 tablespoons of the olive oil in a large nonstick skillet over medium heat. Add the onion and garlic. Sauté for 4 minutes or until brown. Process with roasted peppers, bread crumbs, vinegar, remaining 2 tablespoons olive oil, salt, red pepper and black pepper in a food processor until smooth. Arrange the zucchini and tomatoes in a single layer on broiler pans coated with nonstick cooking spray. Broil for 10 minutes or until blackened. Arrange 3 of the noodles in a 7x11-inch baking dish sprayed with nonstick cooking spray, trimming the noodles as needed. Layer 1/2 of the zucchini, 1/2 of the tomatoes, 1/4 cup basil, 2/3 cup of the roasted pepper mixture and 3 noodles in the prepared pan. Continue layering with the remaining zucchini, remaining tomatoes, remaining basil, 1/2 of the remaining roasted pepper mixture and remaining noodles. Spread the remaining roasted pepper mixture over the top. Bake, covered, at 350 degrees for 30 minutes. Bake, uncovered, for 10 minutes longer. Let stand for 10 minutes before serving. Sprinkle with Parmesan cheese. Garnish with sprigs of fresh basil.

Docking
Desserts

⚓

Windemere

*This lovely brick mansion was built in 1929
by Audrey and Harold Fletcher on the undeveloped land,
now known as Clear Lake shores. The Fletchers frequently
hosted elegant garden parties at their lakeside home.
Professional musicians entertained as guests strolled
the grounds enjoying the beautiful lake vistas.
At the recommendation of Howard Hughes, the Fletchers
moved to Houston in the 1940s and the lake house was closed.
The Fletcher home still stands on Clear Lake,
nearly unchanged since that time. Known as Windemere,
Bal Harbour's clubhouse is still enjoyed by the area residents.*

⚓

Happy Endings
(A Dessert Buffet)

BLANC DE NOIR OR SPARKLING WINE

Peanut Butter Cheesecake

Yield: 12 servings

32	ounces cream cheese, softened
5	eggs, at room temperature
1½	cups packed brown sugar
1	cup creamy peanut butter
½	cup heavy cream
1	teaspoon vanilla extract
10	regular peanut butter cups, broken into small pieces
•	Chocolate Crust (below)
•	Sour Cream Topping (at right)

Beat the cream cheese in a mixer bowl until light and fluffy. Add the eggs 1 at a time, beating well after each addition. Add the brown sugar, peanut butter and cream and mix until smooth. Stir in the vanilla. Fold in the peanut butter cups. Pour into the Chocolate Crust. Press heavy-duty foil tightly over the bottom and up the side of the springform pan to prevent leakage. Set the pan into a larger shallow pan. Pour enough hot water into the larger pan to come 1 inch up the side of the springform pan. Bake at 275 degrees for 1¼ hours or until firm and light brown. Spread with Sour Cream Topping. Bake for 5 minutes. Remove the springform pan from the oven and the water bath to a wire rack. Let cool for 1 hour. Chill, covered, in the refrigerator for 4 hours before serving.

Chocolate Crust

2	cups chocolate sandwich cookie crumbs
½	cup chopped roasted peanuts
¼	cup (½ stick) butter, melted

Process the cookie crumbs and peanuts in a food processor until finely ground. Stir in the melted butter. Pat onto the bottom and up the side of an 11-inch springform pan sprayed with nonstick cooking spray.

Sour Cream Topping

For Sour Cream Topping, combine 6 tablespoons sour cream and ½ cup sugar in a small bowl and mix well. Chill, covered, for 1 hour or longer before using.

Praline Pecan Cheesecake

Yield: 12 to 16 servings

1	(2-layer) package butter recipe cake mix	1	to 1¹/₂ teaspoons rum extract
¹/₂	cup (1 stick) butter or margarine, softened	3	eggs
24	ounces cream cheese, softened	1	(5-ounce) package coarsely chopped toffee candy
¹/₂	cup sugar	¹/₂	cup packed brown sugar
3	tablespoons flour	1	cup chopped pecans
		¹/₃	cup caramel ice cream topping

Beat the cake mix and butter at low speed in a mixer bowl until crumbly. Reserve 1 cup of the crumb mixture. Pat the remaining mixture onto the bottom and 1¹/₂ inches up the side of a 9- or 10-inch springform pan. Beat the cream cheese, sugar, flour and rum extract in a large mixer bowl until smooth. Add the eggs and mix well. Stir in the chopped toffee. Pour into the prepared pan. Combine the reserved crumb mixture, brown sugar and pecans in a small bowl and mix well. Sprinkle evenly over the filling. Bake at 325 degrees for 70 to 85 minutes or until the center is set and the topping is golden brown. Remove from the oven. Drizzle caramel topping over the top. Bake for 8 to 10 minutes or until the topping is set. Cool for 30 minutes. Loosen the cheesecake from the side of the pan with a knife. Let stand until cooled completely. Chill, covered, in the refrigerator for 4 to 12 hours. Remove the side of the pan before serving. Store in the refrigerator.

Apples Baked in Grand Marnier

Yield: 6 servings

6	Golden Delicious apples, cored	1	cup sauterne or sweet German wine
2	cups golden raisins	2	cups Crème Anglaise (page 200)
2	cups sugar		
1	cup Grand Marnier		

Butter a baking dish large enough to hold the apples. Fill the center of each apple with 2 to 3 tablespoons raisins and pack the center of each with sugar. Place in the prepared baking dish. Pour the Grand Marnier and sauterne around the apples. Bake at 325 degrees for 1¼ hours or until tender and golden brown, basting frequently after 30 minutes. Serve with Crème Anglaise.

Chef Cheryl Lewis is a native of California, but after moving coast to coast in the states, she graduated from a high school in the Bay Area. As a graduate with honors from the Culinary Institute of America, she has an impressive record! Former garde manager of the Remington Hotel, sous chef manager at the Park Hyatt in Washington, D.C., executive sous chef at the Park Lane Hotel and executive chef at Barbizon Hotel, both in New York City, are just some of the positions Chef Lewis has held. She now operates a highly successful catering and cooking instruction business. This luscious dessert is one of many mouth-watering creations of Chef Cheryl Lewis.

Poached Pears with Crème Anglaise

Yield: 6 servings

6 pears	½ cup raspberry preserves
• Juice of 1 lemon	1 teaspoon vanilla extract
3 cups dry red wine	• Crème Anglaise (at left)
½ cup sugar	6 mint leaves
3 or 4 lemon slices	

CRÈME ANGLAISE

For Crème Anglaise, bring 2 cups half-and-half to a boil in a saucepan. Beat 4 egg yolks and ½ cup packed light brown sugar in a mixer bowl. Beat in 1 tablespoon cornstarch. Add the hot half-and-half gradually, beating constantly. Return to the saucepan. Cook over medium heat for 8 minutes or until thick enough to coat a silver spoon, whisking constantly. Pour into a bowl and cover the surface with plastic wrap. Chill until ready to serve.

Peel the pears and rub with lemon juice. Remove the cores, leaving the stems attached. Bring the wine, sugar, lemon slices, raspberry preserves and vanilla to a boil in a large saucepan. Add the pears. Return to a boil and reduce the heat. Simmer, covered, for 20 minutes or until the pears are tender, turning the pears occasionally. Remove from the heat and let stand until cool. Drain the pears, reserving the raspberry liquid. Boil the reserved liquid in a saucepan until reduced by ½.

To serve, spoon Crème Anglaise onto each serving plate. Stand a pear in the Crème Anglaise. Spoon 2 tablespoons of the raspberry glaze over each pear, letting it drip into the Crème Anglaise. Place a mint leaf on the top of each pear to resemble a pear leaf. Serve immediately.

Anything-Goes Bread Pudding

Yield: 15 servings

3   eggs
2   cups milk
2   cups half-and-half
7   tablespoons butter, melted
2   tablespoons vanilla extract
1   tablespoon cinnamon

$^1/_2$ teaspoon nutmeg
1   (10-ounce) loaf French bread, torn into bite-size pieces
3   to 5 cups coconut, pecans, raisins or chocolate chips
•   Whiskey Sauce (below)

Beat the eggs in a large mixer bowl until fluffy. Add the milk, half-and-half, butter, vanilla, cinnamon and nutmeg. Fold in the bread and coconut. Mixture should be very moist but not soupy. Pour into a buttered 9x13-inch glass baking dish. Bake at 350 degrees for $1^1/_4$ hours or until golden brown.

To serve, cut the bread pudding into squares and place on serving plates. Serve warm Whiskey Sauce over the bread pudding.

Whiskey Sauce

$^1/_2$ cup (1 stick) butter
$1^1/_2$ cups confectioners' sugar

1   egg yolk
$^1/_2$ cup bourbon or other liqueur

Beat butter and confectioners' sugar in a saucepan over medium heat until the butter is absorbed. Remove from the heat. Blend in the egg yolk gradually. Add the bourbon gradually, stirring constantly. The sauce will thicken as it cools.

Small Steamed Chocolate Puddings

Yield: 4 servings

2	squares unsweetened chocolate	2	eggs, separated
1/3	cup milk	1/3	cup flour
1/4	cup (1/2 stick) butter, softened	1	teaspoon vanilla extract
2/3	cup sugar	1/2	cup whipping cream, whipped

Butter 4 ovenproof 1/2-cup ramekins or custard cups. Line the bottoms with waxed paper. Melt the chocolate in the milk in a saucepan over low heat. Remove from the heat and stir to blend. Beat the butter and sugar in a mixer bowl until creamy. Beat in the egg yolks 1 at a time. Stir in the chocolate mixture, flour and vanilla. Beat the egg whites in a mixer bowl until soft peaks form. Fold into the chocolate mixture. Pour into the prepared ramekins. Place the ramekins in a large pan. Add enough boiling water to the large pan to come halfway up the sides of the ramekins. Bake at 325 degrees for 35 to 40 minutes or until the tops are firm to the touch. Remove from the oven and let stand in the water bath for 20 minutes.

To serve, run a knife around the side of each ramekin. Unmold onto serving plates. Spoon whipped cream on the side of each and serve immediately.

Small Steamed Lemon Puddings

Yield: 6 servings

1 cup sugar	1/4 cup fresh lemon juice
1/2 cup flour	2 tablespoons (1/4 stick) butter, melted
1/2 teaspoon baking powder	
1/4 teaspoon salt	1 1/2 cups milk
3 eggs, separated	1/2 cup sugar
2 teaspoons grated lemon zest	• Whipped cream (optional)

Sift 1 cup sugar, flour, baking powder and salt together. Beat the egg yolks in a large mixer bowl until thick and pale yellow. Add the lemon zest, lemon juice, butter and milk and mix well. Fold in the flour mixture. Beat the egg whites in a mixer bowl until soft peaks form. Add 1/2 cup sugar gradually, beating constantly until stiff peaks form. Fold into the lemon mixture. Spoon into 6 buttered 1-cup ramekins. Place in a 9x13-inch baking dish filled with 1/2 inch water. Bake at 350 degrees for 45 minutes or until set. Let stand until cooled. Top with whipped cream and serve immediately.

ROYAL MOCHA FREEZE

For Royal Mocha Freeze, beat 1 pint whipping cream, 1/3 cup brandy and one 5-ounce can chocolate syrup in a large mixer bowl until thick, but not stiff. Fold in 1 quart coffee ice cream, softened, 1 cup chocolate chips, coarsely chopped, and 3/4 cup chopped almonds. Freeze, uncovered, until firm on top, but still soft inside. Stir to bring the chips and almonds to the top. Freeze, covered, until firm. To serve, spoon into serving dishes and garnish with whipped cream.

Slices of Sin

Yield: 10 to 12 servings

8	ounces semisweet chocolate	4	eggs
1/2	cup strong brewed coffee	1	cup whipping cream
1	cup (2 sticks) butter	2	to 3 teaspoons brandy
1	cup sugar		

Line a 5x7-inch glass baking dish with foil; butter the foil. Melt the chocolate in the coffee in a medium saucepan over low heat. Add the butter and sugar. Heat until the butter is melted, stirring constantly. Remove from the heat. Let stand for 10 minutes. Beat in the eggs 1 at a time. Pour into the prepared dish. Bake at 350 degrees for 35 to 45 minutes or until a crust forms on the top. Set the dish into a larger pan of cool water. Let stand until cool. The dessert will rise and fall. Remove the dish from the water and wrap well. Chill for 2 days or up to 2 weeks.

To serve, beat the whipping cream and brandy in a mixer bowl until soft peaks form. Cut the dessert into slices and serve with the whipped cream.

PRESENTATION MAKES A STATEMENT!

Try this short-cut method of decorating your serving dish and be proud of your display. Chocolate or butterscotch chips can be placed in a plastic sealable food storage bag and melted in the microwave. Snip off a corner of the bag and squeeze the liquid onto dessert plates in a zigzag scroll to add flare to your serving. The size of the hole will determine the width of the liquid. The plate can be lightly dusted with sifted confectioners' sugar to give the presentation more depth.

Grand Marnier Soufflé

Yield: 6 servings

2 cups milk	1/4 cup Grand Marnier
3/4 cup sugar	5 egg yolks
1/3 cup flour	7 egg whites, stiffly beaten
1/4 cup (1/2 stick) butter, melted	• Grand Marnier Sauce (below)

Heat the milk in a saucepan. Add the sugar. Bring to a boil, stirring constantly. Mix the flour into the melted butter. Stir flour mixture into the boiling milk. Cook until thickened, stirring constantly. Remove from the heat. Stir in the Grand Marnier. Beat the egg yolks in a mixer bowl until pale yellow. Add to the mixture, stirring constantly. Fold in the beaten egg whites. Pour into a buttered and sugared soufflé dish fitted with a foil collar. Bake at 400 degrees for 40 minutes. Serve with Grand Marnier Sauce.

Grand Marnier Sauce

5 egg yolks	2 tablespoons sugar
1/2 cup sugar	1 tablespoon freshly grated orange
1/4 cup Grand Marnier	zest (optional)
1 cup whipping cream	

Beat the egg yolks and 1/2 cup sugar in a double boiler over boiling water. Beat for 10 minutes or until thick and pale yellow, scraping around the inside of the pan frequently. Remove from the heat. Stir in 1/2 of the Grand Marnier. Let stand until cool. Chill in the refrigerator. Beat the whipping cream and 2 tablespoons sugar in a mixer bowl until almost stiff. Fold into the chilled sauce. Stir in the remaining Grand Marnier and orange zest.

Pear Rhubarb Trifle

Yield: 12 servings

Pears

2 cups white wine
1/2 cup sugar
2 tablespoons grated fresh ginger
4 large Anjou pears, peeled, cored, quartered
1/4 cup pear liqueur

Pudding
1/2 cup sugar
1/3 cup cornstarch

6 eggs, at room temperature
2 cups heavy cream
1 cup milk
2 tablespoons pear liqueur

Assembly
2 1/2 cups whipping cream, whipped
1 (16-ounce) pound cake, cubed
• Strawberry Rhubarb Jam (page 207)
1/2 cup sliced almonds, toasted

For the pears, heat the wine, 1/2 cup sugar and ginger in a saucepan over low heat. Add the pears. Poach for 20 minutes or until tender. Remove the pears to a bowl. Cook the liquid until reduced to 1/2 cup. Remove from the heat. Stir in 1/4 cup pear liqueur. Pour over the pears. Chill, covered, for 2 hours.

For the pudding, mix 1/2 cup sugar and cornstarch together. Beat the eggs in a mixer bowl until light and fluffy. Add the sugar mixture and beat until pale yellow. Heat the 2 cups cream and milk in a saucepan. Stir 1 cup of the milk mixture into beaten eggs; stir the eggs into the milk mixture. Cook over low heat until thickened and the mixture just begins to boil. Remove from the heat. Let stand until cool. Stir in 2 tablespoons pear liqueur.

To assemble, drain the pears and reserve the syrup. Cut the pears into slices. Fold 1 cup of the whipped cream into the cooled pudding. Place 1/2 of the pound cake in a 3-quart clear glass bowl. Drizzle with 3 tablespoons of the reserved syrup. Spread with 1/2 of the Strawberry Rhubarb Jam. Arrange 1/2 of the pears evenly over the layers. Spread 1/2 of the pudding over the pears. Repeat layers. Spread or pipe the remaining whipped cream on top. Sprinkle with the almonds. Chill, covered, until serving time.

Strawberry Rhubarb Jam

2	cups frozen rhubarb	1	(10-ounce) package frozen
1	cup strawberry jam		sweetened strawberries

Combine the rhubarb, strawberry jam and strawberries in a medium saucepan. Simmer until of a soft consistency, stirring frequently. Let stand until cool.

Zabaglione Cake

Yield: 8 to 12 servings

3	dozen ladyfingers, split	2	cups milk
3	(4-ounce) packages vanilla instant pudding mix	$1^1/2$	cups whipping cream, whipped
		$^1/2$	to $^3/4$ cup marsala wine

Butter a 9-inch springform pan. Line the bottom and side with split ladyfingers. Prepare the pudding mix following the package directions, using only 2 cups milk. Fold in $^3/4$ of the whipped cream. Add the wine and fold in until mixed. Layer $^1/2$ of the pudding mixture, the remaining ladyfingers and remaining pudding mixture in the prepared pan. Spread the remaining whipped cream over the top. Chill, covered with plastic wrap, until serving time.

Espresso Caramel Mousse Tart

Yield: 12 servings

Crust
2   cups peanut butter sandwich cookie crumbs
3   tablespoons butter, melted

Espresso Mousse
1¹⁄₂   cups heavy cream
¹⁄₂   cup coffee beans
¹⁄₄   teaspoon nutmeg
¹⁄₈   teaspoon ground cloves
1¹⁄₃   cups chopped white chocolate
2   egg yolks
¹⁄₃   cup sugar
6   tablespoons (³⁄₄ stick) butter

¹⁄₂   cup whipping cream, whipped stiff

Caramel Mousse
¹⁄₂   cup sugar
2   tablespoons water
¹⁄₄   cup heavy cream
3   egg yolks
1   cup white chocolate, melted
¹⁄₂   cup (1 stick) butter
¹⁄₂   cup whipping cream, whipped stiff
•   Chocolate Glaze (at left)

CHOCOLATE GLAZE

For Chocolate Glaze, melt 1 cup chocolate chips, ¹⁄₂ cup (1 stick) butter, 1 ounce unsweetened chocolate and 2 tablespoons corn syrup in a saucepan over low heat. Cool for 20 minutes before using.

For the crust, mix the crumbs and butter in a bowl. Press in a 9-inch springform pan. Bake at 350 degrees for 8 minutes. Cool.

For the espresso mousse, bring cream, coffee beans, nutmeg and cloves to a boil in a saucepan. Cool for 1 hour or longer. Reheat. Remove the coffee beans and return to the heat. Cook until reduced to ¹⁄₂ cup. Add the white chocolate and remove from the heat; stir until melted. Cool for 5 minutes. Beat 2 egg yolks and sugar in a mixer bowl until thick and pale yellow. Stir in the warm white chocolate mixture and beat until cool. Beat in the butter 1 tablespoon at a time until blended. Fold in the whipped cream. Pour into the crust. Chill until set.

For the caramel mousse, boil the sugar and water in a saucepan until caramel color (about 5 minutes). Remove from the heat. Add the cream and mix well. Beat 3 egg yolks in a mixer bowl until thick. Add the hot caramel and melted white chocolate gradually, beating constantly until lukewarm. Beat in butter 1 tablespoon at a time. Continue beating until cool. Fold in whipped cream.

To assemble, pour caramel mousse over the espresso mousse layer. Chill, covered, for 3 to 12 hours or until firm. Remove the side of the pan. Pour Chocolate Glaze over the top and spread to the side to cover. Chill for 2 to 12 hours before serving.

Almond Angel Cake

Yield: 12 servings

1	cup sugar	2	cups whipping cream, whipped
1/2	cup flour	1	teaspoon almond extract
4	egg yolks, beaten	1	angel food cake, torn into bite-size pieces
1/8	teaspoon salt		
2	cups milk, scalded	•	Whipped Cream Frosting (below)
1	tablespoon unflavored gelatin	•	Raspberry Sauce (below)
2	tablespoons cold milk		

Combine the sugar, flour, egg yolks and salt in a bowl and mix well. Add a small amount of the scalded milk to the egg mixture; add the egg mixture to the scalded milk in a double boiler. Cook over simmering water until thickened, stirring constantly. Soften the unflavored gelatin in 2 tablespoons milk in a cup. Add to the hot custard. Cook until dissolved, stirring constantly. Remove from the heat. Let stand until cool. Fold in the whipped cream and almond flavoring. Chill in the refrigerator. Fold in the cake pieces. Spoon into a buttered 10-inch tube pan. Chill, covered, for 1 to 2 hours or until set.

To serve, wrap the pan briefly in a hot towel. Run a knife around the edges of the pan. Unmold onto a serving plate. Frost with Whipped Cream Frosting. Spoon Raspberry Sauce onto each serving plate; place a slice of the dessert on the sauce.

Whipped Cream Frosting

1 1/2	cups whipping cream	1	teaspoon vanilla extract
6	tablespoons confectioners' sugar		

Beat 1 1/2 cups whipping cream in a mixer bowl until thick. Add the confectioners' sugar gradually, beating constantly. Add the vanilla. Beat until stiff peaks form.

Raspberry Sauce

2	cups fresh raspberries	1 1/2	tablespoons fresh lemon juice
1/4	cup sugar		

Purée the raspberries, sugar and lemon juice in a food processor; strain to remove the seeds. Chill, covered, in the refrigerator.

Chocolate Cream Cheese Cake Bellissimo

Yield: 18 to 20 servings

12	ounces cream cheese, softened	6	tablespoons baking cocoa
1/2	cup sugar	2	tablespoons baking soda
2	eggs	1	teaspoon salt
1	teaspoon vanilla extract	2	tablespoons apple cider vinegar
2	tablespoons flour	3/4	cup corn oil
2	cups semisweet chocolate chips	2	cups water
3	cups flour	•	Chocolate Glaze (below)
2	cups sugar		

Line the bottom of a buttered 12-inch round cake pan with waxed paper. Butter and flour the waxed paper. Beat the cream cheese and 1/2 cup sugar in a mixer bowl until light and fluffy. Beat in the eggs 1 at a time. Stir in the vanilla, 2 tablespoons flour and chocolate chips. Mix 3 cups flour, 2 cups sugar, baking cocoa, baking soda and salt in a large bowl. Combine the vinegar, corn oil and water in a small bowl and mix well. Add to the flour mixture and mix just until combined. Pour into the prepared pan. Spoon the cream cheese mixture onto the batter in dollops, leaving a 1 inch border around the edge. Marbleize with a knife. Bake at 375 degrees for 45 to 55 minutes or until the cake tests done. Cool in the pan on a wire rack. Invert onto a serving plate. Remove the waxed paper and let stand until completely cool. Pour Chocolate Glaze over the cake, spreading evenly over the top and side. Chill, covered, for 2 to 12 hours.

Chocolate Glaze

1/2	cup semisweet chocolate chips	1/4	cup (1/2 stick) unsalted butter
1	ounce chopped unsweetened chocolate	1/2	cup heavy cream

Combine the chocolate chips, chocolate, unsalted butter and cream in a metal bowl. Set over a pan of barely simmering water. Cook until smooth, stirring constantly.

Hot Milk Cake

Yield: 12 to 15 servings

1/2	cup (1 stick) margarine	1	teaspoon vanilla extract
1	cup milk	•	Butterscotch Sauce (below)
2	cups flour	1	cup whipping cream, whipped
2	teaspoons baking powder		
1/2	teaspoon salt	•	Chocolate Curls (at right)
4	eggs	1	cup finely chopped toasted pecans
2	cups sugar		

Bring the margarine and milk to a boil in a saucepan. Sift the flour, baking powder and salt together. Beat the eggs, sugar and vanilla in a mixer bowl until light and fluffy. Add the flour mixture and milk mixture alternately, beating well after each addition. Pour into a greased and floured tube pan. Bake at 325 degrees for 55 minutes or until the cake tests done.

To serve, cut the cake into slices and place on serving plates. Drizzle with Butterscotch Sauce. Top with a dollop of whipped cream. Sprinkle with the Chocolate Curls and chopped pecans.

Butterscotch Sauce

1 1/2	cups packed brown sugar	1	tablespoon (1/8 stick) butter
1/4	cup white corn syrup	1/8	teaspoon salt
1/2	cup heavy cream		

Combine the brown sugar, corn syrup, cream, butter and salt in a saucepan. Bring to a boil. Boil for 2 minutes, stirring constantly. Remove from the heat.

CHOCOLATE GARNISHES

Finishing touches can make all the difference, especially when it's made out of chocolate! Adults and children alike will love these.
To make chocolate leaves, brush several coats of melted chocolate on the underside of non-toxic fresh leaves. Place chocolate side up on a tray lined with waxed paper. Chill until firm. Before using, peel the leaves away from the chocolate.
To make chocolate curls, let a bar of chocolate come to room temperature. Draw a vegetable peeler at an angle carefully across the chocolate.

Doberge Cake

Yield: 12 to 15 servings

2¹/₄	cups flour	3	egg yolks
2	teaspoons baking powder	³/₄	cup milk
¹/₈	teaspoon salt	3	egg whites, stiffly beaten
¹/₂	cup (1 stick) butter or margarine, softened	•	Lemon Filling (page 213)
¹/₄	cup shortening	•	Lemon Icing (page 213)
1¹/₂	cups sugar	•	Finely shredded lemon rind and lemon leaves (optional)
1	teaspoon vanilla extract		

Grease and lightly flour three 8-inch round cake pans. Mix the flour, baking powder and salt together. Beat the butter and shortening in a mixer bowl for 30 seconds. Add the sugar and vanilla and beat until light and fluffy. Add the egg yolks 1 at a time, beating for 1 minute after each addition. Add the flour mixture and milk alternately, beating until blended after each addition. Fold in the beaten egg whites. Pour a generous ³/₄ cup of batter into each of the prepared pans, spreading evenly over the bottom. Bake at 375 degrees for 10 to 12 minutes or until the layers test done. Cool in the pans for 5 minutes. Invert onto wire racks to cool completely. Repeat with the remaining batter in 3 additional greased and floured cake pans.

For the assembly, stack the 6 cake layers on a serving plate, spreading ¹/₂ cup Lemon Filling between each layer. Cover and chill thoroughly. Uncover and spread Lemon Icing over the top and side of cake. Cover and chill for several to 12 hours. Sprinkle the top of the cake with lemon rind just before serving. Garnish with lemon leaves.

Lemon Filling

1¼	cups sugar	3	egg yolks, beaten	
3	tablespoons flour	2	tablespoons (¼ stick) butter or	
3	tablespoons cornstarch		margarine	
•	Dash of salt	½	teaspoon shredded lemon rind	
1½	cups cold water	⅓	cup lemon juice	

Combine the sugar, flour, cornstarch and salt in a saucepan. Stir in the water. Cook until thickened, stirring constantly. Cook for 2 minutes longer. Stir 1 cup of the mixture into the beaten egg yolks; stir the egg yolks into the hot mixture. Bring to a boil. Cook for 2 minutes, stirring constantly. Remove from the heat. Stir in the butter and lemon rind. Stir in the lemon juice gradually. Cover the surface with clear plastic wrap. Cool to room temperature.

Lemon Icing

6	ounces cream cheese, softened	2	teaspoons finely shredded
3	cups sifted confectioners' sugar		lemon rind
1	tablespoon milk	½	teaspoon vanilla extract

Beat the cream cheese, confectioners' sugar and milk in a mixer bowl until light and fluffy, adding additional milk if needed for the desired spreading consistency. Beat in the lemon rind and vanilla.

Double Chocolate Biscotti

Yield: 2 dozen

½ cup (1 stick) unsalted butter	½ teaspoon salt
4 ounces bittersweet or semisweet chocolate, chopped	1 cup sugar
½ cup Dutch baking cocoa	2 eggs
1¾ cups flour	1 teaspoon vanilla extract
1½ teaspoons baking powder	1 cup blanched almonds, toasted

Melt the butter and chocolate in a double boiler over simmering water, stirring constantly. Sift the baking cocoa, flour, baking powder and salt together. Beat the sugar and eggs at medium speed in a mixer bowl until light. Add the vanilla and beat at low speed. Beat in the chocolate mixture and flour mixture. Stir in the almonds. The dough will be soft. Knead the dough slightly on a lightly floured surface. Shape into 3x9-inch logs. Place on a cookie sheet. Bake at 350 degrees for 30 minutes or until set. Cool for 15 minutes or until cool enough to handle. Reduce the oven temperature to 275 degrees. Cut the logs diagonally into ½-inch-thick slices. Place cut side down on a cookie sheet. Bake for 20 minutes or until lightly toasted. Turn over the biscotti. Bake until slightly dry. Cool on a wire rack. Store in an airtight container for up to 2 weeks.

Café au Lait Squares

Yield: 16 or 32 squares

1/2	cup flour	2	eggs
1/4	cup quick-cooking oats	1	cup sugar
1/4	cup packed brown sugar	2	tablespoons Kahlúa or other
1/2	cup (1 stick) butter, melted		coffee liqueur
1	tablespoon instant coffee	3/4	cup flour
1/3	cup butter	3/4	cup chopped toasted walnuts
2	ounces unsweetened chocolate	•	Coffee Frosting (at right)

Combine 1/2 cup flour, oats, brown sugar, 1/2 cup butter and instant coffee granules in a bowl and mix well. Press into an ungreased 9-inch square baking pan. Bake at 350 degrees for 12 minutes. Combine 1/3 cup butter and chocolate in a small saucepan. Cook over medium-low heat until melted, stirring frequently. Remove from the heat. Let stand until cool. Beat the eggs at medium speed in a mixer bowl until thick and pale yellow. Add 1 cup sugar and Kahlúa, beating until blended. Stir in the chocolate mixture, 3/4 cup flour and walnuts. Spread evenly over the crust. Bake for 25 minutes. Cool in the pan on a wire rack.

To serve, spread Coffee Frosting over the brownies. Cover and let stand until the frosting hardens. Cut into 16 or 32 squares. Garnish with chocolate covered coffee beans or chopped chocolate chips.

COFFEE FROSTING

For Coffee Frosting, beat 1/3 cup butter, softened, at medium speed in a mixer bowl until creamy. Add 2 1/4 cups sifted confectioners' sugar and 1 1/2 tablespoons Kahlúa gradually, beating constantly until blended.

French Cookies

Yield: 6 dozen

¹/₂ cup (1 stick) butter or margarine, softened	2 cups chopped pecans
1 cup packed light brown sugar	2 cups semisweet chocolate chips
1 cup half-and-half	• Confectioners' sugar
40 graham crackers, crushed, or 2 packages from a 3-package box	

Beat the butter and brown sugar in a mixer bowl until creamy. Add the half-and-half, graham crackers, pecans and chocolate chips and mix well. Fill well-greased small muffin cups ²/₃ full. Bake at 375 degrees for 12 to 15 minutes or until golden brown. Cool in the muffin cups for 15 minutes. Invert onto wire racks. Sprinkle with confectioners' sugar.

Praline Cookies

Yield: 4 to 5 dozen

¹/₂ cup packed dark brown sugar	1 egg white, stiffly beaten
¹/₂ cup packed light brown sugar	1 teaspoon vanilla extract
2 tablespoons flour	2 cups pecan halves
¹/₂ teaspoon salt	

Sift the dark brown sugar, light brown sugar, flour and salt into a large bowl and mix well. Fold in the stiffly beaten egg white and vanilla. Fold in the pecan halves. Drop by spoonfuls (2 to 3 pecans per spoonful) onto well-buttered cookie sheets lined with parchment paper or foil. Bake at 275 degrees for 30 to 35 minutes or until firm and golden brown. Cool on the cookie sheets. Store in an airtight container.

Note: *These cookies are best served the day of preparation. Do not store for more than 2 days.*

Tri-Chocolate Chip Cookies

Yield: 1 to 1½ dozen

1	cup butter, softened	1	teaspoon salt
¾	cup packed brown sugar	1	cup white chocolate chips
¾	cup sugar	2	cups large milk chocolate chips
2	teaspoons vanilla extract		
2	eggs	2	cups semisweet chocolate chips
2¼	cups flour		
1	teaspoon baking soda	2	cups coarsely chopped pecans

Beat the butter, brown sugar, sugar and vanilla in a mixer bowl until creamy and smooth. Beat in the eggs. Add the flour, baking soda and salt and mix well. Stir in the chocolate chips and pecans. Drop by rounded ¼ cupfuls onto a lightly greased cookie sheet. Bake at 375 degrees for 8 to 12 minutes or until golden brown.

Note: *It is best to bake a test cookie to determine the desired length of baking time for your oven.*

CHOCOLATE

Chocolate ranges from bitter to sweet in flavor. There are several types of chocolate available for use. Semisweet is a flavored mix of chocolate liquor, cocoa butter and sugar that is ideal for baking. Dark is sweeter than semisweet but contains very little chocolate liquor and is also ideal for baking. Bittersweet is half chocolate liquor and half sugar, flavorings, and cocoa butter and is very good to eat. White is cocoa butter combined with sugar, milk and flavoring. It contains no chocolate liquor. The richness of the combined chocolates makes this oversized cookie a must for "chocoholics".

Peanut Butter Fudge Cookies

Yield: 4 dozen

1¹/₄	cups flour	¹/₂	cup packed brown sugar
³/₄	teaspoon baking soda	1	egg
¹/₂	teaspoon salt	¹/₂	teaspoon vanilla extract
¹/₂	cup (1 stick) butter, softened	•	Fudge Filling (at left)
¹/₂	cup creamy peanut butter	2	tablespoons chopped peanuts
¹/₂	cup sugar		

FUDGE FILLING

For Fudge Filling, combine 1 cup milk chocolate chips, 1 cup semisweet chocolate chips, 1 teaspoon vanilla extract and one 14-ounce can sweetened condensed milk in a nonstick saucepan. Cook over low heat until melted and smooth, stirring frequently.

Mix the flour, baking soda and salt together. Beat the butter and peanut butter at medium speed in a mixer bowl until creamy. Add the sugar and brown sugar gradually, beating well after each addition. Beat in the egg and vanilla. Add the flour mixture and mix well. Cover and chill the dough for 1 hour. Shape the dough into forty-eight 1-inch balls using a tiny ice cream scoop. Place in lightly greased miniature 1³/₄-inch muffin cups.

Bake at 325 degrees for 12 to 14 minutes or until light brown. Cool in the muffin cups on wire racks for 5 minutes. Remove cookies to wire racks to cool completely. Spoon ¹/₂ of the warm Fudge Filling into a heavy-duty sealable plastic food storage bag and seal. Snip a tiny hole in the corner of the bag. Pipe a small amount of Fudge Filling onto the top of each cookie. Let stand until slightly firm. Dip each cookie into the chopped peanuts.

Note: *Cookies can be frozen for up to 8 months.*

Cinnamon Oatmeal Cookies

Yield: 7 dozen

3	eggs, beaten	1	teaspoon cinnamon
1	cup raisins	1	cup (2 sticks) butter, softened
1	teaspoon vanilla extract	1	cup packed brown sugar
2¹/₂	cups sifted flour	1	cup sugar
2	teaspoons baking soda	2	cups quick-cooking oats
1	teaspoon salt	¹/₂	cup chopped pecans

Combine the eggs, raisins and vanilla in a bowl and mix well. Let stand, covered, in the refrigerator for 1 hour. Sift the flour, baking soda, salt and cinnamon together. Beat the butter in a mixer bowl until creamy. Add the brown sugar and sugar and beat well. Beat in the flour mixture. Add the raisin mixture and mix well. Stir in the oats and pecans. Drop by teaspoonfuls onto ungreased cookie sheets. Bake at 350 degrees for 10 minutes. Cool on wire racks.

White Chocolate with Raspberry Bars

Yield: 7 dozen

1	cup (2 sticks) unsalted butter	1	teaspoon salt
4	cups white chocolate chips	2¹/4	teaspoons almond extract
4	eggs	1	(10-ounce) jar seedless
1	cup sugar		raspberry fruit spread, melted
2	cups flour	¹/2	cup sliced almonds

Melt the butter in a saucepan over low heat. Remove from the heat. Add 2 cups of the white chocolate chips; do not stir. Beat the eggs in a mixer bowl until foamy. Add the sugar gradually, beating at high speed until pale yellow. Stir in the white chocolate mixture. Add the flour, salt and almond extract. Beat at low speed until just combined. Spread ¹/2 of the batter into a greased and floured 9x13-inch baking pan.

Bake at 325 degrees for 15 to 20 minutes or until light brown. Spread the melted raspberry spread evenly over the baked layer. Stir the remaining 2 cups white chocolate chips into the remaining batter. Spoon gently over the fruit. Sprinkle with the almonds. Bake for 30 to 35 minutes or until light brown. Cool completely before cutting into bars.

ALMONDS

Almonds are one of the most widely recognized "nuts". Correctly speaking, however, almonds are not nuts, but are stone fruits. You are actually eating the seed. Mentioned since Biblical times and known throughout the world, they are used generously by French and Chinese gourmet cooks.

White Chocolate Chip Cookies

Yield: 6 dozen

2½ cups flour
1 teaspoon baking soda
1 teaspoon baking powder
½ cup oats
1¼ cups (2½ sticks) butter, softened
2 cups packed light brown sugar

2 eggs
2 teaspoons vanilla extract
11 ounces white chocolate chips
2 cups pistachios, toasted, coarsely chopped

Mix the flour, baking soda, baking powder and oats together. Beat the butter and brown sugar in a mixer bowl until creamy. Beat in the eggs and vanilla. Add the flour mixture gradually, stirring after each addition. Stir in the white chocolate chips and pistachios. Chill for 30 minutes. Drop the dough by heaping teaspoonfuls 2 inches apart onto ungreased cookie sheets. Bake at 350 degrees for 8 to 9½ minutes. Cool for 2 minutes on the cookie sheets. Remove to wire racks to cool completely.

Antique Show Buttermilk Pies

Yield: 12 to 14 servings

3   cups sugar
2   tablespoons flour
1½   cups buttermilk
5   eggs, beaten
¾   cup (1½ sticks) butter, melted

2   teaspoons vanilla extract
2   unbaked (9-inch) pie shells
1   egg white, lightly beaten
½   to 1 teaspoon freshly grated
     nutmeg

Combine the sugar, flour and ¾ cup of the buttermilk in a bowl and mix well. Add the eggs and remaining buttermilk and mix well. Fold in the butter and vanilla. Brush the pie shells with the egg white. Bake at 425 degrees for 5 minutes. Pour the filling into the pie shells. Bake for 10 minutes. Reduce the oven temperature to 350 degrees. Bake for 30 minutes or until firm. Sprinkle with the nutmeg.

Holiday Cherry Pies

Yield: 12 to 14 servings

1	(15-ounce) can pitted sour cherries	1	teaspoon vanilla extract
1	(8-ounce) can crushed pineapple	1	tablespoon red food coloring
1¹/₂	cups sugar	¹/₂	cup chopped pecans
		5	bananas, sliced
¹/₂	cup plus 1 tablespoon cornstarch	1	baked (10-inch) pie shell
		1	baked (9-inch) pie shell
¹/₂	teaspoon salt	1	cup whipping cream, whipped

Drain the cherries and pineapple, reserving the juice. Add enough water to the reserved juice to measure 2 cups. Combine the sugar, cornstarch and salt in a medium saucepan. Add the juice mixture and mix well. Add the cherries, pineapple, vanilla and food coloring. Cook until thickened, stirring constantly. Let stand until cool. Stir in the pecans and bananas. Pour into the pie shells. Top with the whipped cream.

JAPANESE FRUITCAKE PIE

For Japanese Fruitcake Pie, beat 4 eggs lightly. Add 1 cup (2 sticks) butter or margarine, 1¹/₂ cups sugar, ¹/₂ teaspoon vinegar and 2 teaspoons vanilla extract and beat well. Stir in 1 cup shredded coconut, 1 cup chopped pecans and 1 cup golden raisins. Pour into 2 unbaked 9-inch pie shells. Bake at 300 degrees for 50 to 55 minutes or until set. These pies freeze well.

Margarita Mousse Dessert

Yield: 8 to 10 servings

Crust
1½ cups graham cracker crumbs
⅓ cup unsalted butter, melted

Filling
1 envelope unflavored gelatin
3 tablespoons cold water
2 eggs
3 egg yolks
1½ cups sugar

1 cup fresh lime juice
1 tablespoon lime rind
½ cup tequila
⅓ cup Cointreau
⅓ cup unsalted butter
1 cup whipping cream

Toppings
4 ounces semisweet chocolate
1 cup whipping cream

For the crust, mix the graham cracker crumbs and melted butter in a bowl. Pat into a 9-inch springform pan. Chill in the refrigerator.

For the filling, soften the gelatin in the cold water in a saucepan for 5 minutes. Heat until the gelatin dissolves. Beat the eggs and egg yolks in a large saucepan. Whisk in the sugar. Beat until light and pale yellow. Whisk in the lime juice and lime rind. Cook until thickened, stirring constantly. Add the softened gelatin and liqueurs. Cook until just combined. Add the butter. Cook until melted. Spoon into a bowl and cool to room temperature. Whip 1 cup whipping cream in a bowl until soft peaks form. Fold into the filling. Spoon into the prepared pan. Chill for 4 to 5 hours or up to 12 hours.

For the toppings, melt the chocolate in a double boiler over simmering water. Spoon into a plastic squeeze bottle. Pipe the chocolate into a cactus shape on a tray lined with waxed paper. Chill until firm. Whip 1 cup whipping cream in a bowl until stiff peaks form.

To serve, remove the side of the pan. Pipe or spoon the whipped cream around the edge. Remove the chocolate cactus gently and place on the top of the dessert. Serve on glass plates rimmed with sugar or salt, if desired.

Bayou Fudge Pie

Yield: 6 to 8 servings

24	chocolate wafers, crumbled (about 1¼ cups)	¼	cup rum (optional)
¼	cup (½ stick) butter, softened	¾	cup packed brown sugar
½	teaspoon cinnamon	2	teaspoons instant coffee
12	ounces semisweet chocolate	3	eggs
¼	cup (½ stick) butter	¼	cup flour
		1	cup chopped pecans

Mix the first 3 ingredients in a bowl. Press into an ungreased 9-inch pie plate. Melt the chocolate and ¼ cup butter in a double boiler over hot water, stirring constantly. Add the rum, brown sugar, coffee granules, eggs and flour in the order listed, stirring after each addition. Stir in the pecans. Pour into the prepared pie plate. Bake at 375 degrees for 25 minutes. Cool on a wire rack. Serve warm or at room temperature with whipped cream.

Peanut Butter Satin Pie

Yield: 10 to 12 servings

¼	cup (½ stick) butter, melted	2	tablespoons (¼ stick) butter, melted
¼	cup packed brown sugar		
1½	cups graham cracker crumbs	2	teaspoons vanilla extract
16	ounces cream cheese, softened	1½	cups whipped cream
1	cup creamy peanut butter	3	small Hershey candy bars
2	cups sugar	3	tablespoons milk

Mix ¼ cup melted butter, brown sugar and graham cracker crumbs in a bowl and mix well. Press into a 9-inch springform pan. Bake at 350 degrees for 10 minutes. Let stand until cool. Beat the cream cheese and peanut butter in a mixer bowl until smooth. Add the sugar, 2 tablespoons melted butter and vanilla and mix well. Fold in the whipped cream. Pour into the cooled crust. Chill until firm. Melt the candy bars and milk in a double boiler over hot water. Let stand until cool. Spread over the chilled pie. Chill until serving time.

"To Die For" Low-Fat Pie

For "To Die For" Low-Fat Pie, fill a low-fat graham cracker piecrust with 1 quart fat-free frozen vanilla yogurt. Freeze in the freezer until firm. Microwave one 16-ounce jar fat-free chocolate sauce, 1 to 2 jiggers Kahlúa and cinnamon to taste in a glass dish on High until heated through. Stir in 1 cup roasted pecans. Drizzle over pie. Can add raspberries and strawberries and omit the pecans.

225

Strawberry Almond Tart

Yield: 6 to 8 servings

8 ounces whole blanched almonds	• Tart Shell (below)
3/4 cup sugar	2 pints strawberries, quartered
3/4 cup (1 1/2 sticks) butter, softened	1 1/2 tablespoons confectioners' sugar
2 eggs	• Crème Fraîche (at left)

Process the almonds and 1/4 cup of the sugar in a food processor until the almonds are finely ground. Beat butter and remaining 1/2 cup sugar in a mixer bowl until light and creamy. Add to the almond mixture and process until combined. Add the eggs 1 at a time, processing constantly until smooth. Spread in the Tart Shell. Bake for 45 minutes, covering the crust with foil to prevent over browning.

To serve, release the side of the tart pan. Place the tart on a serving plate. Arrange the strawberries upright on top. Sift confectioners' sugar over the top. Serve with Crème Fraîche.

Tart Shell

1 2/3 cups flour	2/3 cup confectioners' sugar
3/4 cup (1 1/4 sticks) butter	2 egg yolks
• Pinch of salt	

Process the flour, butter and salt in a food processor until the mixture resembles coarse bread crumbs. Add the confectioners' sugar and egg yolks and pulse until the mixture pulls from the side of the bowl. Roll dough into a 12-inch circle on a floured surface. Fit into a 9 1/2-inch fluted tart pan with a removable bottom and trim the overhang. Line the pastry with foil. Fill with pie weights, dried beans or rice. Bake at 350 degrees for 20 minutes or until the edge is light brown. Remove the foil and weights. Bake for 10 minutes longer or until firm. Let stand until cool.

CRÈME FRAÎCHE

For Crème Fraîche, combine 1 cup sour cream and 1 cup heavy cream in an airtight container and mix well. Let stand at room temperature for 12 hours or until thickened. Chill for 24 hours. Crème Fraîche is available in some supermarket dairy cases. For a lighter version, substitute plain yogurt for your sauce. Crème Fraîche is a wonderful alternative to whipped cream on fruit or dessert.

Tortuga Tart

Yield: 10 to 12 servings

Crust
1/2 cup hazelnuts, toasted
2 1/2 cups chocolate sandwich cookie crumbs
1/3 cup butter, melted

Caramel Layer
3 tablespoons butter
3/4 cup sugar
3/4 cup hazelnuts, toasted
3/4 cup heavy cream

Mousse Layer
3 egg whites
1 1/2 tablespoons sugar
8 ounces milk chocolate
1/4 cup brewed coffee
2 egg yolks
1 cup whipping cream, whipped
1/4 cup hazelnuts, toasted
• Chocolate Curls (page 211)

For the crust, process 1/2 cup hazelnuts in a food processor until finely chopped. Add the cookie crumbs and 1/3 cup butter and process until mixed. Press into a 10-inch tart pan. Place on a baking sheet. Bake at 350 degrees for 10 to 12 minutes or until set. Let stand until cool.

For the caramel layer, combine 3 tablespoons butter and 3/4 cup sugar in a small saucepan. Cook over medium-high heat until the butter melts and the sugar dissolves, stirring constantly. Boil until the mixture turns a rich golden amber. Add 3/4 cup coarsely chopped hazelnuts and 3/4 cup cream. Boil for 3 minutes, stirring constantly. Pour into the tart shell. Chill for 1 hour or longer.

For the mousse layer, beat the egg whites in a mixer bowl until soft peaks form. Add 1 1/2 tablespoons sugar gradually, beating constantly until stiff peaks form. Place chocolate and coffee in a mixer bowl over simmering water. Heat until melted, stirring occasionally. Beat the egg yolks lightly in a mixer bowl. Add the warm chocolate mixture gradually, whisking constantly. Whip in 1/4 of the stiffly beaten egg whites. Fold in the remaining stiffly beaten egg whites and whipped cream. Mound on top of the caramel layer. Garnish with additional whipped cream, 1/4 cup hazelnuts and Chocolate Curls.

After-Dinner Coffees

Café Brûlot

- Hot strong-brewed coffee
- 3 tablespoons warmed brandy or cognac
- Sugar to taste
- 3 strips orange rind
- 1 cinnamon stick

Irish Coffee

- Hot strong-brewed coffee
- 1½ teaspoons light brown sugar
- 3 to 4 tablespoons Irish whiskey
- Whipped cream

Hungarian Coffee

- Hot brewed coffee
- 2 tablespoons brandy or cognac
- Whipped cream
- 1 tablespoon grated German's chocolate
- 1 cinnamon stick

Mexican Coffee

- Hot strong-brewed coffee
- 3 tablespoons Kahlúa
- Whipped cream
- Grated semisweet chocolate
- 1 cinnamon stick

After a large dinner party, what better way to send off your guests than with this wonderful display of After-Dinner Coffees (at right). Place all of the ingredients on a silver tray, display written recipes on cards, and let the guests prepare their own unique coffee. With a tray of cookies, this could be the dessert!

Coastal Celebrations

⚓

Johnson Space Center

Pictured in the background of this photo taken on the
grounds of the Johnson Space Center, is the Saturn V rocket.
This type of rocket supported the Apollo flights
to the moon and represents a special kind of "dock."
At the top of the Saturn V is the Command and Service
Module (CSM). Behind that is the Lunar Module (LM).
At the beginning of a trip to the moon the CSM rotates
around to dock with the LM and they stay in that
configuration until they undock prior to lunar landing.
When standing upright, the Saturn V rocket is taller
than the Statue of Liberty and its three million
components weigh as much as the Nautilus submarine.
The Center officially opened in September 1963
and was renamed in honor of the late President
Lyndon B. Johnson in February 1973.

Fireworks Picnic

FIRE CRACKERS, *page 31*
SEAWALL CRAB MEAT IN A BOWL, *page 239*
ASPARAGUS ROLL-UPS, *page 245*

ROCKET COLESLAW, *page 83*
RED, WHITE AND BLUE SALAD, *page 81*
CHICKEN SALAD WITH A TWIST, *page 96*
CHEDDAR CHEESE BREAD, *page 48*

CHOCOLATE PEPPERMINT BROWNIES, *page 258*
CINNAMON BAR COOKIES, *page 259*
SPACE-AGE PEANUT BRITTLE, *page 253*

DELTA MINT TEA, *page 64*

Cranberry Conserve

Yield: 10 to 12 servings

1	pound fresh cranberries	1¹/₂	cups pecans, toasted, coarsely
2	cups sugar		chopped
1	(16-ounce) jar orange	2	tablespoons Grand Marnier
	marmalade		

Rinse the cranberries and place in a bowl. Add the sugar and mix lightly. Place in a 9x13-inch baking pan and cover tightly with foil. Bake at 300 degrees for 1 hour. Remove from the oven. Add the marmalade, pecans and Grand Marnier and mix lightly. Spoon into glass jars with lids. Store, covered, in the refrigerator for up to 3 weeks.

To serve, spoon 1 cup of the conserve on an 8-ounce wheel of Brie cheese with the rind removed and accompany with sliced toasted baguettes.

Kahlúa Pecan Brie

Yield: 8 servings

1	medium wheel Brie cheese	¹/₄	cup Kahlúa
3	tablespoons brown sugar	³/₄	cup chopped pecans, toasted

Cut the top from the Brie cheese. Combine the brown sugar and liqueur in a microwave-safe bowl and mix well. Microwave on High for 30 seconds. Stir until the brown sugar is dissolved. Cool. Add the pecans. Pour over the Brie cheese. Serve with your favorite crackers.

CALIENTÉ CRANBERRY RELISH

To add a southwest Texas twist to your Thanksgiving dinner, prepare Calienté Cranberry Relish. Purée 2 cups canned whole cranberries in a food processor. Combine with the juice of 1 lime, 3 tablespoons tequila, 4 to 5 jalapeños, minced, and ¹/₄ cup chopped fresh cilantro in a bowl and mix thoroughly by hand. Chill for 8 to 12 hours. This recipe has been handed down to several generations and remains a favorite to this day.

Fiesta Cheesecake

Yield: 25 servings

1½ cups finely crushed tortilla chips
¼ cup (½ stick) butter, melted
20 ounces cream cheese, softened
2 eggs
2½ cups shredded Monterey Jack cheese with jalapeño peppers
2 tablespoons chopped black olives
1 (4-ounce) can green chiles, drained, chopped

¼ teaspoon ground red pepper
8 ounces sour cream
½ cup chopped parsley (optional)
½ cup chopped green bell pepper
½ cup chopped yellow bell pepper
½ cup chopped red bell pepper
½ cup chopped green onions
1 medium tomato, chopped
2 tablespoons chopped black olives

Combine the tortilla chips with the butter in a bowl. Press into a lightly greased 9-inch springform pan. Bake at 375 degrees for 15 minutes. Cool on a wire rack. Reduce the oven temperature to 325 degrees. Beat the cream cheese at medium speed in a mixer bowl for 3 minutes or until fluffy. Add the eggs 1 at a time, beating well after each addition. Stir in the Monterey Jack cheese, 2 tablespoons olives, green chiles and red pepper. Pour into the prepared pan.

Bake for 30 minutes. Cool in the pan for 10 minutes. Release the side of the pan and let cool completely. Spread the sour cream over the top. Chill, covered, until serving time.

To serve, remove the side of the pan. Place cheesecake on parsley-lined serving platter. Arrange the bell peppers, green onions, tomato and 2 tablespoons olives on top as desired. Serve with tortilla chips or crackers.

Note: *These toppings can also be used to make decorative arrangements on top of the cheesecake for holidays and other special events, such as a tree for Christmas, a heart for Valentine's Day, etc.*

Parsley Caper Sauce for Tortellini

Yield: 6 to 10 servings

1   to 2 garlic cloves
2   tablespoons sunflower seed kernels
1/4   cup freshly grated Parmesan cheese
2   tablespoons drained capers
3/4   cup packed flat-leaf parsley
1/2   cup extra-virgin olive oil
•   Salt and pepper to taste
8   ounces meat or cheese small tortellini

Process the garlic in a food processor for 10 seconds. Add the sunflower seed kernels, Parmesan cheese, capers and parsley and process until coarsely puréed. Add the olive oil in a fine stream, processing constantly. Season with salt and pepper. Cook the pasta using the package directions and drain. Add the sauce and toss to coat. Spoon into a baking dish. Bake at 250 degrees for 15 minutes or until heated through; do not overbake. Serve in a warm shallow bowl with small skewers or wooden picks.

PASTA

Pasta is an Italian word for dried, hardened dough made in a great variety of shapes and sizes. Try some of these helpful hints for a more successful pasta. Add a tablespoon of olive oil to keep the pasta from sticking together when boiling. Dry pasta takes several minutes longer to cook than fresh pasta. Sauce will stick to the pasta better if the pasta is not rinsed after cooking. Use thick, large pasta when serving a heavy sauce. Use small, thin pasta when serving a light sauce. Use freshly grated cheese on your pasta dishes.

Artichoke Frittata

Yield: 12 servings

8 eggs	2/3 cup seasoned bread crumbs
1 teaspoon salt	1/3 cup grated Parmesan cheese
1/2 teaspoon pepper	1 cup shredded sharp Cheddar
2 (14-ounce) cans artichokes,	cheese
drained, cut into bite-size pieces	

Beat the eggs lightly in a bowl. Season with salt and pepper. Add the artichokes, bread crumbs and Parmesan cheese and mix well. Spoon into a buttered 7x11-inch baking dish. Bake at 350 degrees for 20 to 25 minutes or until a knife inserted in the center comes out clean. Sprinkle with the Cheddar cheese. Bake for 5 minutes or until the Cheddar cheese is melted. Cut into squares and serve warm.

Bacon Tomato Cups

Yield: 30 miniature muffins

8 slices bacon, cooked, crumbled	1/2 cup mayonnaise
1 medium tomato, seeded, chopped	1 teaspoon basil
1/2 small onion, chopped	1 (10-count) can flaky biscuits
3 ounces Swiss cheese, shredded	

Combine the bacon, tomato, onion, Swiss cheese, mayonnaise and basil in a bowl and mix well. Separate each dough round into 3 layers. Press one layer into each miniature muffin cup. Spoon the filling into each cup. Bake at 375 degrees for 10 to 12 minutes or until the edges are brown.

Asparagus Spears with Citrus-Ginger Dip

Yield: 12 servings

2	pounds asparagus, trimmed	1	tablespoon Dijon mustard
3/4	cup mayonnaise	1 1/2	tablespoons grated fresh gingerroot
3/4	cup sour cream		
1	tablespoon distilled vinegar	1	teaspoon soy sauce
1	tablespoon orange juice	1/2	teaspoon sugar
1	teaspoon grated orange zest	•	Salt and pepper to taste
1	garlic clove, crushed		

Peel the asparagus stalks if desired. Bring about 1 inch of water to a boil in a large skillet. Add the asparagus. Simmer, uncovered, for 4 to 5 minutes or until just tender. Drain the asparagus and plunge immediately into iced water. Let stand until chilled. Remove the asparagus and place in a serving dish. Chill, covered, until serving time. Combine the mayonnaise, sour cream, vinegar, orange juice, orange zest, garlic, Dijon mustard, gingerroot, soy sauce, sugar, salt and pepper in a medium mixer bowl and beat well. Spoon into a serving bowl. Chill, covered, until serving time. Serve with the chilled asparagus.

Note: *Dry ground ginger has a completely different taste from fresh ginger and should not be used as a substitute in this recipe or any recipe calling for fresh ginger.*

GINGERROOT

Gingerroot is a plant that is specifically grown for its root. It is most widely used in Asian and Indian cooking and has a spicy, sweet, pepperlike taste. The root can be peeled and sliced for use in cooking. Without being peeled, it can be grated on the small-holed side of a cheese grater and the pulp will be on the inside for your use. Small pieces of dry gingerroot can be broken off and placed into stock or fruit sauces. Fresh ginger should be kept uncovered in the refrigerator. For longer storage, peel and cut the root into small chunks, place them in a jar, and cover with dry sherry. It can be stored in the refrigerator for many months—even years.

Joyeux Shrimp and Crab in Pastry Shells

Yield: 50 servings

2 cups chopped mushrooms	1/2 teaspoon salt
1/2 cup chopped green onions	1/4 teaspoon paprika
1/2 cup finely chopped celery	1/4 teaspoon Worcestershire sauce
1/2 cup chopped fresh parsley	1/8 teaspoon cayenne pepper or
1/2 cup (1 stick) salted butter	Tabasco sauce
6 tablespoons flour	2 cups chopped shrimp
2 cups half-and-half	2 cups chopped crab meat
1/4 cup sherry	50 miniature pastry shells, baked
2 tablespoons lemon juice	

Sauté the mushrooms, green onions, celery and parsley in 1/4 cup of the butter in a skillet until tender. Melt the remaining butter in a large skillet. Add the flour and stir until smooth. Add the half-and-half, sherry, lemon juice, salt, paprika, Worcestershire sauce and cayenne pepper. Cook until thickened, stirring constantly. Adjust the seasonings. Add the shrimp. Cook until the shrimp turn pink. Fold in the crab meat and sautéed vegetables. Cook until heated through. Spoon into the pastry shells.

Note: *Can also serve in tiny toast cups.*

Spicy Orange Hummus

Yield: 1³/₄ cups

¹/₄	cup parsley leaves	¹/₄	teaspoon salt
2	tablespoons chopped onion	¹/₄	teaspoon ginger
1	garlic clove	¹/₄	teaspoon coriander
¹/₄	cup unsweetened orange juice	¹/₄	teaspoon turmeric
2	tablespoons tahini (sesame seed paste)	¹/₄	teaspoon cumin
		¹/₄	teaspoon paprika
2	tablespoons rice vinegar	1	(15-ounce) can chickpeas
2	teaspoons soy sauce		(garbanzo beans), drained
1	teaspoon Dijon mustard		

Process the parsley, onion and garlic in a food processor until minced. Add the orange juice, tahini, rice vinegar, soy sauce, Dijon mustard, salt, ginger, coriander, turmeric, cumin, paprika and chickpeas and process until smooth. Serve with pita triangles.

SEAWALL CRAB MEAT IN A BOWL

For Seawall Crab Meat in a Bowl, cut off the top of 1 round of sourdough bread, reserving the top. Hollow out the center of the bread to form a bowl. Melt 16 ounces cream cheese in a skillet, stirring constantly. Stir in one 10-ounce can cream of mushroom soup, 2 cups crab meat and 1 cup picante sauce. Cook over low heat until heated through, stirring constantly. Pour into the bread bowl and replace the bread top. Cover completely in foil. Bake at 350 degrees for 15 minutes. Serve with toasted baguette slices.

Black-Eyed Susans

Yield: 30 servings

1   cup (2 sticks) unsalted butter,
    softened
1   pound sharp Cheddar cheese,
    shredded, at room temperature
4   shakes Tabasco sauce, or 2 shakes
    cayenne pepper

2   cups flour
1   cup raisins or chopped dates
³/₄ cup sugar

Combine the butter, cheese and Tabasco sauce in a bowl and mix well. Add the flour and mix well. Flatten a scant tablespoonful of the dough in the palm of your hand. Place raisins in the center of the dough; fold over and crimp the edge with a fork. Repeat with the remaining dough and raisins. Place on a baking sheet. Chill in the refrigerator. Bake at 300 degrees for 25 to 30 minutes or until cooked through. Do not brown. Sprinkle with sugar.

Devilish Cheese Straws

Yield: 2 dozen

3	cups flour	1	pound extra-sharp Cheddar
1	teaspoon salt		cheese, shredded, at room
1	teaspoon cayenne pepper		temperature
1	cup (2 sticks) butter, softened		

Sift the flour, salt and cayenne pepper together. Beat the butter and cheese in a mixer bowl until light and fluffy. Add the flour mixture and mix well. Place in a cookie press fitted with a star tip. Press long strips of dough onto ungreased baking sheets. Bake at 325 degrees for 8 to 10 minutes. Do not brown. Cool slightly. Break into desired lengths. Store in an airtight container.

HOLIDAY DATES ON HORSEBACK

For Holiday Dates on Horseback, roll a pitted date in 1/2 slice bacon and secure with a wooden pick. Place on a baking sheet. Repeat with remaining dates and bacon. Bake at 375 degrees for 20 minutes or until the bacon is cooked through.

Peppered Jelly Thumbprint Cookies

Yield: 72 servings

4   cups shredded sharp Cheddar
     cheese, at room temperature
1   cup (2 sticks) butter, softened
2   eggs, separated
•   Dash of Tabasco sauce

2   cups flour
1¹/₂ cups chopped pistachio nuts or
     walnuts
¹/₂ cup pepper jelly

Process the cheese and butter in a food processor until blended. Add the egg yolks and Tabasco sauce and process well. Add the flour and blend well. Whisk the egg whites in a mixer bowl until foamy. Shape 1 tablespoon of the dough into a ball. Roll in the egg whites and then in the pistachio nuts. Repeat with the remaining dough. Place 1 inch apart on baking sheets sprayed with nonstick cooking spray. Make an indention in the center of each ball with your thumb or a thimble. Bake at 350 degrees for 15 to 20 minutes or until the edges are light brown. Cool on a wire rack. Fill each with a dab of pepper jelly.

Pimento Cheese Spread

Yield: 12 servings

2   (4-ounce) jars whole
    pimentos, drained, rinsed
1/2 medium onion, grated
6   hard-cooked eggs, grated
1   pound mild Cheddar cheese,
    finely grated

1/2 cup mayonnaise
•   Juice of 1/2 lemon
•   Finely chopped green onion
    tops to taste
•   Salt and pepper to taste

Process the pimentos and onion in a blender for 2 seconds. Do
not purée. Combine with the hard-cooked eggs and cheese in a
bowl. Add the mayonnaise and mix until of a spreading consistency.
Stir in the lemon juice and green onion tops. Season with salt
and pepper.

Vegetable Sandwich Spread

*Coffees, luncheons, or
Super Bowl parties
always need a lavish
feast to feed a crowd.
This Vegetable Sandwich
Spread is delicious and
light; it is sure to be a
hit. Chop finely:
2 tomatoes, 1 cucumber
and 1 small onion.
Combine with 1 cup
finely chopped celery,
1/2 cup finely chopped
green bell pepper and
1/2 cup finely chopped red
bell pepper and pat dry.
Soften 1 envelope plain
gelatin in 1/4 cup cold
water. Add 1/4 cup boiling
water. Cool. Add
chopped vegetables and
2 cups mayonnaise and
mix well. Spread on
bread or crackers, or use
to stuff cherry tomatoes.*

Tiny Orange Muffins with Smoked Turkey

Yield: 30 servings

1/2	cup (1 stick) butter, softened	1	cup golden raisins
1	cup sugar	•	Grated zest and juice of 1 orange
2	eggs	1/2	cup sugar
1	teaspoon baking soda	8	ounces smoked turkey, thinly sliced
1	cup buttermilk	1/4	cup quince or apple jelly
2	cups flour		

Beat the butter and 1 cup sugar in a mixer bowl until creamy. Add the eggs and beat until fluffy. Stir the baking soda into the buttermilk. Add the buttermilk mixture and flour alternately to the creamed mixture, beating well after each addition. Process the raisins and orange zest in a food processor until ground. Stir into the batter. Spoon into miniature muffin cups sprayed with nonstick cooking spray. Bake at 400 degrees for 12 minutes or until golden brown and firm to the touch. Brush the warm muffins with orange juice and sprinkle with 1/2 cup sugar. Let stand until cool.

To serve, split the muffins into halves. Layer the turkey on the bottom halves of the muffins. Spread with the jelly and replace the muffin tops.

Poppy Seed Ham and Cheese Rolls

Yield: 30 to 72 servings

1	cup (2 sticks) butter, softened	3	(20- to 24-count) packages small party rolls
3	tablespoons poppy seeds		
3	tablespoons prepared mustard or Dijon mustard	1	pound shaved boiled ham or turkey ham
1	tablespoon Worcestershire sauce	12	ounces Swiss cheese, thinly sliced
1	medium onion, grated		

Combine the butter, poppy seeds, mustard, Worcestershire sauce and onion in a bowl and mix well. Cut each package of rolls into halves horizontally. Spread the cut sides of the bottom halves with 1/2 of the butter mixture and place in 8x12-inch pans. Layer with the ham and cheese. Spread the remaining butter on the cut sides of the top halves of the rolls. Place spread side down on the cheese layer. Cut into individual rolls. Wrap the pans loosely with foil. Bake at 350 degrees for 15 to 20 minutes.

Note: *Can freeze the prepared rolls, but thaw before baking.*

ASPARAGUS ROLL-UPS

For Asparagus Roll-Ups, beat 1/2 cup (1 stick) butter, softened, with 4 ounces crumbled bleu cheese until creamy. Trim the crusts from 14 slices white bread. Roll each slice of bread with a rolling pin until flat. Spread with the bleu cheese mixture. Place 1 drained canned asparagus spear on each bread slice and roll up. Brush with melted butter and sprinkle with grated Parmesan cheese. Cut each roll-up into thirds. Place on a baking sheet sprayed with nonstick cooking spray. Bake at 350 degrees for 15 minutes.

Party Puffs with Shrimp Salad Filling

Yield: 3 dozen

3	ounces cream cheese, softened	1½	cups finely chopped, peeled, cooked shrimp
½	cup mayonnaise		
2	teaspoons lemon juice	½	cup finely chopped celery
1	teaspoon Tabasco sauce	•	Party Puffs (below)

Beat the cream cheese, mayonnaise, lemon juice and Tabasco sauce in a mixer bowl until smooth. Stir in the shrimp and celery. Chill, covered, for 1 hour or longer.

To serve, slice off the top of Party Puffs, reserving the tops and discarding the doughy centers. Fill each puff with the shrimp salad and replace the top. Garnish with parsley or pipe additional softened cream cheese in a flower design on top of each.

Party Puffs

1	cup water	•	Dash of salt
½	cup (1 stick) butter, softened	4	eggs
1	cup flour		

Bring the water to a boil in a saucepan. Add the butter. Heat until melted, stirring constantly. Add the flour and salt all at once. Cook until the mixture forms a soft ball, stirring constantly. Cool slightly. Add the eggs 1 at a time, beating well with a wooden spoon after each addition. Continue to beat until the mixture is shiny. Drop by teaspoonfuls onto lightly greased baking sheets. Bake at 375 degrees for 50 minutes. Let stand until cool.

Silver Tea Cucumber Sandwiches

Yield: 6 dozen

8	ounces cream cheese, softened	1	to 1½ loaves thinly sliced white bread
1	garlic clove, minced		
2	tablespoons mayonnaise	2	medium cucumbers, peeled, thinly sliced
2	teaspoons milk		
2	dashes Worcestershire sauce		

Beat the cream cheese, garlic, mayonnaise, milk and Worcestershire sauce in a mixer bowl until creamy. Trim the crusts from the bread. Cut the bread into 4 sections per slice. Spread each with the cream cheese mixture. Arrange a cucumber slice on ½ of the bread slices. Top with the remaining bread slices, spread side down.

To store, layer the sandwiches in an airtight container with waxed paper between each layer. Cover the top layer with a slightly dampened paper towel. Chill, covered, until ready to serve.

ROMA TOMATO ROUNDS

For Roma Tomato Rounds, slice 1 French baguette into ¼-inch-thick slices and place on a baking sheet. Broil until toasted and firm, but not brown. Spread the toasted side of the bread with a mixture of ½ cup sour cream, ½ cup mayonnaise and 1 teaspoon dillweed. Top each with a thin slice of Roma tomato. Garnish each with a sprig of basil.

Fresh Fruit Salad with Mimosa Sauce

Yield: 6 to 8 servings

1/3	cup sugar
4	teaspoons cornstarch
•	Pinch of salt
1	cup pineapple juice
1/4	cup orange juice
1/4	cup fresh lemon juice
2	eggs, beaten

1/2	cup whipping cream, whipped
•	Fresh fruit of choice, such as sliced bananas, sliced strawberries, blueberries, seedless grapes, chopped apples and pitted cherries

Combine the sugar, cornstarch and salt in a double boiler. Add the pineapple juice, lemon juice and orange juice. Cook over warm water for 20 minutes, stirring constantly. Stir a small amount of the hot mixture into the beaten eggs; stir the eggs into the hot mixture. Cook for 5 minutes, stirring constantly. Remove from the heat. Let stand until cool. Fold in the whipped cream and fruit. Spoon into a serving bowl. Chill, covered, until serving time.

Mimosa Dip

For Mimosa Dip, blend 3 ounces whipped cream cheese into the sauce (at right) instead of whipped cream. Serve with a fresh fruit tray for a coffee or tea.

Spicy Pecans

Yield: 12 servings

1/2 cup sugar	1/2 teaspoon cayenne pepper
3 tablespoons water	2 cups pecan halves
1 teaspoon salt	

Combine the sugar, water, salt and cayenne pepper in a medium saucepan. Cook over medium heat until the sugar is dissolved, stirring constantly. Boil for 2 minutes; do not stir. Add the pecans and stir until coated. Spread on a buttered large baking sheet. Bake at 350 degrees for 13 minutes or until toasted. Remove to waxed paper to cool. Store in an airtight container for up to 1 week.

Lemon Curd

Yield: 5 1/2 cups

4	lemons	2	cups sugar
1/2	cup (1 stick) butter	6	eggs

Rinse the lemons and pat dry. Grate the lemon rinds onto a plate. Cut the lemons into halves. Squeeze the juice into a strainer over a pitcher, discarding the seeds and pulp. Melt the butter in a double boiler. Add the sugar, lemon juice, lemon rind and eggs. Cook for 20 minutes or until thickened, stirring constantly. Pour into a container with a tight-fitting lid. Store, covered, in the refrigerator for up to 10 days.

Crescent Dainties

Yield: 3 dozen

1	cup (2 sticks) butter, softened	2	cups flour
3/4	cup sour cream	3/4	cup sugar
1	egg yolk, lightly beaten	1	teaspoon cinnamon
1/2	teaspoon vanilla extract	•	Finely chopped pecans to taste

Beat the butter, sour cream, egg yolk and vanilla in a mixer bowl until smooth. Add the flour and mix well. Divide the dough into 3 portions. Chill, covered, for 8 to 12 hours. Mix the sugar, cinnamon and pecans in a bowl. Roll each chilled ball into an 8-inch circle. Sprinkle with the cinnamon mixture. Cut into wedges. Roll up from the wide end. Shape into crescents on buttered cookie sheets. Bake at 375 degrees for 17 minutes. Cool on the cookie sheets on a wire rack.

Sweet Tooth Pralines

Yield: 48 servings

2¹/4	cups packed brown sugar	2	cups pecan halves
1	cup heavy cream	1	tablespoon (¹/8 stick) butter
2	tablespoons corn syrup		or margarine

Mix the brown sugar, cream, corn syrup and pecans in a large microwave-safe bowl. Microwave on High for 13 minutes. Add the butter. Stir for a few minutes or until the glossy mixture has a dull finish and is thick. Drop by spoonfuls onto waxed paper.

PERRIER PUNCH

For Perrier Punch, combine a 750- milliliter or 25.4- ounce bottle of dry white wine, 25 ounces Perrier and 20 ounces white grape juice in a large punch bowl. Add ice cubes and 8 ounces green grapes, frozen. Ladle into punch cups to serve.

Jungle Pieces

Yield: 20 servings

3   cups white chocolate chips
1½ cups chunky peanut butter

2   cups chocolate chips

Microwave the white chocolate chips with the peanut butter in a microwave-safe dish until melted using the package directions on the white chocolate chips. Stir until smooth. Pour onto a buttered 10x15-inch baking sheet. Microwave the chocolate chips in a microwave-safe dish until melted using the package directions. Pour over the white chocolate layer and swirl with a knife. Chill until set. Slice or break into pieces to serve.

Space-Age Peanut Brittle

Yield: 1 pound

1   cup raw peanuts
1   cup sugar
½   cup white corn syrup
⅛   teaspoon salt

1   teaspoon butter
1   teaspoon vanilla extract
1   teaspoon baking soda

Combine the peanuts, sugar, corn syrup and salt in an 8-cup glass measure. Microwave on High for 4 minutes; stir. Microwave for 3 to 4 minutes longer. Add the butter and vanilla and blend well. Microwave for 1 minute. Peanuts will be light brown. Stir in the baking soda until light and foamy and amber in color. Pour immediately onto a flexible baking sheet, spreading mixture quickly. Let stand for 30 minutes. Break into small pieces. Store in an airtight container.

Almond Cake Squares

Yield: 12 servings

2	eggs	1	cup (2 sticks) butter, melted
1	cup sugar	•	Almond Topping (below)
1	cup flour		

Beat the eggs and sugar in a mixer bowl until thick and pale yellow. Do not overbeat. Stir in flour and melted butter. Pour into a greased and floured 9x13-inch baking pan. Bake at 350 degrees for 30 minutes or until the cake tests done. Spread Almond Topping over the hot cake. Broil 4 inches from the heat source for 3 to 5 minutes or until the top is brown and bubbly. Watch carefully. Cool on a wire rack. Cut into desired shapes with a sharp knife.

Almond Topping

½	cup sugar	1	tablespoon flour
½	cup (1 stick) butter	1	tablespoon milk
½	cup sliced almonds		

Combine sugar, butter, almonds, flour and milk in a small saucepan. Cook over low heat until thickened and the sugar is completely dissolved, stirring constantly.

Decadent Fudge Muffins

Yield: 4 dozen

1¹/₃	cups sifted flour
6	tablespoons baking cocoa
¹/₂	teaspoon baking soda
¹/₂	teaspoon salt
6	tablespoons (³/₄ stick) butter, softened
1	cup sugar
2	egg yolks
1	teaspoon vanilla extract
1	cup milk
2	egg whites, stiffly beaten
1	cup chocolate chips
1	cup chopped pecans
•	Cream Cheese Topping (at right)

Mix the flour, baking cocoa, baking soda and salt together. Beat the butter and sugar in a mixer bowl until light and fluffy. Add the egg yolks and vanilla and beat well. Add the flour mixture alternately with the milk, beating well after each addition. Fold in the stiffly beaten egg whites. Fold in the chocolate chips and pecans. Spoon into well-buttered miniature muffin cups. Bake at 350 degrees for 15 minutes. Remove from the pans onto wire racks to cool completely.

To serve, place Cream Cheese Topping in a pastry bag fitted with a rosette tip. Pipe rosettes onto each muffin. Garnish with a candied flower or cherries.

CREAM CHEESE TOPPING

For Cream Cheese Topping, beat 3 ounces cream cheese, softened, with 1 tablespoon (¹/₈ stick) butter, softened, in a mixer bowl until light. Beat in enough confectioners' sugar (¹/₂ to ³/₄ cup) for a stable consistency. Stir in vanilla extract to taste.

Cranberry Upside-Down Cake with Orange Custard Sauce

Yield: 6 to 8 servings

9	tablespoons (1 stick plus 1/8 stick) butter, softened	1/4	teaspoon salt
1	cup sugar	1	egg
1	(12-ounce) package fresh cranberries	1	teaspoon vanilla extract
		1	teaspoon grated orange zest
1 1/4	cups flour	1/2	cup milk
1 1/4	teaspoons baking powder	1/3	cup currant jelly, melted
		•	Orange Custard Sauce (below)

Spread 3 tablespoons butter on the bottom and side of a 9-inch round cake pan. Sprinkle 1/2 cup of the sugar evenly in the bottom. Cover with the cranberries. Mix the flour, baking powder and salt together. Beat the remaining 6 tablespoons butter and remaining 1/2 cup sugar in a mixer bowl until light and fluffy. Add the egg, vanilla and orange zest and mix well. Add the flour mixture alternately with the milk, beating constantly at low speed until just combined after each addition. Pour over the cranberries and smooth the top. Bake at 350 degrees for 45 to 60 minutes or until brown. Cool in the pan on a wire rack for 20 minutes. Invert onto a serving plate. Brush with melted currant jelly. Serve with Orange Custard Sauce.

Orange Custard Sauce

1	cup milk	6	egg yolks
1	cup half-and-half	1/4	cup sugar
1	(1-inch) piece vanilla bean	2	tablespoons Grand Marnier
3	(1/2x3 1/2) pieces orange zest		

Bring the milk, half-and-half, vanilla bean and orange zest to a simmer in a small saucepan. Remove from the heat and let stand for 15 minutes. Strain into a bowl. Beat the egg yolks in a mixer bowl. Add the sugar. Beat for 3 minutes. Add the strained milk mixture and mix well. Pour into a saucepan. Cook for 7 to 10 minutes or until thickened over low heat, stirring constantly. Remove from the heat. Stir in Grand Marnier. Let stand until cool. Pour into a sauceboat.

Orange Honey Cake

Yield: 12 servings

2	teaspoons instant coffee	1³/4	cups flour
1/2	cup warm water	1	teaspoon baking powder
2	large eggs	1	teaspoon baking soda
3/4	cup sugar	1/2	teaspoon cinnamon
1/2	cup honey	1/2	teaspoon allspice
3	tablespoons vegetable oil	1/8	teaspoon salt
1/3	cup thawed frozen orange juice concentrate		

Dissolve the coffee granules in the warm water. Beat the eggs, sugar, honey and vegetable oil at medium-high speed in a mixer bowl until blended. Stir in the coffee and orange juice concentrate. Add the flour, baking powder, baking soda, cinnamon, allspice and salt. Beat at low speed until combined. Beat at high speed for 1 minute or until smooth. Pour into a 5x9-inch loaf pan sprayed with nonstick cooking spray. Bake at 300 degrees for 1¹/4 hours.

Note: *Can divide the batter between 4 miniature loaf pans and bake for 35 to 40 minutes or until the loaves test done.*

Honey Cake

Honey Cake, or Lekahh in Yiddish, is an Eastern European cake that is traditionally served on Rosh Hashana, before or after Yom Kippur, or any other happy occasion to ensure a "sweet year."

Chocolate Peppermint Brownies

Yield: 24 servings

1/2 cup (1 stick) butter, melted	1/2 cup flour
2 ounces unsweetened chocolate, melted	1 teaspoon vanilla extract
	1/2 cup chopped pecans
2 eggs	• Peppermint Filling (at left)
1 cup sugar	• Chocolate Icing (below)

Melt 1/2 cup butter and 2 ounces chocolate in a saucepan over low heat, stirring constantly. Let stand until cool. Beat the eggs and sugar in a mixer bowl until light and fluffy. Add the chocolate mixture and mix well. Add the flour and vanilla and mix well. Stir in the pecans. Pour into a greased 9x13-inch baking pan. Bake at 325 degrees for 20 to 25 minutes or until the edges pull from the sides of the pan. Let stand until cool.

To assemble, spread Peppermint Filling over the cool brownies. Drizzle with Chocolate Icing. Let stand until cool. Cut into squares.

Chocolate Icing

2 tablespoons (1/4 stick) butter	2 ounces unsweetened chocolate

Melt 2 tablespoons butter and 2 ounces chocolate in a saucepan over low heat, stirring constantly.

Cinnamon Bar Cookies

Yield: 4 dozen

1 cup (2 sticks) butter, softened
1 cup sugar
1 egg, separated
1 teaspoon vanilla extract

1 teaspoon cinnamon
2 cups flour
1 cup chopped pecans

Beat the butter and sugar in a mixer bowl until light and fluffy. Add the egg yolk, vanilla and cinnamon and mix well. Beat in the flour. The dough will be thick. Spread the dough in a 10x15-inch baking pan. Whisk the egg white in a bowl. Brush over the dough and sprinkle with pecans. Bake at 325 degrees for 15 to 20 minutes or until light brown. Remove from the oven and cut into bars while still warm.

Marvelous Macaroons

Yield: 80 cookies

1	cup sugar	$1/16$	teaspoon salt
8	cups shredded sweetened coconut	$1/4$	cup ($1/2$ stick) butter, melted
6	egg whites	1	teaspoon almond extract
		1	teaspoon vanilla extract

Combine the sugar, coconut, egg whites and salt in a large bowl and mix well using your hands. Add the butter, almond extract and vanilla extract and mix well. Place in the freezer for 30 minutes. Line a 9x13-inch cookie sheet with parchment paper. Roll 1 tablespoon of the coconut mixture at a time into a ball, squeezing to make compact. Place 1 inch apart on the prepared baking sheet. Bake at 350 degrees for 16 to 17 minutes or until the edges and bottoms are golden brown. Remove the parchment paper with the macaroons to wire racks to cool. Store with waxed paper between layers in an airtight container for 8 to 10 days.

SPICED CRANBERRY APPLE GLÖGG

For Spiced Cranberry Apple Glögg, bring 3 cups cran-apple juice cocktail, 7 cups dry red wine, 1/2 cup sugar, 2 cinnamon sticks, 2 whole cloves and orange rind strips to just below a simmer in a large saucepan. Cook for 1 hour. Strain and ladle into mugs. Can be prepared ahead and served warm.

Gulf Coast Orange Eggnog

Yield: 24 servings

6	egg yolks, beaten		1/4	teaspoon cinnamon
3/4	cup sugar		1	cup orange juice
2	cups half-and-half		6	egg whites, beaten
1	cup milk		•	Grated orange zest to taste
1/2	teaspoon nutmeg		1	tablespoon nutmeg

Beat the egg yolks in a mixer bowl until light and fluffy. Beat in the sugar gradually. Add the half-and-half, milk, 1/2 teaspoon nutmeg and cinnamon. Pour into a double boiler. Cook until the mixture is thickened and coats the back of a spoon, stirring constantly. Remove from the heat. Chill until cool. Stir in the orange juice. Fold in the beaten egg whites and orange zest. Sprinkle with 1 tablespoon nutmeg. Chill until serving time.

Cranberry Punch

Yield: 25 servings

1	(3-ounce) package cherry gelatin		3	cups cold water
1	cup boiling water		1	quart cranberry juice cocktail, chilled
1	(6-ounce) can frozen lemonade or pineapple-orange juice concentrate		1	(12-ounce) bottle ginger ale, chilled

Dissolve the gelatin in boiling water in a large pitcher. Stir in the lemonade concentrate. Add the cold water and cranberry juice cocktail.

To serve, place 24 ice cubes or a molded ice ring in a large punch bowl. Pour the punch over the ice. Add the chilled ginger ale in a fine stream.

Holiday Open House

Cranberry Punch, *page 261*
Champagne Punch, *page 262*
Coffee

Joyeux Shrimp and Crab in Pastry Shells, *page 238*
Poppy Seed Ham and Cheese Rolls, *page 245*
Tiny Orange Muffins with Smoked Turkey, *page 244*

Roma Tomato Rounds, *page 247*
Asparagus Spears with Citrus-Ginger Dip, *page 237*
Silver Tea Cucumber Sandwiches, *page 247*
Fiesta Cheesecake, *page 234*
Cranberry Conserve with Brie Cheese, *page 233*
Parsley Caper Sauce for Tortellini, *page 235*

Fresh Fruit Tray with Mimosa Dip, *page 248*

Spicy Pecans, *page 249*
Marvelous Macaroons, *page 260*
Peppered Jelly Thumbprint Cookies, *page 242*
Texas Tarts with Lemon Curd, *page 250*
Decadent Fudge Muffins, *page 255*
White Chocolate with Raspberry Bars, *page 220*
Cranberry Upside-Down Cake with
Orange Custard Sauce, *page 256*
Sweet Tooth Pralines, *page 252*

CHAMPAGNE PUNCH

For Champagne Punch, combine 1/2 cup Triple Sec, 1 cup vodka, 2 quarts ginger ale, chilled, and 2 bottles inexpensive Champagne in a large punch bowl and mix well. Add 1 bunch frozen seedless green grapes.

Contributors

ASSISTANCE LEAGUE® of the Bay Area expresses grateful appreciation to those contributors who have spent countless hours and/or dollars to provide us with the quality recipes featured in *Settings on the Dock of the Bay*. We hope we have not inadvertently excluded anyone from the following list:

Fatin Abdalla
Patricia Abele
* Atiya Abouleish
Shirley Alderman
Susan Alterman
* Nayla Aneed
* Shaun Anzaldua
* Christine Arlitt
Kathy Arthur
* Pamela Bagley
* Jackie Bailey
Jan Bailey
Janet Ballard
Robert Barge
Mary Ann Baxter
Beth Beatty
* Ruth Beecher
* Carol Bergman
Mae Berlin
Lilia Bilbao
Louis J. Bilbao
Mary Ann Bishop
* Maureen Blanding
* Carol Bobo
* Suzanne Bonner
Susan Bonora
John Bosso
* Dianne Bowman
Patty Branch
* Lucinda Breck
* Troy Bredthauer
Barbara Brewer
* Dana Brown
* Lynn M. Brown
* Sharon M. Brown

Grace Burns
Dan Burt
* Joan Burt
Katie Burt
* Betsy Bush
Joe Byrd
* Linda Byrd
Tony Caliva
* Marion Callahan
* Lisa Callner-Schulte
Frances Campbell
Meg Campbell
Lisa Cannon
Jacque S. Caplan
Karyn Carmical
Dorothy Carroll
* Nancy Chen
Dee Dee Cherry
Matt Clevenger
Diane Clear
* Barbara Coleman
* Brenda Concienne
Nancy Cotton
* Ebby Creden
* Gloria Cruz
* J. Pamela Culpepper
* Georgette McMillan-
   Curran
* Kathie Curry
Martha Daniel
Mary Davis
Sheila Dell'Osso
* Belva Dewey
* Sharon Dillard
Louise Dillon

* Dina DiMaria
* Judy Doggett
Margie Dolin
Anne Dowbekin
* Linda DuBose
* Diane Duff
Alexis Dunn
Libby and Patrick Dunn
* Mary Alice Dunn
* Jailane Ebeid
Elaine Ebner
* Leslie Edmonson
* Annie Epstein
* Pat Escue
* Ann Marie Falbo
Linda Falco
* Judie Ferguson
* Sheila Fichtner
Melissa Field
Iris Fisherman
Mrs. John Foltz
Betty Forsten
* Lynda Forsthoffer
Rina Friley
* Sheree Frede
Lonore Fredrichs
* Debi Frieden
* Dianne Friel
* Mary Kay Gaido
Tom Gallagher
Marge Gannon
* Donna Gartner
* Fran Gentry
* Cathy Giesinger
John Gillespie

* Rae Gillespie
Deb Gittin
* Elizabeth Glenn
* Lil Glynn
Marcy Golden
* Linda Goodman
* Debbie Gorenstein
Jennie Gorenstein
Woodfield Gormet
Sharon Graham
Dick Gregg, Jr.
* Lynette Mason Gregg
* Louise S. Gregory
Laura Grossman
Rhonda Guzzetta
* Katherine Moser Haden
* Carole Haider
* Sharlet Hairr
Nancy Hammerle
* Jennifer Hampton
* Cheng Hang
Elsie Hardy
Doris Durbin Heard
* Melba Heselmeyer
* Suzanne Hicks
Delores Holcomb
* Barbara Holderman
Deborah Holstein
J.B. Holstein, CWC
* Mary Sue Holstein
Patricia Holstein
* Cherre House
Kay Howard
* Leslie Huff
* Becky Huffeldt
* JoNell Hunter
* Lisa Hurwitz
* Katherine Incalcaterra
Marie Inkofer
Hanan Ismail

* Laura Jachimiec
* Karen Jackson
* Lucy Jacobson
* Donna James
* Jinny Jarrell
* Sue Ellen Jennings
* Emily Johnson
* Sally Jordan
* Michele Jowid
* Sue Kazda
Henrietta Kidd
* Faye R. Kidder
Richard Kidder
Stella Kiefer
Jane Kochuba
* Diane Konick
* Carole Krist
* Diane Krist
* Kimberly Krist
* Gayle Kuoni
* Sue Laabs
Adele Landry
* Sheryl Lane
Nancy Laura
* Joan Lindsay
Diane Little
* Carole Loomis
* Connie S. Lopez
Laurie Lowery
Jeanne Mack
Arlene Mader
Catherine Maenza
Charleen Magliolo
* Jeana Magness
Ruth Mann
* Melinda Marcum
* Johanna Mathera
Gia McAllister
* Pat McAllister
Ann McAndrew

* Cathy Fetzer McDaniel
Mrs. McDaniel
Burnice McDonald
* Darla McKitrick
Ellen McKitrick
* Diane McLaughlin
Mary McMullen
Mary McMurray
* Suzanne Meyer
* Ceci Miglicco
* Lynda Milan
* Janet Miller
Margie Miori
Brigette Miori-Hogsed
Virginia Mladinch
Jan Moates
Pam Morneau
Jolie Morrow
* Peggy Morrow
Tommy Morrow
Debbie Moyle
* Barbra Mouton
* Joy Muniz
* Sandra Munz
* Casey Myers
Beverly Beatty Nester
* Donna Leigh Newland
* Pat Nichilo
* Charlotte Nicks
Evelyn Noack
* Ulrike Nordhoff
* Nancy O'Dowd
Ann O'Malley
* Cathy Osoria
Bev Overhauser
Debbie Potter Parker
* Jan Parks
Judi Passon
* Sanjukta Pattanaik
* Betsy Pennington

Holly Peery
* Debra Perry
* Wendy Peters
Judy Pfeiffer
* Barbara Phillips
* Georgia Piwonka
Sherry Pomykal
* Cindy Porterfield
* Maureen Powell
* JoLynn Puff
Marilyn Quinn
* Judy Raiford
* Joy W. Rayne
Charlotte Reem
* Sylvia Resch
Madeline Reymond
* Rebecca Gentry Richey
* Delinda Richman
Mona Roberts
* Patty Rodgers
* Betsy Rogers
* Suzie Rogers
Metta Rone
Teresa Rosenberg
Anne Rosenthal
* Barbara Rosenthal
Marianne Rouse
Lana Royal
* Marcia Safirstein
* Sooky Sarabia
Dorothy Moser Sawin
* Sarah Sawin

Joan Scheel
Maxine Schneider
Peachy Schneider
Tyna and Mark Schultze
Leslie Schwanke
Cindi Sharp
Diane Sheridan
* Sandra Sellers
* Elise Sher
* Roberta Sherer
* Carol Short
* Sharon Siddons
* Bertina Smith
Ruth Smith
* Joy Smitherman
* Lynda Smythe
* Elaine Stacha
* Jackie Stallings
* Janice Starko
* Becca Stout
Elaine Strahan
* Patti Sulkin
* Bernie Sullivan
Meridy Tabackman
Dot Tate
Mary L. Taylor
* Sharon Taylor
Libby Tomasi
* Charlotte Teeter
* Lucille Terraso
* Toinette Tillinghast
* Pat Trampe

* Barbara Visser
* Bobbye Volentine
Gene Volentine
Mary K. Walden
Doug Walt
* Linda Walt
Cleo Ward
* Janet Watkins
* Nancy Watson
Robyn Watts
Susan Weaver
Marion Webber
* Arlene Weinberg
* Angie Weinman
* Jennifer Whatton
* Owen Whitlock
* Sally Wigginton
Kara Williams
Kathy Williams
Robin Williams
Sonny Williams
* Pat Wilson
* Gloria Wong
* Renate Wood
Virgie Woodward
* Linda Wright
* Jimetta Wright-Eudey
* Elaine Wynegar
Rori Yager
* Rosanne Zarcaro
* Sarah Zarcaro

* denotes members of ASSISTANCE LEAGUE® of the Bay Area

265

Settings on the Dock of the Bay

ASSISTANCE LEAGUE® of the Bay Area
P.O. Box 590153 • Houston, Texas 77259-0153
Toll-Free Phone: (877) 277-3452
Fax Number: (281) 333-9157
Visit our webpage at www.albatx.org

Please send _____ copies of *Settings on the Dock of the Bay* @ $22.95 each $ _____

Texas residents add 8.25% sales tax $ _____

Postage and handling $3.50 for the first book $ _____

$2.00 for each additional book $ _____
(delivered to the same address)

Grand Total $ _____

Mr. _____   Mrs. _____   Miss _____   Ms. _____

Name _____

Address _____

City/State/Zip _____

Daytime Telephone Number _____

VISA _____   MasterCard _____   American Express _____

Account Number _____

Signature _____   Exp. Date _____

Make checks payable to: ALBA Cookbook

Look for our new cookbook, *Settings, Sunrise to Sunset,* in October 2006.

Proceeds from the sale of this cookbook are returned to the community through projects of ASSISTANCE LEAGUE® of the Bay Area.

Photocopies accepted